D0518300

THE *BERNESE MOUNTAIN DOG* TODAY

Dr Malcolm B. Willis

Howell Book House

HOWELL
BOOK
HOUSE

New York

Copyright © 1998 by
Ringpress Book, PO Box 8, Lydney,
Gloucestershire GL15 6YD, United Kingdom.

HOWELL BOOK HOUSE
A Simon & Schuster / Macmillan Company
1633 Broadway
New York, NY 10019

MACMILLAN is a registered trademark of Macmillan, Inc.

Library of Congress Cataloging-in-Publication Data
Willis, Malcolm Beverley.
    The Bernese mountain dog today / Malcolm Willis.
            p.   cm.
        ISBN 1-58245-038-2
        1. Bernese mountain dog.   I. Title.
    SF429.B47W55   1999
    636.73--dc21   98-12405
                                                                                    CIP

Manufactured in Singapore

10 9 8 7 6 5 4 3 2 1

In Memory of
CH. CARLACOT GENESIS AT NELLSBERN (BOGIE)
The finest dog to live with that I will ever know
and of
NELLSBERN CASABLANCA (one CC three Res. CCs) (Cas)
taken too soon with so much to give

*A*CKNOWLEDGEMENTS

Thanks are due to Mrs Diane Cochrane for a large number of photographs without which this book would be much the poorer. To Margret Bartschi and Hansjoachin Spengler for the gift of a copy of their excellent book and for permission to use drawings made for that book. To Martin Packard and the Berner-Garde officers and helpers for data on hips that filled in gaps. To Kim and Kelley Behrens of the Ledgewood kennels for organising American photos and to all those who helped with pictures. To Yvonne Fison-Bates for some New Zealand and Australian data, and to Shirley and David Franks for carting information. All these and others have helped to improve this book and I am most grateful. I am also grateful to my wife Helen who has helped and was to have been joint author, but who changed her mind – a woman's prerogative! The occasional use of "we" is not intended to be the "royal we", but to avoid the use of "I" when it is Helen who does more of the practical work than I do. Any deficiencies that remain in this book are mine.

CONTENTS

INTRODUCTION

Although there are several books on the Bernese Mountain Dog in English, and as many again in other languages, I make no apology for producing a new one since this book is, in many respects, very different from those that have gone before. There are ten chapters, beginning with the origins and spread of the breed around the world. The Standards of Britain, America and the FCI are then detailed and interpreted and there are chapters on feeding, living with and training a Bernese, and on showing and judging the breed. The principles of breeding are dealt with, followed by a chapter on the genetics of specific features and also diseases of the breed. There is an index, glossary and list of references cited, as well as details of all the books known to have been written about the breed.

Outside of the history, I have made minimal reference to breeders, so that, in tabulations of leading sires or top winners, I have given the dogs and their breeding, rather than, as in some books, their owners and breeders. This is not to diminish the skills of breeders and owners, but to emphasise that, however successful we may be, we are all transitory, whereas the dogs themselves leave a legacy (for good or ill) within the breed that can last for many decades. It is the dogs that we need to know about and to understand, and the more we become involved in breeding, the more true this becomes.

At times, this book may require careful thought and it is not intended as bedtime reading. Within the limitations of space I have sought to make a serious study of the breed, within which I feel that the beginner will glean information and the experienced breeder will perhaps find new ways to look at the breed and how it can be developed and advanced.

At its best, the Bernese is a very beautiful dog to look at, it is also a beautiful breed to live with. I have been a German Shepherd man all my adult life and have lived with some fine dogs, but the finest dog I have ever lived with was a Bernese, Ch. Carlacot Genesis at Nellsbern, who had a great zest for life and who was as bright and intelligent as I could have hoped for. Too many Bernese are not developed mentally as well as they could be and it behoves their owners to try and bring out the best in them. They have a great love of their owners and an eagerness to please that deserves to be cultivated. If this book can help those of you who own and breed Bernese to do it that bit better, then it will more than serve its purpose.

I would be pleased to hear from anyone who feels that additional information should be included and especially from owners who can add to the information on specific dogs named.

1 ORIGINS OF THE BERNESE MOUNTAIN DOG

CANINE EVOLUTION

It is widely accepted that the domestic dog goes back some 14,000 years and that it is the first species to be domesticated by man. In fact, the bones of wolves, in conjunction with those of early man, have been dated back some 300,000 years (Olsen, 1985) which suggests that the two species (man and wolf) overlapped in territorial terms. The domestic dog (*Canis familiaris*) is one of 38 species of the family *Canidae*. The wild species of *Canidae* are all land-based, fast-running and mostly nocturnal. They differ in hunting habits, ranging from solitary operators such as the fox through to social pack hunters like the wolf.

The domestic dog has 39 pairs of chromosomes and, in this context, is identical with the wolf (*Canis lupus*), the coyote (*Canis latrans)* and the golden jackal (*Canis aureus*). Although there has been debate about the origins of the domestic dog, with both wolf and jackal being cited as the precursor, it is now generally accepted by most authorities that all canine breeds trace back to some form of wolf. It has generally been supposed that the wolf was domesticated as an aid to hunting, but, as

Manwell and Baker (1984) pointed out, present uses may not always have been the initial use. They argue that, in addition to hunting capabilities, the early dogs might have been a source of food, an emotional object or pet or even a bed-warmer. They also suggest that, rather than man becoming impressed by the wolf's hunting capabilities, it was the reverse situation. Wolves were impressed by man's capacity in this endeavour and hung around his camps.

In a recent DNA study, Vila (1997) showed that domestic dogs do not share the DNA of coyotes and jackals but that of the wolf. It may be that more than one type of wolf was involved in canine domestication, but it is certain that the wolf was the origin of all domestic dog breeds. Once a small population is established and is kept isolated from others, as would happen with domestication, then problems of inbreeding and genetic drift would arise and differentiation between canine groups would result. Thus dogs would develop into distinct types or breeds.

In fact, the modern dog shows greater variability than any other mammalian species with a range in size from a Chihuahua through to a St Bernard. It does seem (see Clutton-Brock, 1995) that breeds, or, more correctly, differing types of domestic dog, began to appear around 3,000-4,000 years ago. Paintings from the Middle East and Western Asia show that animals resembling sight hounds and types similar to the Greyhound seem to have been the earliest domestic breeds. By Roman times, many of the three main breed types known today were in existence and dogs were used for war, hunting, herding, guarding and as lap dogs. Proliferation of breeds started about the 13th to 15th centuries AD. Peters (1965) reported that the first classification of dogs in the English language was published in 1486, and listed the Greyhoun and Mastif (spelt in this way) among others. By the 1600s, breeds akin to the modern King Charles Spaniel existed, though none of today's dogs could have pedigrees traced so far back. A listing of 42 pedigree breeds was published in 1859 by a body called the Kennel Club of Great Britain. In 1873, the Kennel Club (British) was formed, and the American Kennel Club (AKC) soon afterwards, in 1884. Probably the first authoritative book on canine breeds of the world was published by the AKC in 1939. Pedigree (or Pure) breeds, as we know them, can normally trace back their ancestry only as far as the latter decades of the 19th century, which encompasses some 25-30 generations.

ORIGINS OF THE BREED
Many breeds were developed relatively recently, within the past 100-150 years, and the Bernese Mountain Dog may be no exception. Until this century, the average man was limited in terms of how far he might travel. Just as people tended to seek their spouse from within a narrow limited

The Appenzeller Sennenhund.

The Entlebucher Sennenhund.

The Great Swiss Sennenhund.

area, so breeds of dog would develop in specific regions. This would be all the more likely in a country such as Switzerland, with high mountain ranges dividing the country into somewhat isolated regions.

There are four so-called Swiss Mountain breeds, all tricolour (black, white and tan) with the same basic marking pattern, and it is logical to assume that all four derived from similar origins and that they developed distinctly in different semi-isolated areas or regions. The Great Swiss is a large breed (about 70 cms or 27.5 ins to the shoulder) with a short coat, and is thought to have arisen near Burgdorf, while the Entlebucher (about 56 cms or 22 ins) has, usually, a stumpy tail and is said to derive from the region of Entlebuch. The Appenzeller (about 59 cms or 23.4 inches) is short-coated like the other two, but has a distinctive curled tail and derives from north-east Switzerland in the region of Appenzell. The Bernese, the only long-coated breed of the four, is larger than the Appenzeller and Entlebucher and is thought to have arisen in the Canton of Bern in central Switzerland. Indeed, the region of Durrbach, south of Bern, is said to be the original home and the breed is often called Durrbachler. The first mention of the Swiss Sennenhund appears to be in a German book by Von Tschudi (1853) dealing with animals that live in the Alps.

It was originally claimed by the German author Strebel in 1904 that the Bernese – and, presumably, the other three – derived from dogs of the Mollossus (Mastiff) type imported by the Romans, a view accepted by Professor Albert Heim (1849-1937), who is often regarded as the father of the breed. Bartschi (1986) and Simonds (1989) argue, correctly in my view, that there was little need for the Romans to import dogs of this

kind, since local dogs certainly existed already in the countries occupied by the Roman armies. Undoubtedly, the Romans used Mastiff-type animals as dogs of war, but the idea that these remained behind in Switzerland to form the four Sennenhund breeds is fanciful. Skeletons of large breeds found in the region are known to trace back to pre-Roman times and may be from Bronze Age years (Bartschi, 1986).

As far as the antecedents of the Bernese are concerned, Bartschi (1984) is probably correct in seeking a mixed explanation, with local farmers keeping different kinds of dog of varying sizes according to the objective desired, as well as their financial standing, since large dogs were expensive to keep. There was likely to be Roman influence in the period 300-100 BC, and a German influence from the Alemannen from 400 to 700 AD. Culturally, the peoples of the Bernese region are a mixture of Celt, Roman and German influences. Why not the dogs? Bartschi (1986) suggests that the origins of the Bernese breed can go back no more than to about 800-1000 AD. However, as Simonds (1989) points out, there is no proof that the Bernese as we know it today goes back very far into history. Russ and Rogers (1993) refer to a painting from 1651 that shows a Bernese-type dog, as well as to a Swiss painting dated 1773 also showing this type of dog. These may be forerunners of the modern breed but it does not take us into the realms of proof.

As shown by Peters (1965), breed types were developing during the 14th century and onwards and Swiss breed types might have been in existence from this time. However, the concept of breed would not have existed in the sense of a unique group of isolated animals of similar shape and construction,

Nelly v Burgdorf (Bari – Prisca): Swiss bitch born at the start of the 20th century and typical of the breed at that time.

bred as a separate entity. Swiss farmers certainly developed dogs that would have been used to herd cattle as well as to protect their farms from thieves and brigands. Such dogs would also have been useful in discouraging wolves and bears, which still existed in mainland Europe. There is no evidence that farmers selected dogs for specific physical appearance or colour, and they would have been more likely to be concerned with size and with character than with 'purity' of race. It seems to me that the breed's origins are less important than its immediate past and its future. Whether the Bernese Mountain Dog goes back several hundred years or merely a century does not alter its appeal. Many breed enthusiasts seem to want to claim antiquity for whatever breed it is that they admire. The reality is that no breed can really trace its history back very far.

The Bernese is black, tan and white, due to the recessive gene combination creating black with tan points combined with the gene causing Irish spotting. Once created, such a colour combination would be perpetuated if bred together. However, it is known that yellow/red and white dogs also occurred – forerunners of the other famous Swiss breed, the St Bernard.

FORMATION OF SWISS BREED CLUBS

The Swiss Kennel Club was formed in 1883, some ten years after the English, and for the previous few decades breed types had been emerging. The St Bernard was certainly attracting interest beyond Swiss borders, but little attention was paid to the smaller Swiss breeds with the tricolour pattern. A Burgdorf innkeeper called Franz Schertenlieb is said to have brought back a Durrbachler and become enthusiastic about preserving and extending the importance of the 'breed'. What is known is that some dogs were exhibited by Schertenlieb at Bern in 1902, and that the Swiss KC show at Bern in 1904 saw six males and one female exhibited. From then on, Durrbachlers were registered with the Swiss KC irrespective of pedigree status, provided that they were approved by Schertenlieb and two of his colleagues. Two members of the Swiss KC, Gottfried Mumenthaler (one of Schertenlieb's expert team) and Albert Heim, professor of geology at Zurich University and a Newfoundland breeder, took a serious interest in the breed, especially Heim. It was Heim's enthusiastic writings which helped to increase the Bernese's popularity, though it was still called the Durrbachler.

According to Bartschi (1984), a club with 14 members was formed in 1907, called the Schweizerischer Durrbach Klub, and a year

Ch. Carlo vd Grandfeybrucke (Bari v Belfaux – Erna v Schneggenberg): An important dog found in most UK pedigrees.

9

Swiss females owned by Margrit Bartschi. Pictured (from left to right): Aila vd Hagrasse (b 1980), Bina vd Hagrasse (b 1981), Prisma v Hichels Hof (b 1978, foundation bitch of the kennel), and Perri vd Hagrasse. Aila and Bina were sired by Hondo v Bernetta, and Perri by Gaston v Nesselacker.

later over 20 animals were exhibited at two shows. A Standard was established about this time and has been little altered in the years since. The terms Appenzeller or Entlebucher Sennenhund were in vogue by this time and Professor Heim proposed the name Berner Sennenhund to match these names. Initially, the members of the Durrbach club were opposed to the name change. The term "Senn" refers to alpine cattle herdsmen, who probably did not use a dog of the size of the Durrbachler for this purpose. However, the club was persuaded by Heim and, about 1908, it became the Berner Sennenhund Club. In 1910, 107 dogs were shown at Burgdorf and 80 of these were said to be good enough to breed from (Bartschi, 1984). Prof. Heim was the judge at this remarkably large event.

Numerous faults were present at this time which, bearing in mind the motley assortment of dogs and the absence of pedigrees in many cases, was not surprising. Curly tails, still present today, were commonplace but the split nasal cleft, often accompanied by a cleft palate, was the most serious, albeit not common, fault. Some

breeders felt that this trait made the dogs appear more ferocious, but Heim, rightly, persuaded breeders to avoid this serious failing and it gradually died out. Blue eyes, a feature frowned upon today, were said to be highly prized in some quarters. Gradually, with selective breeding being encouraged by Heim, animals began to conform to the Standard and markings increasingly moved towards the modern type in which the white neck band did not extend around the neck.

SPREADING THE BERNESE

English-speaking fanciers of the Swiss breeds termed them Swiss Mountain Dogs, which is not the literal translation of the names. In France and the French-speaking part of Switzerland, the breed is known as the Bouvier Bernois, while in German-speaking regions it is the Berner Sennenhund, and, in English, it is the Bernese Mountain Dog. Gradually, the Bernese became increasingly popular and began to extend outside its native country. The Swiss breed club had reached over 2,000 members by the mid-1980s; the German club was of similar size and is now larger. Clubs are also found in

Some of the puppies born in 1936 from the first litter bred in Britain.
Photo: Thomas Fall.

many other countries. The first imports to Britain were made in 1936 by Mrs D.L. Perry who had the Kobe kennels of Samoyed. She brought in the bitch Senta v Sumiswald and several others later, advertising the male Dani v Kleinegg in the *Our Dogs* annual of December 1938. One bitch, Laura v Haslenbach, whelped a litter of four males and one female in March 1937, the first Bernese litter on British soil. However, the advent of World War Two put a stop to breeding activities and the breed died out in Britain. Importation did not occur again until 1969, when Mastiff breeder Irene Creigh (affix Kisumu) brought in two puppies, Oro de coin-Barre and Dora v Breitenhof, followed by Karin v Hinterfeld. Oro and Dora produced two litters and the breed was established and has flourished in Britain since that time.

According to Chesnutt Smith (1994), America first saw the Bernese in about 1926 when Isaac Schiess imported Donna vd Rothohe and Poincare v Sumiswald from Switzerland. This pair produced a litter in March 1926 but it was registered only in Switzerland. The American KC only recognised the breed in 1937. Glen Shadow of Louisiana brought in a show-winning

Dora v Breitenhof of Nappa (Galan v Mattenhof – Briska v Grunenmatt): An early import to post-war Britain.

bitch, Fridy v Haslenbach, in 1936 and a male, Quell v Tiergarten, the same year. Chesnutt Smith (1994) argues that Shadow was the only Bernese owner/breeder in the USA until 1949 when other dogs began to come over, since which time the breed has remained relatively popular. However, a club for the breed was formed on the West Coast in 1967, had 33 members the following year, reached 100 by 1971, and became the Bernese Mountain Dog Club of America (BMDCA) in 1972. Its membership now exceeds 7,000. The BMDCA held its first match in 1973 and its first specialty in 1976, which has now grown to become the largest Bernese Mountain Dog show in the world.

In Canada, the Bernese Mountain Dog Club of Canada was formed in 1979 and the breed may have first appeared in British Columbia some ten years previous to that. However, according to Russ and Rogers (1993), one Ron Smith from Ontario is credited with the first importation in 1974 and the Canadian KC recognised the breed in 1977. The population is small and show entries minuscule by UK standards, but a Canadian male, Bigpaws Yoda, went BOB at the 1985 BMDCA specialty.

Germany imported Bernese prior to World

Tawajah's Leopold (Int. Ch. Gallo v Leubschimoos – Ch. Tawajah's Ibis): A Belgian import to Britain.

Int. Ch. & Nordic Ch. Foursomels Rex Ramses. Photo: Steinar Moen.

War One and there is a breed club, the SSV (Schweizer Sennenhund Verein), founded in 1923, which caters for the four tricolour breeds and which currently has a membership of over 3,000. Recently, a separate club catering solely for Bernese has been established. According to Russ and Rogers(1993), the first import was Senn v Schlossgut, a Swiss dog imported by Herr and Frau Behrens. Germany has strict controls on breeding, as do many European countries.

The breed is popular in Scandinavia. Norway first saw Bernese Mountain Dogs in the Second World War accompanying Italian troops, but the first attempt to establish the breed began in 1956. The breed club was formed in 1988, though an earlier club catering for large breeds, including the Bernese, had been started 26 years earlier. Finland was the first Nordic country to import the breed, in 1950, and the combined club (catering for the four breeds) was set up in 1965. The Swedish club was formed in 1968, some 13 years after the first importation. The Danish club was formed in 1979. Scandinavia is an important area for the breed, not only in terms of the quality of

the dogs, but because it is where much of the scientific research on the breed has taken place, notably in Sweden.

Holland was one of the first countries to import the Bernese, in 1924, with the first litter some two years later, and a club was established (for the four breeds) by the late 1930s. An outbreak of unprovoked aggression among Bernese Mountain Dogs (see page 152) in the 1970s did great harm to the breed in the Netherlands but a new club was set up towards the end of that decade. The Bernese came to Belgium during the 1970s and a club was established (for the four breeds) in 1979.

According to Fison-Bates (1986), the breed started in New Zealand with imported stock from Britain. Doreen Murdoch imported Kisumu Achilles (Oro de coin-Barre ex Karin v Hinterfeld) in 1973 and established the Durrbachler kennels. Others came in, including Forgeman Fancy in 1977.

Aust. Ch. Forgeman Folkhero (Glanzberg Blue Wind – Foldance At Forgeman), born 1980. An early import to Australia from Britain. Photo courtesy: Fison-Bates.

Both Fancy and Achilles became NZ Champions. The Balahu kennel of Yvonne Fison-Bates was begun in 1978 with Durrbachler China (who made an NZ title) and Durrbachler Merlin. About this time, Mrs Murdoch gave up the breed, so Balahu was virtually the only NZ kennel from about 1980 to 1985. With Barbara Tate of the Escarp kennels, Fison-Bates brought in NZ Ch. Meiklestane Dusky Emperor and later NZ Ch. Claishady Winged Dagger. Among others, Dagger sired Aust. and NZ Ch. Balahu Amazing Grace CDX ET, one of the few Bernese to gain a working qualification. New Zealand was among the first countries to establish an elbow scheme and it uses a hip scheme similar to that used in Britain.

In 1978 the first Bernese Mountain Dog went to Australia. The importer was Renee Edwards who brought in Durrbachler Shiralee from New Zealand. In the same year a British import, Aust. Ch. Millwire Clockwork Soldier, was imported by Miss M. Clayton. He eventually went to Lyn Brand and helped in establishing the Branbern kennels. Subsequently, Malcolm Smith established his Anderbern kennel in Victoria with the importation of Forgeman Folkhero, Forgeman Figaro and Attila Snowprincess, who all made Aust. Ch. titles. Only some 28 imports have reached Australia, of which possibly the most influential was initially Aust. and UK Ch. Choristma Monch of Vindissa who was taken out in 1985 when his owners, Ann and David Waterman, emigrated. In recent years, dogs have come in from other locations, notably Norway and the USA. An American import was Aust. and Am. Ch. Abbey Roads Echo in Orbit, whose father, Am. Can. Ch. Dallybecks Echo

NZ Ch. Balahu Jazzmatazz (Aust. Ch. Vindissa Night Voyager – Balahu Twelve Bar Blues), born 1994.

Photo courtesy: Fison-Bates.

NZ Ch. Clashaidy Winged Dagger (Gillro Flapjack Of Forgeman – Tarncred Tattoo Of Clashaidy), born 1985. An early import to New Zealand from Britain.   Photo courtesy: Fison-Bates.

Int. Ch. Alex v Angstorf.

Jackson, is also to be found in a few British bloodlines. A Norwegian import was Aust. Ch. Jojans Woody, whose father was Nor. Ch. Tertzo's King Shahzamana, a top winning Danish dog imported into Norway. Woody came in as a puppy.

Neither country has large numbers of Bernese and, in Australia, the size of the country militates against effective clubs and breed spread. Nor is the breed particularly suited to hot climatic conditions. Nevertheless, enthusiastic breeders exist in both countries. Relaxation of quarantine laws in March 1996 should help Australian breeders to make greater use of European and other bloodlines in the future.

Table 1.1 shows the registrations of certain countries for various periods and for most recent years.

Table 1.1 BMD registrations in selected countries

Period	SHSB	USA	UK	DKK
pre 1910	4			
1910-19	198			
1920-29	1048			
1930-39	1595	3		
1940-49	1542	19		
1950-59	2545	29		
1960-69	3859	210		
1970-79	7813	2215	506	102
1980-89		6739	4291	2062
1990-97		12707	5900(1)	686(2)
TOTAL		21922	10967	

(1)includes 1st quarter of 1997   (2)1990-92
SHSB = Switzerland DKK=Denmark

THE NEWFOUNDLAND 'BLOOD'
In December 1948, the Bernese bitch Christine v Lux gave birth to a litter sired by the Newfoundland Pluto v Erlengut. Most writers (Cochrane, 1987; Simonds, 1989; Chesnutt Smith, 1994) argue that the mating was an accident resulting from Pluto jumping over a fence to mate. However, Chesnutt Smith used the term "supposed" accidental mating and seems to hold the view that the mating might have been deliberate. She argues that, in the late 1940s, Swiss Bernese were in need of new blood and that temperaments were poor with many aggressive temperaments. A touch of Newfoundland blood might have been just the thing the breed needed. Whether accidental or intentional, there is no doubt that this mating had a profound effect upon the breed worldwide.

The Pluto/Christine litter produced four dogs and three bitches and, with Pluto being a pure-breeding black carrying neither Landseer nor brown, all seven were largely black with a few small white markings. One bitch (Babette) was bred from, being backcrossed to the Bernese Mountain Dog Aldo v Tieffurt.

This produced a litter, in March 1951, of four males and four females. The colours were approaching Bernese colours in most cases, but with minimal white except for three of the bitches. One of these (Christine v Schwarzwasserbachli) was mated to the Bernese Mountain Dog Osi v Allenluften and a litter of one male and four females was born in March 1952. These were typical Bernese-type animals since, by this stage, they were 87.5 per cent Bernese Mountain Dog. Only one dog, Alex v Angstorf, and his sister Bella v Angstorf were reared. Alex became World Champion at the

1956 Dortmund show and appears to be a typical Bernese of that period.

There was some opposition to the use of Alex v Angstorf but, under control from the club, he sired 51 litters and is to be found in almost all Bernese pedigrees in the world today. Cochrane (1987) states that the introduction of Newfoundland blood was desirable and useful, leading to wider, deeper chests, a black shining coat and a good Newfoundland temperament. She also argues that, after a couple of generations, the Newfoundland would be bred out completely since no blacks appeared in the litters that descended from Alex. This view is self-defeating and incorrect. In reality, black coloration could not appear, since it is a dominant allele (B), as is the absence of white (S). Alex could not have carried either allele since, if he had done so, he would not have been tricolour but solid black. Of course, other genes coming from the Newfoundland would still exist in the breed but, because there are many similarities in broad construction between the two breeds, it is the colour issue which is most obvious. The fact that Pluto v Erlengut appears at the back of many lines in almost all Bernese Mountain Dogs in the world does, however, emphasise the importance of the Newfoundland infusion and this may well have increased size and substance compared with Bernese from the first few decades of the 20th century. The case for continuing with Newfoundland 'blood', as one breeder in Britain is doing, has nothing to recommend it. It might give rise to an increase in size and substance, but it could add little to character, would undoubtedly harm hip status, and could introduce heart conditions not currently found in the Bernese. Alex was a lucky fluke and we should not tempt providence.

Figure 1.1 shows the pedigree of Alex v Angstorf, showing the line of descent from Pluto v Erlengut the Newfoundland. Note that Alex's sire, Osi v Allenluften, was the result of a father/daughter mating.

SO YOU WANT TO BUY A BERNESE? PROBLEMS AND VIRTUES AT A GLANCE

If you are potential buyer of a Bernese Mountain Dog, then it seems appropriate, in this first chapter, to give you a short summary of the breed. It is a large breed – a

Alex v Angstorf	Osi v Allenluften	Athos v Berghaus	Senn v Tiergarten
			Xantippe v Haslenbach
		Farandole v Allenluften	Athos v Berghaus
			Bella vd Schorenmatt
	Christine v Schwarzwasserbachli	Aldo vd Tieffurt	Eiger v Waldheimat
			Cilli v Ruglen
		Babette v Schwarzwasserbachli	PLUTO v ERLENGUT
			Christine v Lux

Figure 1.1 Pedigree of Alex v Angstorf SHSB 45178, born 15.3.1952. Breed/owner Fritz Mischler.

full Standard-sized male can be as big as 70 cms (27.5 ins) to the withers, with the smallest female being 58 cms (22.8 ins). It has a striking colour and the Standard demands a specific pattern, so mismarks do occur along with things like blue eyes. These features would not affect the suitability of a dog as a pet but would affect showing / breeding potential.

In broad terms, the breed is a friendly, laid-back dog but, as with any breed, exceptions can occur. European dogs are probably tougher, on the whole, than British or American animals. The breed is generally not long-lived and, though individuals may reach 13 or 14 years, the mean age at death is nearer to seven years, with cancers being a major killer of the breed. You will find those who will argue that their lines are long-lived or that the cancer theories are just theories; but you would be foolish to listen to such siren voices, because it is simply not true. Cancer is a major killer of this breed and the Bernese Mountain Dog is one of the worst breeds in the world for this problem. Mouth faults are common, ranging from the odd missing tooth to bite defects. In most cases, this would not affect the suitability of a pet but would affect show potential.

In their book on dog breeding, Walcowicz and Wilcox (1994) listed a series of defects that are known to exist within the breed and some of these are discussed in detail in Chapter Ten along with other problems. Some are very rare, others more common, but, if you are thinking of buying a Bernese, do not ignore the comments I have made against each item in the following list.

• **Cataract:** Rare, possibly inherited.
• **Cleft lip/Cleft palate:** Rare, dog is usually destroyed or dying at birth so not something you are likely to buy.
• **Entropion, also Ectropion:** Not uncommon.
• **Fragmented Coronoid Process:** Elbow arthroses feature very commonly in the breed. Do not buy from unscored parents under any circumstances, whatever the breeder tells you. Will lead to juvenile lameness and arthritis.
• **Gastric Torsion:** Not uncommon. Can kill.
• **Hip Dysplasia:** Common. Again, do not buy from parental stock that has not been graded or scored through a national scheme. Avoid breeders who do not assess hips, regardless of what they tell you – or you could be heading for long-term trouble.
• **Histiocytosis:** Inherited cancer. Not uncommon.
• **Hypoadrenocorticism:** Rare. May be inherited.
• **Hypomyelinogenesis:** Trembler. Rare inherited disease. Usually visible by three

Casparov v Hohen Gripfel (Int. Ch. Pilatus – Anouk vd Sandenburg).

months of age.

• **Progressive Retinal Atrophy:** Rare disease in the breed but common in dogs in general. Inherited. Leads to total blindness.

On the credit side, the breed is not only very beautiful to look at but is, in the main, very good with people and other animals and very affectionate. It is a quiet breed, compared with some, and very loyal.

Discuss these problems and virtues with the breeders of the litter you are looking at. If they dismiss them as irrelevant or appear to know nothing about them, then think twice about buying from such breeders. The fact that someone has a litter does not mean that the person in question is a skilled breeder or knows the first thing about the breed. Go to a breeder who is prepared to tell you about failings as well as virtues and who is going to make a contract of sale in which you know exactly what you are getting. Use only breeders who make an effort to test for things like hips and elbows, who can tell you something about their results in this field and who can fill in such data on the pedigree. Always ask to see hip and elbow score/grading sheets or certificates.

Even the best breeder can produce faulty stock, but the breeder who does nothing about testing for such things is unsafe as a source of puppies – so avoid him or her. Make sure that breeders are interested in what will happen to the puppy you buy and are prepared to rescue him/her should the need arise. If all they want is your money and the puppy off their hands, are they the sort of people you should be going to? We have a lifetime commitment to our puppies and will bring them back at whatever age. Rescue procedures do exist with many breed clubs in several locations, because some breeders do not accept their own breeding back and the whole thing is left to clubs. My view is that, if you will not rescue, then you should not be breeding!

2 THE BREED STANDARDS

INTRODUCTION

All pedigree (or pure-bred) dogs have a Breed Standard which is, in effect, a kind of blueprint of what the breed should look like. These Standards were usually first written by the originators of the breed club and, in the case of the Bernese Mountain Dog, these were the founders of the Swiss club – the Schweizerischer Klub für Berner Sennenhund – or a sub-committee of that body. Following normal procedure, the Swiss Kennel Club would adopt this and the Standard would then usually be accepted with minor modifications by the FCI (Fédération Cynologique Internationale), which controls dog breeding in most of the world, and by the UK Kennel Club (KC) and American Kennel Club (AKC) as well as other bodies that are outside FCI control (such as the Australian Kennel Union). The FCI headquarters are in Thun in Belgium.

At a meeting some years ago, kennel clubs agreed to accept the Standard of the country of origin of the breed, but universal adoption of this policy is still not in force, though there have been moves in this direction. In the following discussion, each clause of the FCI, UK and American Standards is given, together with an interpretation of them. Since the three Standards do not have the same headings throughout, the British KC version is used. Alternative headings are also given, together with the clause from the relevant Standard. The purpose of listing Standards clause by clause and of having the three together is to allow comparison of the three versions when seeking to interpret the breed blueprint. In essence, all are trying to achieve the same objective but some express it better than others. Certainly, the AKC version is better written and more explicit than the other two, which are too brief in some areas.

If you, the reader, are a would-be first-time owner, then you may wonder what the purpose of a Standard is and see little to be gleaned from a detailed examination of its

Ch. Forgeman Folksong At Tarncred (left), handled by Brenda Griffiths, becoming the first British Champion, under W.E. Foster at the SKC Championship Show, May 1977. The dog CC winner was Meiklestane Dark Ace, handled by Cynthia Totty (now Bailey). Dark Ace eventually made up.
Photo: William Moores.

meaning. Nevertheless, a good and conscientious breeder, from whom, hopefully, you have purchased, will be using the Standard as the criterion against which his or her breeding stock will be measured. The Standard is aimed at producing a beautiful, agile, functional dog that has an ideal character for a family companion. Although it will take a long time before you can assess a puppy and see in it the potential adult it will become, some appreciation of what breeders are trying to achieve, especially in functional features, will be of benefit.

THE BREED STANDARDS : CLAUSE BY CLAUSE

In the following discussion, the Standards (in bold type) are those of the KC, AKC, and FCI. The AKC used one Standard from 1937 to 1980. A revised version was adopted in August 1980 and a second revised version in March 1990, which is still in vogue today. It is the 1990 version which is used here. The FCI version is dated March 1993 and the British KC version 1985.

GENERAL APPEARANCE

KC: Strong, sturdy working dog, active, alert, well boned, of striking colour.

AKC: The Bernese Mountain Dog is a striking tri-coloured, large dog. He is sturdy and balanced. He is intelligent, strong and agile enough to do the draft and droving work for which he was used in the mountainous regions of his origin. Dogs appear masculine, while bitches are distinctly feminine.

FCI: Longhaired, tricoloured working dog of above medium size, sturdily built, yet agile; well balanced in all parts.

In broad terms, the three Standards seem agreed that the breed is a large one (a relative term) and of striking appearance, which its colour and strength ensures. The most important issue is probably the fact that the breed should be strong but mobile, and that it is an active breed. At a time when many British Bernese are overweight, seeming (and being) quite incapable of doing more than a couple of laps of the show ring, it is expedient that breeders and exhibitors go back to basics and read the three Standards, all of which are seeking an active, mobile dog. It is not a tricolour Newfoundland or a miniature Shire horse, but the Bernese is, and must be, a working dog capable of jumping, droving and pulling a cart. Being active does not mean that it cannot have good bone or that it should be like a large Border Collie, but agility and fitness should be a feature of *all* Bernese.

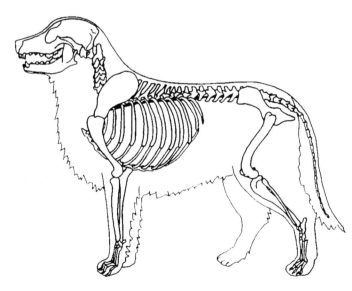

Skeleton of the Bernese Mountain Dog.

All drawings (from Bärtschi & Spengler, 1992), adapted By Viv Rainsbury.

CHARACTERISTICS
KC: A multi-purpose farm dog capable of draught work. A kind and devoted family dog. Slow to mature.

The Bernese Mountain Dog was developed as a farm dog, mainly to drive cattle and to be a guard. Subsequently it became a carting dog. Carting is not permitted upon the highway in Britain, as it is in Switzerland, but it can and does take place on private land quite legally. Note that the breed is described as slow to mature. It is thus surprising that some judges give high awards to young animals under 12 or 18 months of age. Selecting young animals in this way encourages early maturity and it is time that awards such as CC and Res. CC should not be given to youngsters. There is some restriction in parts of Europe as regards CACs or CACIBs, but a liberal and unwise approach exists in both the UK and USA.

TEMPERAMENT
KC: Self-confident, good-natured, friendly and fearless. Aggressiveness not to be tolerated.

Irish Ch. Annealdon Early Eclipse illustrating a typey animal with good markings, showing desirable cross and rich pigment.

Photo: Kelly.

AKC: The temperament is self-confident, alert and good-natured, never sharp or shy. The Bernese Mountain Dog should stand steady, though may remain aloof to the attentions of strangers.

BEHAVIOUR/TEMPERAMENT
FCI: Self-confident, attentive, vigilant, fearless in situations of everyday life, good-natured and devoted to his own people, self-assured and friendly towards strangers; of average and docile temperament.

All three Standards are agreed that the breed is self-confident, friendly and fearless. Aggressiveness is equally agreed upon as being undesirable. The breed does require confidence and, to that end, judges should think very carefully about placing dogs that lack this confidence, are blatantly fearful or who back away. Of course, an owner has to accept that a young puppy at his first show may not respond exactly as the owner hopes. Nevertheless, the animal should be penalised if he shows fear and to excuse him is unfair on other animals that are sound in character. Some dogs are reluctant to let their teeth be examined. This may be not so much fear as lack of training, and such animals should be given an opportunity to rectify their reluctance, but shy animals must be penalised. Aggression is not desired and there was a serious problem in the breed in Holland during the 1970s stemming from uncontrolled aggression, However, aggression that is unprovoked is not the same as defensive aggression. I would see no problem with a dog who is threatened or who sees his owner threatened and goes to the defence of himself or his owner. In some parts of Europe, many Bernese males at shows can and do demonstrate some degree of dominance. Quite often males around the ring will grumble at one another and I have been to continental shows and witnessed fights among males. This would be an extreme rarity at British shows and may reflect a difference in the type of character sought in distinct countries.

HEAD AND SKULL

KC: Strong with flat skull, very slight furrow, well defined stop; strong, straight muzzle. Lips slightly developed.

AKC: Expression is intelligent, animated and gentle. The eyes are dark brown and slightly oval in shape with close-fitting eyelids. Inverted or everted eyelids are serious faults. Blue eye color is a disqualification. The ears are medium sized, set high, triangular in shape, gently rounded at the tip, and hang close to the head when in repose. When the Bernese Mountain Dog is alert, the ears are brought forward and raised at the base;

Irish Ch. Annealdon Early Eclipse illustrating the dark eye, clean lips, and correct medium-sized, white head markings.   *Photo: Kelly.*

the top of the skull is flat on top and broad with a slight furrow and a well-defined, but not exaggerated, stop. The muzzle is strong and straight. The nose is always black. The lips are clean and, as the Bernese Mountain Dog is a dry-mouthed breed, the flews are only slightly developed. The teeth meet in a scissors bite. An overshot or undershot bite is a serious fault. Dentition is complete.

FCI: Head: Strong. Skull viewed from front and in profile very slightly rounded. Facial-cranial depression (stop) well defined without being too pronounced. Frontal furrow slightly marked. Nose: Black. Muzzle: strong, of medium length, nasal bridge straight. Lips: not much developed; well fitting to the jaws; with black pigmentation.

The head is the crowning glory of a beautiful Bernese and few would doubt the beauty of a strong male head. Nevertheless, the head should not be gross or overdeveloped but must fit the size of the dog. Despite the Newfoundland ancestry, we are not seeking a pronounced stop though a stop should be obvious. Excessive flews are not wanted. A Bernese should have a clean mouth without overdeveloped lips, and the sort of hanging lips seen in breeds like the St Bernard are not desired. The top of the skull should be flat with a slight furrow down the centre towards the front. Note that the latest FCI Standard seeks a slightly rounded skull, the reason for which change is unclear. The muzzle should be about as long as the skull and broad and deep (see below for eyes and ears). Note that a Bernese is not a head breed. Some judges are carried away by a beautiful head and fail to see limitations in the dog. In show ring terms, the head should be kept in perspective. Important it may be, but it is only part of the dog – not its whole.

MOUTH
KC: Jaws strong with a perfect, regular and complete scissor bite, i.e. upper teeth closely overlapping lower teeth and set square to the jaws.

FCI: Strong, complete dentition; scissor bite.

All dogs should have 28 deciduous teeth, which are lost in early puppyhood, and then have 42 teeth when adult. The number of teeth as a puppy is no indication of teeth in the adult; missing teeth can occur and should be faulted in relation to the number missing. Using I for incisors, C for canines, PM for premolars and M for molars, the pattern can be described for the upper and lower jaw on one side which is then multiplied by two to give the total number. Missing incisors in the Bernese are a rarity and almost always will be the result of an accident. The same is true of canines, which may have been knocked out or may be broken, but premolars and molars are often missing and there is a genetic basis to some of this. As a consequence, some penalty should be imposed in the case of missing PM and M teeth. In Switzerland a dog missing several PM or M cannot be graded higher than Good and it is a breeding disqualification. A dog with two missing PM as well as an undershot or overshot bite cannot rate higher than Very Good.

Faulty bites are not uncommon in Bernese. These can range from a minor misalignment of the incisors which, in Switzerland, would be tolerated and allow a grading of Excellent (provided that overall quality merits this grading) through to undershot, overshot and wry mouths.

As described in the Standard, the bite should be a scissor one in that the upper incisors should come in front of the lower ones, with the back of the upper ones touching the front of the lower ones. Deviations from this are failings and should be penalised according to severity. Overshot bites have a gap between the upper and lower incisors which can be relatively small or as much as 0.5 cm or more. This is a more serious fault than misalignment, but much will depend upon how far the animal is overshot. Often an overshot animal will show such misalignment of the teeth that the canines on the lower jaw may start to dig into the upper gums and lower canine(s) could need to be removed to prevent pain to the dog.

An undershot animal has the lower incisors in front of the upper and this is a still more serious fault, though it can range from a reverse scissor arrangement through to a bite akin to a Boxer or Bulldog. A wry mouth is a twisted bite and is relatively rare.

The deciduous pattern is:
$$\text{I}\,\frac{3}{3}\quad \text{C}\,\frac{1}{1}\quad \text{PM}\,\frac{3}{3} \times 2 \;=\; 28$$

The permanent pattern is:
$$\text{I}\,\frac{3}{3}\quad \text{C}\,\frac{1}{1}\quad \text{PM}\,\frac{4}{4}\quad \text{M}\,\frac{2}{3} \times 2 \;=\; 42$$

EYES
KC and FCI: Dark brown, almond shaped, well fitting eyelids.

A gentle expression is typical of a Bernese Mountain Dog and is achieved by an almond-shaped eye of dark brown colour.

A lighter colour is faulty but it is a minor fault relative to constructional ones. That is not to say that light eyes should not be penalised, but I would not agree with placing a dark-eyed but poorly constructed animal ahead of a well-constructed dog with a light eye. Some judges do tend to become fanatical about eyes and will penalise any animal, however good, if the eyes are not dark brown or even black – which latter mars the expression in any event. One must assess the whole animal and not become over-zealous in the pursuit of so-called perfection.

Entropion (inward-turned eyelids) and ectropion (outward-turned eyelids) are serious failings, but both can be corrected surgically with such skill that the original failing may be disguised. Judges should thus be careful. Unpigmented third eyelid is a relatively common fault in the breed. Usually it is specialist judges who become fanatical about things like eyes and they have to learn to keep such views in perspective.

EARS

KC: Medium sized, set high, triangular shaped, lying flat in repose, when alert brought slightly forward and raised at base.
FCI: Triangular shape, slightly rounded at the tips, set high, medium sized, in repose hanging flat and close to the head.

When aroused or alert the ears will be brought slightly forward and raised at the base, though the upper part will still hang forward. Low-set ears will detract from that alert look and are penalised on the Continent. It is important to trim out the long hairs (streamers) from the ears with a comb. Failure to do so will result in the impression of a thicker, shorter neck and an inability to distinguish the clean lines of the ears. Some people seem to like streamers, but they do detract and may often be there simply because it was less work to leave than to remove them!

NECK

KC and FCI: Strong, muscular and medium length.

NECK, TOPLINE, BODY

AKC: The neck is strong, muscular and of medium length. The topline is level from the withers to the croup. The chest is deep and capacious with well-sprung, but not barrel-shaped ribs and brisket reaching at least to the elbow. The back is broad and firm, the loin is strong. The croup is round and smoothly rounded to the tail insertion. The tail is bushy. It should be carried low when in repose. An upward swirl is permissible when the dog is alert, but the tail may never curl or be carried over the back. The bones in the tail should feel straight and should reach to the hock joint or below. A kink in the tail is a fault.

Bernese should have a medium-length neck. This is a relative term but it certainly means that short, stuffy necks are not desired. Often the short neck will be seen when the lay of the shoulder blade (scapula)

23

*Nellsbern Casablanca 1991-1998 (Ch.
Carlacot Genesis at Nellsbern – Redinka
Rose at Nellsbern): Winner of one CC
and three Reserve CCs. Pictured at 18
months and illustrating a correct shoulder
and excellent length of neck with a good
topline. Sire of Ch. Materas Ready Teddy
Go and the two CC winning Nellsbern
Elsa.*   *Photo: Hartley.*

FOREQUARTERS

**KC: Shoulders long, strong and sloping,
with upper arm forming a distinct angle,
flat lying, well muscled. Forelegs straight
from all sides. Pasterns flexing slightly.**

is too steep. Ideally, the scapula should lie
back at an angle approaching 45 degrees to
the point of the shoulder. The steep angle of
the scapula can be described as a forward
placed shoulder. It will alter the perspective
of length, may limit reach, though that is not
certain, and could make the dog put its head
upwards rather than forwards as is the
correct position.

**AKC: The shoulders are moderately laid
back, flat lying, well muscled and never
loose. The legs are straight and strong
and the elbows are well under the
shoulder when the dog is standing. The
pasterns slope very slightly but are never
weak. Dewclaws may be removed. The
feet are round and compact with well-
arched toes.**

SHOULDERS AND WITHERS
(From Bärtschi & Spengler 1992)

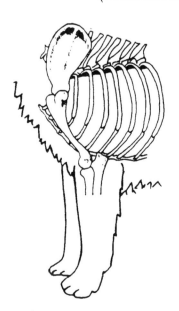 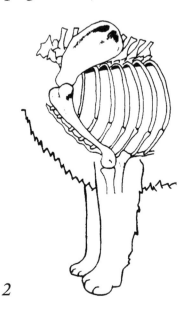

1   2

*Dog 1 has a short scapula and short humerus (upper arm), with the former laid too far forward. This
would probably lead to the appearance of a short neck and also to lack of chest development. Dog 2 has
a well laid back scapula and a longer upper arm than dog 1. The chest is well developed, and there
would be no shortage of neck.*

FRONT STANCE
(From Bärtschi & Spengler)

1

Correct stance.

2

Standing narrow across the chest and legs too close together.

3

Correct width, but the feet are turned outwards.

4

Standing tied in at the elbows, and with the feet turning outwards.

5

(5) Standing out at elbow, with the feet turned in. Examples 4 and 5 could indicate a dog with elbow problems, though it is not always the case. It is probable that dogs 2-5 would demonstrate some problems in movement, especially 4 and 5. Dog 1 should move correctly, but this is not guaranteed.

FCI: <u>Forequarters</u>: forelegs standing rather wide apart, straight and parallel. <u>Shoulders</u>: shoulder blades long, strong and well laid back, forming a not too open angle with the upper arm, well attached to the chest, well muscled. <u>Pasterns</u>: almost vertical, firm. <u>Feet</u>: short round and tightly bunched; well arched toes.

The lay of the shoulder has been described in the previous section above. The British Standard states that the shoulder blade and upper arm (humerus) form a distinct angle, which is rather a vague definition. The Swiss Standard asked for an obtuse angle (over 90 degrees) and many breeders would be seeking a right angle that was 90 degrees. It is probable that the best angle for movement is slightly more than 90 degrees, but the

Two 12-month-old males from the same litter of two, illustrating faulty fronts. The dog on the left is standing with legs splayed outwards, and the dog on the right has a narrow chest with both legs appearing to 'come from the same hole'.

Queen Of Clubs b 1986 (Gin Fizz – Ch. Lotsolove From Meadowpark): This bitch won her fourth Reserve CC at the Festival of Bernese in 1991, and the following day she won the CC at Bath under the author. Sadly, she died relatively young.

most crucial issue is that the scapula and humerus should be long. Not as long as in a trotting dog like the German Shepherd, but certainly of good length and of more or less equal lengths for the two bones. If the humerus is appreciably shorter than the scapula, then, in motion, the dog is likely to drop on the forehand (run downhill). Shoulders should be clean and flat-lying, with loaded shoulders not desired. Dogs who are aged or carry too much muscle around the shoulder may give a loaded impression. The forelegs should be straight and powerful and they should look straight from front and side, with powerful bone that matches the overall strength of the animal. There is a slight angle to the pasterns so that they are inclined forward. Dewclaws are likely to be present in all dogs and can be removed, though they do not need to be and frequently are not. The angle to the pastern helps in reducing force when the dog is moving.

FEET
KC: Short, round and compact.

Feet should be rounded with tightly arched toes though, on a soft surface, the feet may appear to flatten out and create some space between the toes. A good Bernese foot will rarely require nails to be trimmed as they will wear in normal movement.

BODY
KC: Compact rather than long. Height to length ratio, 9:10. Broad chest, good depth of brisket reaching at least to elbow. Well ribbed; strong loins. Firm straight back. Rump smoothly rounded.

FCI: <u>Body</u>: compact and sturdy. <u>Chest</u>: broad and deep, reaching to the elbows; forechest well developed; chest and ribcage of wide oval cross-section. <u>Back</u>: firm, straight and level. <u>Loins</u>: broad and strong. <u>Rump</u>: slightly rounded. <u>Belly</u>: not tucked up. <u>Tail</u>: bushy, reaching at least to the hocks; hanging straight down when at rest; carried level with back or slightly above when moving.

The Bernese is a 10:9 dog; that is to say, the length from point of chest to back of thigh is 10 units compared with the height from ground to wither of 9. Thus a dog that is 64 cms in height should be about 71 cms long, while a large 70-cm male should be about 78 cms long. Dogs of these extremes will certainly differ, obviously in length, but both would be of ideal proportions. It is important that the dog has a long ribcage so that the loin is short, as this can be a source of weakness. The chest should be broad but it should not be excessively so. Narrow dogs, who give the impression of both legs coming from the same place, are not wanted – but neither is a dog that is very wide in chest and stands wide as a consequence. The claim that the chest should reach at least to the elbow is badly worded, since the implication is that if the chest were to come down to the pastern it would be acceptable. The ideal chest depth should be about 50 per cent of the wither height with the chest reaching to about the elbow (which is now the FCI wording). The backline should be level from withers to croup with a long rounded croup and a relatively low-set tail. Few Bernese Mountain Dogs are high at the wither but many are overbuilt, i.e. the rump is higher than the withers. This is a failing, but much will depend upon age. Some puppies grow with level backs all through their development while others grow higher at the rump. However, once adult, the Bernese should be level-backed and an overbuilt rump is a failing.

HINDQUARTERS
KC: Broad, strong and well muscled. Stifles well bent. Hocks strong, well let down and turning neither in nor out. Dewclaws to be removed.

AKC: The thighs are broad, strong and muscular. The stifles are moderately bent and taper smoothly into the hocks. The hocks are well let down and straight as viewed from the rear. Dewclaws should be removed. Feet are compact and turn neither in nor out.

1 Correct hindquarter with good lay of pelvic bone giving good croup, long femur and good curve of second thigh.

2 Flat lie of pelvic bone giving a short, flat croup, a rather straight femur, and hence a lack of hind angulation. This dog will probably fly its tail in motion.

3 Good lay of pelvic bone, but slightly short femur length and a short second thigh so that the dog appears to have minimal hind angulation.

4 Very similar to dog 1, but the femur is slightly shorter, but with a longer tibia and fibula. Some judges might prefer dog 4, but dog 1 has the better curve of stifle.

1. Correct

2. Standing with feet turned out.

3. Cow hocked

4. Standing too narrow.

5. Bow legged

Dogs 2-5 would possibly demonstrate problems in movement, particularly numbers 3 and 5, though some dogs which stand cow-hocked (3) do not move that way.

FCI: <u>Hindquarters</u>: seen from the rear straight and not too narrow; hocks and feet neither turning in nor out. Dewclaws to be removed. <u>Thighs</u>: rather long, strong, broad and well muscled with well bent stifles. <u>Hocks</u>: strong, well angulated.

The hind limb should be broad-thighed and muscular. There should also be some length of stifle such that there is a degree of angulation. Many Bernese have very short second thighs. The hock should be well let down, i.e. the rear pastern should be relatively short. A long rear pastern (often incorrectly called the hock) is unsightly and will affect the way the dog moves as well as often creating a tendency to kick up when moving. Long rear pasterns are common in Britain, less so in America, though there some animals have ultra-short rear pasterns. In stance, the rear pasterns should be parallel and this should also be true of movement, but a dog that moves close at speed may be acceptable. Dewclaws on the rear foot is a dominant genetic trait and their absence recessive. Most Bernese do have hind dewclaws and they should be removed. Some have a fifth toe which should not be confused with a dewclaw and should not be removed.

Some dogs stand cow-hocked, often because they are excessively angulated or their rear pasterns are too long, but sometimes because it is the most comfortable way for that dog to stand. A dog which stands cow-hocked but corrects when moving is less seriously faulty than one which stands and moves in this fashion.

TAIL
KC: Bushy, reaching just below hock. Raised when alert or moving but never curled or carried over back.

The tail should reach at least to the hock joint and preferably slightly longer, but should not be so long that it touches the ground. Tail carriage in the Bernese has always been a variable trait with a variety of failings being seen, ranging from a tight curl rather like some Spitz breeds through to a tail that arches over the back. Ideally, the tail in repose should hang in a sabre-like format. In movement, the tail should be carried straight out or can be elevated above the horizontal but it must really get no higher. A high tail carriage may result from a high-set tail and obviously an excited dog may elevate the tail, but, carried too high, the tail carriage will adversely affect hind action.

GAIT/MOVEMENT
KC: Stride reaching out well in front, following well through behind. Balanced stride in all gaits.

AKC: The natural working gait of the

Bernese Mountain Dog is a slow trot. However, in keeping with his use in draft and droving work, he is capable of speed and agility. There is good reach in front. Powerful drive from the rear is transmitted through a level back. There is no wasted action. Front and rear legs on each side follow through in the same plane. At increased speed, legs tend to converge towards the centre line.

FCI: Sound and balanced movement in all gaits covering a lot of ground; free stride reaching out well in front, with plenty of drive from behind; at the trot, coming and going, legs moving forward straight and parallel.

Many Bernese owners seem to have a phobia about moving their dogs at a trot. Many feel that once round the ring is more than enough, and judges who seek longer gaiting are frowned upon. Such judges are right. The Bernese is, or should be, an active breed and it should not be beyond its capability to move around a ring several times. Ideally, the dogs should be assessed at the walk and at the slow trot. However, many Bernese will pace when asked to walk. The breed is not a fast trotter but, as the AKC Standard states, should be capable of

Redinka Rose At Nellsbern 1985-1991 (Ch. Duntiblae Dark Protector – Forgeman Folksinger); Foundation bitch of the Nellsbern kennels. Note the excellent hindquarters and the beautiful topline. She had 3:3 Hips (near Normals). Photo: Trafford.

Ch. Clashaidy Nordic Fire, handled by owner Virginia Stenner, in the group Ring at Crufts 1989. He was made up on the day. In this photo, he shows his excellent side gait, reaching out well in front whilst holding his topline.   Photo: Dalton.

varied gaits. Most of the power should come from the hind limbs, which is then transmitted through a strong, powerful, muscled back. A dog that is overweight and/or soft in back is unlikely to transmit power. The front legs should reach out with good extension which will depend upon the length of the bones of the forelimb. The angle of the shoulder may have some bearing on front reach but the shoulder is not stationary in motion, and thus it is the length of the humerus, and of the radius and ulna, which influence reach. The dog should not drop in front which it is likely to do if it is short in foreleg, short in upper arm or kicks up too high at the back. A dog that is tied in

at the elbows – possibly because of elbow arthrosis or some other elbow problem – will tend to toe in and will be unable to move correctly, and will no more be able to move correctly than a dog that is out at elbow.

COAT
KC: Soft, silky with bright natural sheen, long, slightly wavy but should not curl when mature.

AKC: The coat is thick, moderately long and slightly wavy or straight. It has a bright, natural sheen. Extremely curly or extremely dull-looking coats are undesirable. The Bernese Mountain Dog is shown in natural coat and undue trimming is to be discouraged.

FCI: Long, smooth or slightly wavy.

The breed is long-coated compared with its three cousin breeds. However, it is not, and should not be, a Rough Collie, and excessive coat is neither functional nor desirable. The coat should be only moderately long, straight rather than wavy and certainly not curly. The UK Standard requirement of soft and silky is an aberration which has crept in and for which there is no justification. A soft, silky coat would have no place in the Bernese Oberland. A bright sheen is desired and enhances the beauty of the dog. However, the construction of the dog should not be overlooked because of lack of coat, nor should a thick, long coat be allowed to hide constructional failings. A dog needs only as much coat as is functional and profuse chest hair detracts from shape and from function.

Ch. Folkdance at Forgeman, 6. 1977), (Ch. Tarncred Puffin – Ch. Forgeman Folksong At Tarncred), winning her sixth CC at the Championship Show of the BMD Club of Great Britain under Tom Horner in 1981. Note the high-quality hind angulation, the rear drive, and the correct tail carriage.   Photo: Kennedy.

The Breed Standards

COLOUR

KC: Jet black with rich reddish brown on cheeks, over eyes, on all four legs and on chest. Slight to medium sized symmetrical white head markings (blaze) and white chest markings (cross) are essential. Preferred but not essential, white paws, the white not reaching higher than pastern, white tip to tail. A few white hairs at nape of neck, and white anal patch are undesirable but tolerated.

FCI: Jet black with rich tan markings on cheeks, over the eyes, on all four legs and on the chest, and with white markings as follows: clean white symmetrical markings on the head: blaze extending towards the nose on both sides to a muzzle band; the blaze should not reach the tan markings above the eyes, and a white muzzle band should not extend beyond the corners of the mouth. Moderately, large, unbroken white markings on throat and chest. Desirable: white feet, white tip of tail. Tolerated: small white patch at nape of neck, small white anal patch.

COLOR AND MARKINGS

AKC: The Bernese Mountain Dog is tri-colored. The ground color is jet black. The markings are rich rust and clear white. Symmetry of markings is desired. Rust appears over each eye, on the cheeks, reaching to at least the corner of the mouth, on each side of the chest, on all four legs and under the tail. There is a white blaze and muzzle band. A white marking on the chest typically forms an inverted cross. The tip of the tail is white. White on the feet is desired but must not extend higher than the pasterns. Markings other than those described are to be faulted in direct relationship to the extent of the deviation. White legs or a white collar are serious faults. Any ground color other than black is a disqualification.

Markings vary in this breed only as to the extent of the white and the distribution of the tan, in that the same basic pattern is seen in all specimens. The Standard is, however, quite clear that the markings on the head – which encompass the blaze and the muzzle – are slight to medium. An overmarked dog who has a large white muzzle, a very wide blaze and with white on the muzzle that extends back beyond the mouth has a series of failings. Contrary to popular belief, the absence of white on the feet or of a white tip to the tail are not failings, although the AKC Standard seems to suggest that the latter is. Such features are preferred, but their absence is not a fault. Thus a dog with white feet should not be placed above one without white feet if the latter is better constructed. Only in the event of equality of merit should the white feet/tail tip be taken into account. White feet markings extending higher than the pasterns are not desirable.

The KC Standard seems to suggest that a white chest cross is essential, in which event many excellent dogs would be penalised. The cross pattern is desirable but the white chest markings should not be excessive. The clause has now gone from the FCI Standard.

The white pattern of the Bernese is termed 'Irish spotting' and in some breeds, e.g. Boxers, the white neck band is desirable. In the Bernese Mountain Dog, however, there has been selection to restrict this so that it does not extend around the neck. If it does, it is penalised. Unfortunately, breeders have

HEAD AND CHEST MARKINGS
(From Bärtschi & Spengler 1992)

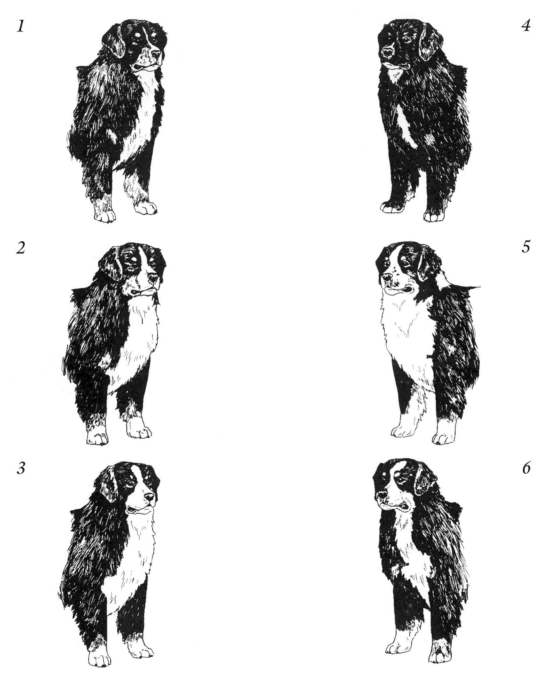

Dogs 1, 2 and 3 all fit the requirements of the Breed standard in respect of markings, and thus are equally acceptable. I would personally prefer Dog 1 to 2 and 3, but this choice would only come into play if I were trying to split hairs. None of these three dogs should be penalised for markings. Dog 4 is decidedly undermarked and, to that extent, should be penalised. Dog 5 is overmarked. It has rather too much chest white, the muzzle markings extend beyond the mouth, and there are flecks on the muzzle. The nape mark is too large, and white runs up the inside of the left leg. Dog 6 is satisfactory on chest markings, but has too much white on the muzzle, and the left leg markings extend too far up the leg so that , as with dog 5, the tan markings on the leg have almost gone. Dog 6 is also not symmetrically marked.

not completely eliminated modifier genes which increase or decrease the extent of the colour. Thus, at intervals, white collars can occur, as can totally white heads. These are failings, but breeders should understand the genetics behind such events. A few white hairs on the back of the neck are tolerated. Note that, in puppies, more white appears at birth than will eventually endure. Although rare (I have not seen one), it is possible to get Bernese that do not have black ground colour but are red and tan and white. This has nothing to do with St Bernard ancestry (improbable), but is the recessive bb combination which prevents black pigment on coat and nose.

SIZE
KC: Dogs: 64-70cms (25-27.5 ins). Bitches: 58-66cms (23-26 ins).

FCI: Dogs: 64-70cms at withers; ideal size 66-68cms. Bitches: 58-66cms at withers; ideal size 60-63cms.

SIZE, PROPORTION, SUBSTANCE
AKC: Measured at the withers, dogs are 25-27.5 inches; bitches are 23-26 inches. Though appearing square, Bernese Mountain Dogs are slightly longer in body than they are tall. Sturdy bone is of great importance. The body is full.

Size is very explicit and essentially the same in all three Standards, but the FCI version gives ideal sizes of 66-68 cms for males and 60-63 cms for females. Thus the clamour for very big dogs is unjustified by this Standard. Looking at the overall range, it is feasible for a bitch to be larger than a dog because the two height ranges overlap to the extent of two centimetres. It is thus perfectly

Moor Of Venice b 1995 (Nellsbern Casablanca – Jona v Mont-Dedos) illustrating white markings that have gone too far up the legs. Note that the head markings are very good. White markings are not essential on the feet, but they should not extend over the pastern.

acceptable to have a best bitch that is larger than the best dog, without this being in any way wrong. It is, however, important that Bernese breeders fully understand size. In Britain, most people grossly overestimate the size of their dogs, because most breeders do not have a measuring stick and have never used one. Their dogs are unused to being measured and breeders are unable to accurately estimate size because they so rarely measure any dog. This would be less likely in Europe where breeders breed survey, and thus measure, dogs regularly. The use of measuring sticks would help breeders to better understand size in the breed. Details of size in surveyed dogs appear on page 142. Increasing size is likely to bring about straighter hind angulation and breeders would do well to stick to the ideal sizes recommended in the FCI Standard.

FAULTS

KC and AKC: Any departure from the foregoing points should be considered a fault and the seriousness with which the fault should be regarded should be in exact proportion to its degree.

FCI: Light bone structure, undershot or overshot bite, absence of teeth other than one or two PM. PM1 (first premolar); M3 (third molar) not to be considered. Entropion, ectropion, sway back, rump higher than withers, sloping backline, curled tail, kink tail, distinctly curled coat. Faults of colour and markings – absence of white on head. Blaze too large and/or muzzle band reaching noticeably beyond the corners of the mouth. Large white patch at nape of neck. White collar. White markings on forelegs reaching distinctly beyond half-way point of pasterns (boots). Disturbingly asymmetrical white markings on head and chest. Black ticks and stripes on white of chest. Dirty white (strong spots of pigmentation). Black coat with a touch of brown or red. Weak temperament, aggressiveness.

The FCI has a long list of undesirable failings and Swiss breeders have a long series of failings that would not be accepted in a breeding animal. Blue eyes are inherent in the breed and many famous animals have had blue eyes in their ancestry. This is a feature often associated with large amounts of white, though not necessarily with white breeds.

Certainly, the British tendency in some quarters to like lots of white is not justified by the Standard, nor is it desirable.

NOTE

KC and FCI: Male animals should have two apparently normal testicles fully descended into the scrotum.

Although the KC now allows castrated males to be shown, this is a retrograde step. If a dog is castrated, it is uncertain whether he originally had two testicles or whether he was a unilateral or bilateral cryptorchid. Since the purpose of shows is to identify suitable breeding stock and compare it with those of other breeders, the exhibition of neutered males (or females) is somewhat pointless. Of course, one cannot identify the neutered female, though she may well be more heavily coated.

DISQUALIFICATIONS

AKC: Blue eye color, any ground color other than black.

DISQUALIFYING FAULTS

FCI: Split nose, wall eye, short coat, double coat (stockhaar), other than tricoloured coat, other than black main colour.

Although only the AKC and FCI Standards list disqualifications, most judges would probably cull animals from the prizes along the lines mentioned above, all of which are self-explanatory.

3 *FEEDING THE BERNESE*

NUTRIENTS AND ENERGY

To keep a dog healthy it needs to be given the right amount of food of the right composition. Dog breeds vary in size more than any other species, from a Chihuahua at just over 1kg (2.2lbs) in weight to a St Bernard which may weigh over 110kg (242lbs). The Bernese Mountain Dog, depending upon size and sex, is around the 45kg (99lbs) mark (though a large range occurs around this figure). Clearly, the amount of food needed will depend, in part, upon the size of the animal being fed, but the composition of the diet could be identical. Nutrients can be divided into five basic component parts. They are:

Carbohydrates: these provide energy and include sugars and starch.

Fats: these also provide energy but they do so in concentrated form, in that they carry more energy per unit of weight than do carbohydrates. Fats help in the absorption of certain vitamins and they provide essential fatty acids (EFA), which are substances that are required if certain bodily functions are to take place.

Proteins: these provide amino acids, which help in the growth of the animal and in the repair of cells and body tissues. Proteins can be broken down by the animal to provide energy akin to that provided by carbohydrates.

Vitamins: these are divisible into fat-soluble and water-soluble vitamins. They help to regulate bodily functions and some are essential to the health of the dog.

Minerals: calcium and phosphorus are the two principal minerals required in nutrition and they are needed not only for the growth of bones and teeth but also in growth and repair of tissues. Other minerals are called trace elements in that they are needed in small or minute quantities but, without them, the animal would exhibit deficiency symptoms.

In addition to these five nutrients the animal requires access to water. It would be wrong to call water a nutrient but it is essential to life and, without adequate amounts of water, the dog's health would be impaired. Most of the feeds offered to a dog contain several of these nutrients as well as water. The energy content of a food is measured in kilocalories (kcal) where 1 kcal is the amount of heat required to raise the temperature of 1kg of water by 1 degree C. The more recent method is to use joules, and 1 kcal is equivalent to 4.2 kilojoules (kJ).

Energy is required simply to maintain the animal. An animal that is doing nothing will require a set amount of energy simply to maintain itself because, although the animal may appear to be doing nothing, it is breathing, its blood is still circulating, its digestive system is still functioning and it is repairing or replacing cells. What the animal requires to do this would be termed its maintenance requirement. If an animal is fed more than this basic requirement then, although some of the energy will go through the body unused and hence be wasted, some will be used by the animal which would therefore increase in weight. Many Bernese are overweight and this is largely because they are given more energy in their diet than they require for the activities in which they indulge.

If your dog is engaged in some activity, such as running, carting, tracking etc., then he will expend more energy than he would if he was just lying around. Accordingly, he will require more energy. By the same token, if your bitch is pregnant or lactating (nursing a litter) then she will require more energy, and the amount of energy she will need will depend upon the stage of pregnancy, the number of puppies being carried, and later, the number of puppies being nursed.

In essence we can say that, for any given size of dog, there will be a specific energy requirement needed for maintenance and also that the energy requirement will increase as the dog indulges in other activities such as those described in the previous paragraph. Quite apart from energy, the dog will need to be fed the correct amount of other nutrients, especially vitamins and minerals. Some of

these are produced by the dog himself; others must be given in the diet. An excess of some minerals or vitamins would obviously be wasteful but might have no adverse effect on the dog. In contrast, an excess or deficiency of other vitamins or minerals can be harmful.

DIGESTION
The dog is usually thought to be a carnivore by most owners but, while this is certainly true of the cat (a genuine carnivore), the dog is more of an omnivore. This is illustrated by the dentition of the dog. A true carnivore does not need grinding molars (which the dog has), while a herbivore (grass eater) has no piercing and ripping teeth (canines). Many dogs bolt their food, an action which, if undertaken by their owners, would almost certainly result in indigestion. This is because humans need to produce saliva in the mouth to begin the digestion of starch. The enzyme responsible does not appear to exist in the dog, so that digestion does not have to be started in the mouth. Dogs do possess salivary glands and will salivate, as Pavlov demonstrated at the start of the 20th century. However, saliva is mostly water.

From the mouth, food passes to the oesophagus through which matter passes by peristaltic action (wave-like contractions) into the stomach. This organ stores food and allows it to pass into the small intestine at a controlled rate. The stomach also initiates digestion by producing acid and the enzyme pepsin. At the entrance to the stomach is the cardiac sphincter, and the dog has a capacity to stimulate this sphincter by signals from the brain. This allows the stomach to empty the contents back via the mouth (vomiting). This is a common feature of the dog and is useful since it allows the animal to get rid of anything toxic. The Cape hunting dog or African wild dog (*Lycaon pictus*) uses this ability to bring back food for its cubs, while in the domestic dog it can act as a safety mechanism. Dogs with a tendency to bloat may save their own lives if they have the capacity to vomit up the contents of their stomach.

In the stomach, food is digested in part by gastric juices and then passes on to the small intestine. Here, digestion and absorption continues, breaking down carbohydrates into their component sugars and making a start on other food components. It is beyond the scope of a general book like this to delve deeply into the canine nutritional process which could occupy a large book on its own, but readers with an interest in delving deeper are recommended to read Burger (1995).

A feature that must be discussed is the action of the pancreas. This acts as an exocrine and endocrine gland. That is to say, it secretes enzymes into the small intestine (proteases, lipases and amylases) and also secretes hormones into the bloodstream (e.g. insulin). The pancreas is much more active in the dog than the cat but, in some animals, it can be faulty, leading to pancreatic insufficiency, a possible genetic disorder discussed elsewhere.

From the small intestine food digesta passes to the large intestine which principally absorbs salt and water. Food passes through this section rather slowly. Most bacteria are found in this section of the digestive tract and these help break down the ingesta into components that the dog can utilise. Bacteria are part of the intestine of a healthy dog and are not usually other than beneficial, though sometimes problems can occur. Fat is harmful to these bacteria and one of the problems of pancreatic insufficiency is that it

causes fat to leave the small intestine undigested which thus harms bacterial activity.

From the large intestine ingesta pass through to the rectum which is evacuated under voluntary control. If food passes too quickly through the digestive tract so that it is not properly digested and absorbed, then diarrhoea can occur and, if persistent, can lead to dehydration. Usually, diarrhoea is short-lived and not particularly harmful but, if it persists, veterinary treatment needs to be sought or it can result in death.

VITAMINS
The role of vitamins is important and can be crucial. Their role and the consequences of deficiencies or excesses are shown in Table 3.1.

In Table 3.1, the water-soluble vitamins have no effects given for excess amounts. This is because it is believed that toxicity does not occur or that extremely high abnormal levels would be required. It should be noted that Vitamin C is synthesised by the dog, so claims that it is implicated in hip dysplasia are ill-founded.

In Table 3.2, the role of minerals and the consequences of deficiencies or excesses are listed.

BALANCING THE DIET
Dogs can be fed in a multiplicity of ways and it is possible to provide a balanced diet via a large number of routes. A balanced diet is one which maintains the body in a state of metabolic equilibrium. A balanced diet should provide all the essential nutrients needed by that dog for a healthy, hopefully long, life. These nutrients will enable the functions that you expect of that dog to be carried out. Any diet will require energy

Table 3.1 The role of Vitamins in the dog

Vitamin	Useful for	Deficiency	Excess
FAT-SOLUBLE			
A	Sight, Bones, Teeth	Eye disorders Respiration	Bone disorders Teeth problems
D	Bones	Rickets	Calcification of soft tissues
E	Fertility	Numerous Blood, Nerves, Fertility etc	May be none
WATER-SOLUBLE			
Thiamin (B_1)	Carbohydrate Metabolism	Metabolism problems	
Riboflavin (B_2)	Cellular growth	Eye disease Skin disorders	
Pantotheic acid	Growth	Depression Fatty liver, ulcers [very unlikely to occur]	
Niacin	Digestion	Oral ulcers Blacktongue	
Pyridoxine (B_6)	Metabolism	Weight loss Anaemia	
Biotin	Metabolism	Scaly skin [very unlikely to occur]	
Folic acid B_{12}	DNA production Fat metabolism	Anaemia Neurological problems Pernicious anaemia	
Choline	as B_{12}	Kidney/liver dysfunction	

Ascorbic acid (C): Not required as dog synthesises its own.

which will be released by proteins and carbohydrates and by fat, though the last named will produce more energy than the first two.

Table 3.3 shows the typical nutrient content of several kinds of dog food. The major differences between these is the moisture content. A tin of meat jelly may contain 83 per cent water, whereas a complete dry food may have only 6 per cent, and the ingredients are given as percentages in the actual feed as fed. This may make comparisons difficult to draw. A level of 30 per cent protein in a dry food that has a moisture content of 6 per cent and thus is 94 per cent dry matter may, at first glance,

Table 3.2 The role of minerals in the dog

Mineral	Useful for	Deficiency	Excess
PRINCIPAL MINERALS			
Calcium (Ca)	Bones, teeth, blood clotting, nerve impulses	The ratio of Ca:P should be about 1:1 and if Ca is less there are bone deficiencies	High ratios linked to bone problems
Phosphorus (P)	Bones, teeth, enzyme systems		
Potassium (K)	Nerves, muscles	Muscular weakness, heart and kidney lesions	Unlikely
Sodium (Na) and Chloride (Cl)	Involved with electrolytes	Unlikely	
Magnesium (Mg)	Soft tissues, heart, skeletal muscle. Na/Cl metabolism	Muscular weakness Convulsions	
TRACE ELEMENTS			
Cobalt (Co)	Part of Vit. B_{12}		
Copper (Cu)	Linked to Zn Enzyme systems, Pigment, melanin	Anaemia Bone disorders	Anaemia Toxicosis
Iodine (I)	Thyroid hormones	Goitre	Anorexia Fever
Iron (Fe)	Blood haemoglobin and myoglobin	Anaemia	Anorexia Weight loss Poor growth
Manganese (Mn)	Enzyme systems		
Selenium (Se)	Linked to Vit. E	Muscle degeneration	Toxic
Zinc (Zn)	Skin/growth	Skin disorders, testicular degeneration	None

appear much higher than 9 per cent protein in a meat jelly that is 80 per cent moisture (20 per cent dry matter). However, in dry matter terms, the two feeds have protein contents of 31.9 per cent and 45 per cent respectively.

If you are feeding raw meat then, depending upon the type (species), you are dealing with a feed that is about 75 per cent water and about 20 per cent protein. If using offal, then the water content may vary from 68 per cent (fresh liver) to 88 per cent (tripe) with protein content ranging from 9 per cent (tripe) to 21 per cent (liver). In broad terms, meats are low in calcium relative to phosphorus and, if fed alone, would almost certainly be deficient in minerals. Some meats lack vitamins A and D, but liver would be a good source of both.

Table 3.3 Nutrient content of feeds

Type of food	Moisture %	Protein %	Fat %	Carbohydrate %	Ca %	P %
Complete dry	6	30.0	11.0	46.0	1.3	1.1
Mixer biscuit	6	13.0	7.5	66.5	1.3	0.5
Meat in jelly	83	7.0	4.5	4.0	0.3	0.2
Meat chunks in jelly	79	7.0	4.5	7.0	0.5	0.4
Meat in jelly (pups)	80	9.0	6.0	2.5	0.4	0.3
Semi-moist food	21	17.0	8.0	45.0	1.3	1.1
Mixture of meaty dog food and biscuit at 3:1 ratio	63	10.0	6.0	18.0	0.6	0.5

(after Earle and Smith, 1995)

FEEDING YOUR PUPPY

Most people will buy their Bernese at about eight weeks, so we will begin with nutrition at that age and deal with nutrition prior to this point in the chapter on mating and whelping. At eight weeks your Bernese puppy will weigh around 10kg (22lbs). It will have been weaned from its mother and will be on a diet fed probably four times per day: first thing in the morning, about midday, around five and then about eight or nine at night. Individual owners will vary as to time of feeding but it is necessary to feed the dog several times per day in order that the digestion of nutrients can be spread out and thus the best use be made of the feed. The amount fed will determine the speed of growth and the size of the puppy during its early life. However, provided that an animal is not deficient in nutrients, it will eventually reach its genetically determined size.

Whether the dog gets there quickly or more slowly will not have much bearing upon final weight. A Bernese should reach some 50 per cent of its adult weight (i.e. about 20-25kg [44-55lbs]) by the time he is around six months of age. The breed is, however, a large

one and slow-maturing, and owners should not be eager to see rapid growth.

It is important that the new owners faced with feeding the eight-week-old puppy do not immediately change his diet. Regardless of the type of diet being fed, a sudden change could lead to problems of diarrhoea. It must be remembered that the puppy has had the trauma of a change of home, possibly a long journey and has left behind his littermates. He may well be reluctant to eat at his new home and may take a couple of days to adjust. The new owners should seek to feed the puppy on the same diet as was fed at the breeder's establishment. To this end, prior communication should have been made so that the new owners have already got the correct food to hand.

A puppy has a higher energy requirement

A nice typey and even litter sired by Majanco Tamaro ex Majanco Quitanara, bred by Doris Lenden. Feeding individually is an excellent idea – if the puppies will stick to their own dishes.

Ch. Alyngarn Adversity (left) as a puppy, and Alyngarn Cheri Amour, dam of Ch. Alyngarn Amourette and Amitie, a multiple Reserve CC winner.

Table 3.4
Energy needs of a BMD puppy

Body weight kg (lbs)	Age Months	Energy need kJ/day
10 (22)	2	7348
15 (33)	3	9961
20 (44)	5-6	7411
35 (77)	12	9769
45 (99)	24	8840

after Legrand-Defretin & Munday(1993).

than an adult per unit of body weight and will have higher protein and calcium needs because of the rate of bone growth. Calcium level must be related to that of phosphorus so as to avoid imbalances which can, in a large breed like the Bernese, lead to growth problems and complications with bone conditions like OCD (osteochondritis dissecans), At this age, a puppy needs an energy-dense feed that is highly palatable and easily digestible. Our own personal preference is to use complete diets. This is not to imply that similar diets cannot be concocted from a variety of ingredients but simply that a complete diet is, by definition, complete and does not require any additions. One animal may eat more than another but both would be eating the same composition.

Legrand-Defretin and Munday (1993) have put forward energy requirements of puppies, based on age and weight, and these are summarised in Table 3.4 for a Bernese puppy, using approximate body weights and extrapolating where necessary.

Puppy complete foods tend to be small-grained and most Bernese would require a larger-grained feed long before their junior (12-month-old) days. We tend to put a puppy on to junior complete feed by six months or slightly older. In the early days, we might moisten a complete diet but very quickly Bernese seem to want to have something to crunch and thus prefer the diet dry. If you were feeding meat chunks in jelly for a puppy of 20 kg (44lbs) then it would need about 7411 kJ per day (7.4 MJ) which, with meat chunks containing some 0.39 MJ per 100g means about 2 kg (4.4lbs) of food or about five normal-sized cans. This is likely to be more expensive than a complete diet. You should not skimp on the feeding of puppies but, by the same token, you do not need to spend more than is needed to achieve the same task.

By about four to five months a puppy would be down to three meals per day and then down to two meals by six months of age. By this stage, the puppy would be on a junior complete diet and would move on to an adult diet by about nine to twelve months. Most manufacturers recommend weighing out feed and some argue that their diets, which may appear more costly than others in absolute terms, are cheaper in that you have to use less feed because of energy density. We have no argument with this view but find that, with many dogs, weighing out feed is a time-consuming business. We prefer to assess the amount fed in relation to the condition of the dog. If a dog looks slightly overweight, then it is either eating too much or not being exercised sufficiently. The policy works in that, of the 16 dogs (mostly German Shepherds and Bernese) that we have at the time of writing, none are overweight and all are hard and fit. In the past ten years I cannot recall having a fat dog on the premises.

You can produce acceptable-quality diets using a mixture of ingredients but, the more you move away from good-quality proprietary foods, the more you are placed in the position of calculating ingredients and particularly working out correct calcium/phosphorus ratios and vitamin/mineral contents. This is far from easy, and miscalculation can result not only in waste, but in excesses or deficiencies of specific ingredients.

There are those who argue that complete feeds are dangerous, based on anecdotal 'evidence', but I do not subscribe to this view though I do feel that you should buy feeds of high quality from reputable manufacturers. Buy by the sack (usually in sizes of 10, 15 or 20 kg [22, 33 or 44lbs]) and do not buy loose. Leaving food in a sack and selling it loose does run the risk of it being contaminated by rats or mice. If you have several dogs, it is easier to keep feedstuffs in large plastic containers (dustbins!) but, in that event, you should empty them completely before refilling or make sure that the new food goes at the bottom and the old is placed on the top of the pile so that it is used first.

FEEDING THE ADULT DOG

Once a dog is an adult, I tend to feed once or occasionally twice per day and to feed a less energy-dense diet unless the dog is being shown, bred from, lactating or is actively worked. Dogs being shown or worked are fed high-quality, energy-dense diets, but those ticking over in retirement, or old dogs, are fed differently. Old age is a relative term and a Bernese at six would be considered older than a German Shepherd (our other breed) at the same age. The average age at death of Bernese is around seven, though some do live longer, while German Shepherds live to nearer ten. Older dogs must usually be fed less because they are less active and their basal metabolic rate will tend to decline. Older animals may have a higher protein requirement, but this can be met by the use of higher-quality proteins rather than simply feeding more. Clearly, one cannot generalise, as some older dogs remain very active and I have known German Shepherd stud dogs siring puppies in their twelfth year.

Highly active dogs will require more food than less active dogs, sometimes two to three times the normal adult quota. This, of course, would be for a highly active dog such as a sled dog. A Bernese who was carting would certainly need a higher feed intake than one doing little or nothing, but carting is not the same as a Siberian Husky pulling a sled, in which case the activity takes place over a long period. A Husky in those circumstances would probably need a high fat content in the diet in order to provide the energy needed to permit the exercise and at the same time maintain body temperature. In contrast, a racing dog active for a relatively short duration would require a higher carbohydrate intake.

4 *LIVING WITH YOUR BERNESE*

Living with a dog has little to do with its beauty or lack of it, but rather with its character and temperament. There is, of course, much pleasure in living with a beautiful dog and, certainly, beauty costs no more to keep than does the lack of it but, in the end, the character of the dog is what we live with. Those of us who show dogs are often inclined to look at the beauty aspect of a dog first and we sometimes forget that showing is just a temporary aspect of a dog's life. Life in a kennels is not ideal for any dog – especially not a sensitive breed like the Bernese – but the crucial thing is the human contact. Sleeping in a kennel is not really important if the dog gets lots of human contact during the working day.

From the classic work of Scott and Fuller (1965) it is generally agreed that there are several stages in a dog's life that have a bearing upon behaviour. In a project that began in 1946 and was reported in detail in their 1965 book, they argued that the neonatal stage (0-21 days) has little effect upon the puppy. From 21-28 days, daily handling is important and puppies become increasingly responsive to their surroundings. From 4 to 12 weeks, socialisation was deemed crucial, in that exposure to all kinds of new experiences is desirable for the correct development of the dog. The final stage from 12 weeks to sexual maturity tends to reinforce what had been learned in the 4 to 12 weeks period.

The Bernese Mountain Dog is no exception to this rule and I believe that puppies should be in close contact, not only with their mother (certainly up to six weeks), but also with humans throughout the first eight weeks of life, at which age they are normally sold. In that respect, Bernese are no different from other dogs, but, just as Scott and Fuller found similarities between the breeds they studied, they also found differences, and that is no less true of the

Bernese as a breed. From eight weeks they need to be increasingly exposed to all sorts of new experiences so that they become well-adjusted dogs.

Bernese tend to be very 'into' people. Pet a Bernese at any age and he or she will be on your lap or attempting to get there. Caress him and then stop, and he will be pushing his head against your hand or putting up a paw to encourage you to restart the action. But, equally, they can also lie around while you do something without molesting or pestering you – until you show signs of wanting to go somewhere and then they will be at your side eager to be off. They tend to prefer living in the house to living in kennels, though this is by no means a global situation and one of our males preferred the cool outdoors to the central heating of the house. These dogs can be very laid back, be deaf when they want to be and be attentive if it suits them. But, by the same token, Bernese seem to be highly susceptible to stress. Left to their own devices, some Bernese can become nervous and hesitant and it may be that their predisposition to cancer is, in part, a reflection of their adverse reaction to stress. In the character testing described elsewhere (page 141), one of the tests involves fastening the dog on a long chain in the centre of a field and the owner then walking out of sight. It is significant that a number of

Bernese show signs of stress with this simple test, whereas most of the other breeds tested tend to settle down and wait for the owner to return.

In these character assessments, I have found that many Bernese will not 'play' with an object such as a piece of rope. Their owners frequently say that they will do so at home, but not in the confines of the hall where testing is being undertaken. On the same tests, I find that many Bernese will not exhibit instincts to retrieve. Similarly, in a 'find the owner' test, some dogs will do this readily enough while others seem totally lost. In Bernese testing, I have found only two dogs in 100 tested who used their noses to identify where the owner was hidden. All the others sought to locate the owner (and mostly succeeded) by the initial call. In contrast, every German Shepherd that I have tested or seen tested, even those with decidedly poor temperaments, has had no trouble whatsoever in locating its owner in quick time using its nose.

Falt et al (1982) suggested that tests undertaken on eight-week-old German Shepherd puppies revealed the following: Fetch (the ability to chase a ball and pick it up) was highly inherited (73 per cent), whereas the willingness to Retrieve (bring it back) was only 19 per cent heritable. Thus, it is easier to train a dog to chase than to bring back, and many police forces will not take a dog unless it can retrieve instinctively.

WORKING POTENTIAL

In Britain, few Bernese are to be found in Obedience competition and even fewer, if any, in Working Trials. Yet in Switzerland some members of the breed are trained to Schutzhund, and in the USA many Bernese, even breed Champions, gain working test

Am. Can. Ch. Jacy's Wyatt v Hund See (1982-1991): Sire of 23 American Champions. He spent his first two years herding cattle in Canada.

qualifications. Schutzhund tests come in three grades abbreviated as SchH I, SchH II and SchH III. All three tests involve a Tracking component, an Obedience component and a Man Work element, together with an assessment of character or courage. The extent of the work and its exactitude increases as one goes from I through to III. The testing is rather stereotyped, in that each dog does the same exercises and each exercise is done in a set form. To that extent, it is not like British Working Trials, at which qualifications such as PD (Police Dog), TD (Tracking Dog), WD (Working Dog), UD (Utility Dog) or CD (Companion Dog) are awarded. For example, in the Man Work component of Schutzhund, the 'criminal' wears a protective sleeve. Many Schutzhund dogs become very excited as soon as the sleeve is produced but would not grip an arm unless it was wearing a sleeve. This stereotypical action is not realistic since 'real' criminals do not usually wear protective sleeves, and a real protection dog would have to be capable of tackling a man regardless of the equipment worn, if any.

Pfleiderer-Hogner (1979) found low heritabilities for the components of SchH I, but this almost certainly reflected the testing rather than the intrinsic inheritance of the ability to work. There is no doubt that to train a dog to Schutzhund tests or to Working Trials does require some ability on the part of the trainer – and some innate ability on the part of the dog. I have seen a SchH III Bernese in Switzerland perform Man Work to a very effective level, suggesting that it is not beyond the breed. During the period 1987-96 in Switzerland, there were 47 Bernese who graded SchH I, 20 who were SchH II and 23 who graded

A series of photos of a Bernese guarding property (a coat) while under threat. Such training should be undertaken with care, and the 'criminal' should wear protective clothing.

A dog undertaking 'manwork'. Note that the 'criminal' is well protected. This type of work constitutes part of the Schutzhund trials.

SchH III. However, only eight graded FH, which is the top tracking award. There is an international version of Schutzhund, termed the Internationale Prüfungsordnung or IPO, which also has three grades but which uses Arabic numbers. Over the 1992-96 period, six Bernese gained IPO titles, two of them IPO 3.

In America, the interest in Obedience testing of Bernese is higher than in Britain where carting is the main activity for the breed. Carting is called Draft Testing in America. These features will be discussed later. Whether the Bernese is not trained through a lack of interest on the part of owners or because of some innate problem in the breed is difficult to say. Certainly, the enthusiastic Obedience competitor is unlikely to think of a Bernese Mountain Dog as the first choice for Obedience training when there is a plethora of working breeds with established reputations. There is no doubt that Bernese can be, and are, successfully trained to a variety of activities which they do well. Many have an extreme eagerness to

please and will demonstrate this eagerness in a variety of ways. At the time of writing, we have a teenage bitch returned for allegedly being destructive in the house to which she was sold. Since returning to us, she has never done an ounce of damage, has fitted like a glove into a multi-dog household, gets on with our cats, has demonstrated an extraordinary eagerness to retrieve and is a fantastic jumper. Having a jumper can be a dubious advantage, since she can get over two-metre (6ft) fences, but at least this demonstrates the agility the breed is supposed to possess.

Bernese tend to be quiet dogs, certainly compared with the German Shepherds or terriers which we also have. Perhaps an archetypal description of what is best in the breed is given in the following letter sent to my wife and myself when we had just lost Nellsbern Casablanca from the almost inevitable cancer at just-gone six years of age. The lady writing the letter had a Cas son called Storm (not bred by us), and a bitch out of Storm's sister. She expressed sympathy for our loss and said: "... of all our dogs, Storm has a very special place in my heart. He is simply the best dog I have every known and I have lived and worked with dogs for many years. He is not a big winner in the show ring, but most definitely a big winner at home, loyal to me at all times, lovely kind nature (except when he spies a chicken or rabbit!). He is also a great clown and makes us smile every day. We lost a young Bernese last year and Storm was the one that kept me going through the following months."

That is a Bernese, and I rest my case.

ELEMENTARY TRAINING

When you get your eight-week-old puppy home, he will be somewhat disorientated having left the home he was born in, his mother, and his siblings all in one fell swoop. He will, however, tend to be very adaptable and should soon adjust. It is said that a puppy's best home is the second one it has – which means you, the buyer. It is therefore up to you to develop the dog's character in the next few months. To do this it will need lots of human contact and, if you are out at work for long periods so that the dog is left alone, then I would not sell you a puppy nor should you be thinking of buying one. Left alone for long periods, dogs become bored and puppies make their own entertainment by being destructive to furniture, wires and basically anything that takes their fancy. If you have to go out and leave a puppy for short periods of time, which everyone has to do, then crate him. There are many manufacturers of crates and very many sizes. Buy one that will suit an adult in a standing position. If used sensibly, they are not seen by the puppy as a prison cell, but they do ensure that, while you are out, no harm

comes to the home *or* to the puppy. In my experience, crated dogs grow up well-adjusted and will, when adults, go into a crate of their own volition, regarding it as a place to be alone.

HOUSE TRAINING

Your first task with a new puppy is to house train. At this stage, the puppy is probably living in the kitchen or the utility room and will only be in other rooms under guidance Most people would start with newspapers spread on the floor (hopefully tiled, not carpeted) onto which the puppy is encouraged to relieve himself. If he does so, then he is praised, either by a verbal "Good boy!" type of approach, or by the use of tidbits. Bernese, having a liking for food, tend to respond well to the tidbit approach. Gradually, the area of newspaper is reduced and is moved closer to the exit. Eventually, the puppy is migrating in that direction and will eventually sit there waiting to be let out. Once that happens and he relieves himself outside, use liberal praise and you should have cracked it. Most dogs will respond within a week to ten days, but you must be around during this period and you must let the puppy out last thing at night and first thing in the morning. Encouragement is essential and the use of some commands such as "Quickly!" or "Hurry up!" can be helpful, once the dog associates the command with the action. Thereafter the dog will respond to the same instruction by relieving himself, even when an adult. It will be useful if you can get your puppy to relieve himself on different surfaces like tarmac or concrete, and not just on grass. The latter may not always be available, and dogs conditioned to only one surface can be a slight problem.

47

RECALL/COME
Getting a dog to return when called is crucial if you expect to have control over the dog. You want to achieve a situation in which the animal will return instantly on command because there may come a time when it is vital for the dog's safety. If you walk into a field after your dog and see that the field contains livestock, you need the instant Recall to prevent any incident. To succeed in this area, the dog must know its own name.

This may sound obvious, but many dogs do not actually know their name because they have a multitude of names. Suppose your dog is called Bill. Not only will he get called that name, but he will probably also get Billy or even William, or he may be called Old Boy, or Old Lad. "Come on, Boy!" is not the same instruction as "Bill, Come!" You may call him one name, your spouse another and the kids a third. The dog does not cotton on, so he may respond to none of the names. Therefore all of your family must stick to one name for the dog all of the time. An older dog will respond readily to a variety of names, but only if trained the right way. I once had a German Shepherd bitch who responded to Spanish and English commands, though she was originally trained in English.

To teach Recall, you can start with the puppy on a lead or, better still, a flexi-lead and let him run around. Then call the puppy's name and give an instruction such as "Come!". Immediately, pull gently on the lead or start retraction of the flexi-lead and, when the puppy returns, praise him. Do it a couple of times, then stop. Overdo it, and the puppy gets fed up and bored. A sensitive Bernese can well stay 'put off' for a while. Once the puppy seems to respond well, even without a tug on the lead, try the exercise in

the garden with the puppy free and heap praise upon any success. Like all training, always finish on a successful note. Praise is of the essence. Similarly, training must be in short bursts on a regular basis – not for long periods and infrequently.

If a dog will not come, then two things might make him return. One is to retreat so that he may be tempted to follow, and the other is to lie down, at which point he may investigate and so return. However, eventually, he has got to learn to come on command.

SIT
Most owners will try to teach this along with house training. The puppy is given his name and the command "Sit!" follows. At the same time, the puppy is gently pushed down at the rump until he is sitting, at which point start the praise. Abundant praise, coupled with food, and most Bernese will pick this up quickly. Cheese is a good 'sweetener'. Keep him seated for a few moments, then release him with a step backwards and a command "Come!".

STAY
Having got your puppy to Sit, and to Come on command, introduce the Stay. Start with your puppy sitting, then give his name and the command "Stay!", then step away from the puppy for a short distance, holding up your hand with the flat palm facing the dog. Keep repeating the instruction. Then return relatively quickly and praise the dog if he stays seated. Some will try to jump up as you return, but "No!" should be your response. A couple of successful tries, then stop; but repeat this each day, moving further away each time. After a while, incorporate "Sit! Stay!" with "Come!" and have the dog

return to you. If you have aspirations to Obedience, the returning dog should sit in front of you and then go around you to heel. However, if what you want is actual obedience to your commands, then the dog returning when called will suffice.

DOWN

Down is, or should be, relatively easy. Bernese take kindly to lying around, so, when given the command "Down!" (initially from a sitting position), either your pushing down on the back or pushing the forelegs forward should get the dog to lie down. Leave him a while, then issue praise but give him the command to Stay. Some Bernese will baulk at lying down since it is a submissive posture and they will resist being made to be submissive, but you have to enforce it without being too rough. Try to make training interesting and rewarding for the puppy and vary the order of different commands, and their combinations.

These basic commands should give you control over your dog, even at a distance, but you will have to test it out in varying conditions with distractions around – especially other dogs. Properly trained, a dog should drop on command even at a distance

and stay if told, but that is not as easy as it may seem. Anyone wanting to train a dog would be wise to attend a training course which can be at the local breed club (in the case of numerically strong breeds with clubs in most large cities), or at an all-breed club. Anyone wanting to take part in Obedience competitions will need to attend such a location to give his or her dog the opportunity to be trained and tested in the company of other dogs, as well as exposure to various situations.

It is not the objective of this book to seek to give guidance on competition training, but rather to illustrate to a pet owner the basic essentials of minimal obedience. All training needs to be done on a daily basis for short periods of time (15-20 minutes) and to be kept honed, but competition work is rather different and may not be the objective sought by a pet owner.

RETRIEVE

An ability to retrieve is a highly desirable attribute in any dog and is the first stage of training to track. Many Bernese seem poor at retrieving, yet our own dogs all seem to retrieve; this may well be because we encourage it from an early stage. Playing with puppies is paramount, and providing them with toys that they can carry around is essential. Most of our dogs will carry something around and thus it is relatively easy to couple this with the command "Come" and find that the dog brings the object back. You have to take care in removing the object from the dog's mouth so that he does not become disillusioned and stop bringing it to you. But, once taken, throw the object for the dog to chase and pick up again and the Retrieve is all but cracked. This may sound much easier than it

A dog retrieving a dumb-bell over the high jump.

can be in practice. As explained earlier in this chapter, Retrieve is less heritable than Fetch, and an instinct to chase and pick up is desirable in a retrieving dog. If you are to succeed, then your dog must be willing to carry an object. We have found that even puppies of six weeks of age will happily carry objects and even pick up something like a bunch of keys – which, being metal, is not an easy thing for the average dog.

CARTING

Carting is a tradition in the Bernese, though it is doubtful that it was the first work performed by the breed. In their homeland, the breed pull carts for a living, so to speak, and the BMDCA have a video in which two not-particularly-large Bernese pull a cart weighing 800kg (1,760lbs) – no mean feat.

In Britain, dogs are not permitted to pull carts on the public highways so it is not feasible to use them as in Switzerland. However, pulling carts on private land is quite legal and many Bernese Mountain Dog enthusiasts have got involved in carting. Originally, these carters tended to be seen at the Great Britain Club's garden party or fun days. Not many people owned carts, which were often quite expensive. Shirley Franks, Public Relations officer of the Northern BMD Club, runs Northern Carters and said that her first two carts (East European) cost over £300 ($480) each back in the early 1980s – and she had to make a round trip of over 600 miles to get them. Later, carts were located for about £130 ($210) and,

eventually, a dealer who imported in bulk was located and carts priced at £100-120 ($160-190) became available. Some people do, of course, make their own carts.

Carting tended to be based on simple competitions such as 'The Best-decorated Cart', but, in 1989, Northern Carters appeared at a National Pet Week organised at Harewood House (an English stately home). The club was then asked to provide carts for steam engine rallies, and the idea of public relations with Bernese Mountain Dogs was born. To date, the Northern Carters – who do allow other breeds to cart, though the vast majority are Bernese – have raised over £30,000 ($48,000) at such events, most of which has gone to the Animal Health Trust for research into canine cancer. Midland Carters and Pennine Carters now exist and, in Scotland, Mr and Mrs J. Ross do their bit raising money for children's hospices.

Most people get into carting for the social side and for the charity work, but, increasingly, cart courses are being run with a view to one day having some sort of carting award. This can be an added interest to the use of the breed, but I would not like to see carting become compulsory as an adjunct to a title in the way that field tests have become for gundogs in Britain.

PRACTICAL TIPS FOR CARTING

If you are going to cart, then a harness is the first thing to obtain and this should be of good quality and cause no rubbing on the dog. A full harness involves three back straps and leather traces, while a quarter harness has two back straps and chain traces. Carts can be of variable size, but must be free and easy runners and appropriate in size for the dog. They can be two- or four-wheeled.

The Swiss-type four-wheeled cart has front

wheels under the cart and is easier, since the dog has to pull but not balance. On East European carts, the front wheels lock on the side of the cart and thus they are less manoeuvrable. A two-wheeled cart has to be pulled and balanced and thus requires greater concentration from dog and handler. It also needs a well-distributed load so as to minimise strain. In Britain, carts can be obtained from antique dealers – but do ensure that they have sound wheels. Moreover, most of these have a single handle so there is a need to construct suitable shafts.

The dog needs to get used to wearing a harness before being introduced to pulling, and it is not an ideal occupation for a dog that is cowardly or nervous. Dogs should usually be about 15 months before they start carting and, given the right character, can probably be trained within a day. Once the Bernese is used to the harness, the next stage is to apply tension on the traces by someone walking behind and pulling back slightly as the dog is walked forward on a lead. Then progress to hand-held shafts or small carts. Some people use training rigs (like an American Indian medicine bed, but with small wheels). According to Shirley Franks, most dogs socialised with a carting group make the transition readily enough.

Most breed club shows have some time devoted to carting and usually there is some competition, such as 'Best-Decorated Cart', judged during the luncheon interval. Increasingly, obstacle courses are being created through which the cart is led, serving as a test of dog and owner and not dissimilar from horse-and-carriage contests, though the dog handler does not sit in the cart.

The Swiss system of using carts and dogs to actually work is not a feasible option in Britain because of legal limitations, but there

The long jump.

Forima Festivity, aged four and a half, taking the A-frame.
Photo: Russell Fine Art.

is no doubt that many Bernese seem to actually enjoy pulling carts and the successful charity work of Northern Carters implies that the general public finds carting fascinating.

In the USA, draft work is the term used for carting and Draft titles are awarded by the BMDCA. The exercises involve lead-free work ranging from basic control through to harnessing, traction with specific loads, manoeuvering in circles and right-angled turns, as well as doing all this while distractions are in evidence. Except for the harnessing, the handler does not touch the dog, and the dog has to pass all the exercises

Training a dog to track.

at one time, though repeat testing is possible. Dogs who pass are given a DD (Draft Dog) title, but it is not AKC/CKC recognised. The weight pulled is up to 35 per cent of the dog's weight, which would not be very onerous for most draft dogs.

TRACKING

The most satisfying training, in my experience, is tracking. My first German Shepherd Dog back some 45 years ago was a natural sheep-herder and had a very good nose. Had I known more about tracking (I was a total novice in everything at that time), he might have been even better than he was but I recall one occasion when, on a long morning walk through open country and woodland, I lost a valuable fountain pen and did not realise until later that day. I had no idea where I had lost it, but I put Karl on his harness and tracked back in the general direction that I had walked. He realised he was on a track, probably thought the morning walk had been track-laying, and found the pen some two miles into the walk!

A natural retriever will be an aid to tracking. While walking with your dog, drop something like a glove and let him see you

drop it, then encourage him to go back and retrieve it. He will probably enjoy this and, as you develop the 'game', make the article smaller and more hidden. Drop it without his knowledge, then send him back. In due course, progress to using a harness and a rope so he realises it is tracking work and serious business. Leave your dog in one location and walk away some 50 yards or so and leave an object. Then retrace your steps, harness him up and send him off to track with a command such as "Seek!" which you have probably been using on the searches thus far. If the dog follows your track, he will find the object and then should receive praise or food – whichever turns him on.

Gradually make longer tracks and even vary the shape from a straight track to an angled one. Given a good nose, the dog will follow – though he may do so at a slight distance from the track you walked, depending upon the wind direction and air flow. If you can get a helper, progress to a situation where the helper walks off, and then get your dog to follow the scent and locate the helper. In due course, move on to tracks laid some hours previously, building up the difficulty of the track and the age of the track-laying, as well as the weather conditions under which tracks are followed.

Qualifications such as Tracking Dog (TD) exist in both the USA and Britain and the FH test exists in Europe. All involve specific testing and a high degree of proficiency, but to many people the sheer joy of following a dog who is patently following a track and who reaches a successful conclusion is pleasure enough.

If you are going to track, the use of a harness and a rope is essential and, in due course, your dog will associate these with the work ethic and tracking.

ASSISTANCE DOGS

In recent years, it has been a policy to allow dogs into some hospitals and hospices on the grounds that their presence and the opportunity to pat such animals has been shown to be beneficial to patients. This is an extension of the well-established finding that people who have suffered a heart attack have longer lives if they have pets than if they do not. In Britain, dogs going into hospitals to visit patients have become known as PAT dogs, and in North America they are called Therapy Dogs. Bernese Mountain Dogs, being highly friendly, person-motivated dogs, suit this type of activity. Ch. Forgeman Footpad was well-known for this, and his sister, Forgeman Fandango, a blue-eyed bitch who produced Ch. Brick Kiln Matilda, was owned by a doctor and indulged in PAT dog work for most of her life. Some of the Bernalpen dogs have been involved, as was Abbeycot Christophe, but it is not possible to mention all those involved.

Further extensions of the idea of assistance dogs are Hearing Dogs for the Deaf, Wheelchair Assistance dogs for those incapacitated in movement and wheelchair-bound, and, of course, the long-established Guide Dogs for the Blind. Some of the very early Bernese born in the 1970s in Britain were used as the Guide Dogs. Dora v Breitenhof, one of the early imports to Britain, ended up with the Guide Dogs and some of her progeny were trained for the role.

One problem with Bernese as Guide Dogs is their very rarity and their good looks. A Labrador, Golden Retriever or German Shepherd guide dog is a fairly commonplace sight and unlikely to induce passers-by to stop and comment or distract the dog. That might not be the case with a Bernese Mountain Dog, and such distraction would not help a Bernese, some of whom have a low concentration threshold. It may be for this reason that the early work with Bernese by the Guide Dog Association in Britain did not continue.

Whether Bernese have featured in other activities is uncertain, but, in the USA, Hampshire College, Massachusetts, has had a canine project since 1976, initially based on Livestock Protection Dogs (not the forte of the Bernese) and more recently on Wheelchair Assistance. Data have been produced under the guidance of Professor Raymond Coppinger (1995) showing the sort of work done in the wheelchair assistance programme. Golden Retrievers have been used and I am sure that Bernese could be trained along similar lines.

Forgeman Fandango, born 1980 (Mustang v Nesselacker – Ch. Folkdance at Forgeman). She had a blue eye, but became a treasured PAT dog, seen here visiting a patient in hospital. Owned by Dr Ann Francis.   Photo: Brenda Grifiths.

5 *SHOWING*

Most people's first dog is purchased as a companion animal or pet and that may be as far as the owner goes or wants to go, though most will probably train the dog to undertake some basic obedience. Unless you have gone into the breed in some detail before purchase, it is highly likely that you will not buy a very good animal the first time, unless you are particularly fortunate. Breeders will not usually sell their best, and beginners are not usually equipped to pick the best anyway.

The problem with first-time buyers is that people within the breed do not know who they are or where they are, which means that, unless advisers are approached, they cannot help. In Britain, some of the newer monthly magazines such as *Dogs Today* have tried to build up a number of experts within the various breeds who can be contacted for advice. If the expert really is one (and some simply are not) then would-be buyers can be given sound advice, even to the extent that they may realise that the particular breed being sought may not, after all, be the best choice.

However, let us assume that you have got your first Bernese Mountain Dog at eight weeks and are busy trying to rear, socialise and understand what it is you have bought. The first thing you should do is join a breed club. In most European countries, there is only one club for the breed (often looking after the four tricolour Swiss breeds). In Britain, there are several clubs, as there are in North America, and you can join one or more of these. The advantage of joining a club is that you may be able to get help and advice from established and experienced members, and many clubs publish magazines at regular intervals which can help to inform and interest beginners. Most clubs run shows and showing is something that a proportion of first-time buyers indulge in.

If you are going to show, then it is obviously important that you know about grooming and handling and that you are equipped with a showable dog. In reality, an owner can exhibit any dog, even a very poor one, so that the term 'show dog' may be rather meaningless. It can apply to the world Champion or to a dog that has been placed last every time it was exhibited. However, you may have been lucky and actually got a very nice animal for your first one, and people may suggest that you exhibit the animal. Showing dogs can be time-consuming, expensive what with the cost of entries and travelling, and frustrating when judging is not to an owner's liking (or even blatantly dishonest or incompetent, and there is a lot of that around!). However, it is interesting to the initiated and is actually a means by which breeders can exhibit and compare their stock with those of others. Certainly, if you are ever interested in breeding, then having a successful, winning animal is going to be more useful than having a dog which has never been seen outside your premises or one which has been exhibited with no measure of success.

If showing appeals to you and your first dog is not successful then by the time you seek a second you should have learned a bit more about where to go and what to look for. However, not even the best breeder in the world can guarantee success for an eight-week-old puppy, though his or her chances of being right likely to be better than those of one who has only a beginner's knowledge. An intelligent and interested breeder will learn more the longer they are in a breed and become more knowledgeable with time, so experience is valuable and not to be decried. A person who has really learned will be obvious to those asking the questions and 'time served' is then much less crucial. However, there are those who will tell you that they have been in the breed for 20, 30 or 40 years, but, in reality, they have simply learned for one year and repeated it 20, 30 or 40 times!

If you are going to exhibit your dog, then understanding shows and how they operate is important. There are differences between countries and the following discussion looks at the UK system, the American system and the Danish system, which latter approximates

to the procedure followed in many FCI countries of Europe.

SHOWING IN BRITAIN

All shows in Britain are under the jurisdiction of the Kennel Club. They are classified in two ways. The first category is what are called all-breed shows which, while they may not actually cater for every breed on the KC's books, will have multi-breeds

ABOVE: Crufts 1980. Ch. Folkdance at Forgeman winning the Group. Pictured (left to right): Mr K. Butler (KC), Brenda Griffiths (handling) and Fred Curnow (judge).

RIGHT: Ch. Collansues Brigitta b 1987 (Gillro Flapjack Of Forgeman – Heidi Of Collansues). Winner of six CCs and five Reserve CCs.

The littermates Ch. Choristma Bliss (left) and Ch. Choristma Einselmutz b 1987 (Gillro Flapjack Of Forgeman – Ch. Choristma Jungmutzi), Bliss won five CCs, and Mutz won three CCs.

scheduled. A version of the all-breed event is a group show. The KC divides breeds into six categories or groups: Gundog, Hound, Terrier, Toy, Utility and Working, with the Bernese Mountain Dog in the last named. Many all-breed shows will cater for the Bernese by having classes for it. Similarly, a Working Group show will cater for breeds from the Working Group. The KC is soon to subdivide the Working Group into a Pastoral or Herding Group so that there will be seven groups.

The second category and an alternative to all-breed or group shows is a specialist or breed show. These are shows which cater for only one breed and they are run by a breed club. In Britain, we have the Bernese Mountain Dog Club of Great Britain, the Northern Bernese Mountain Dog Club, the Southern Bernese Mountain Dog Club and the Scottish Bernese Mountain Dog Club, all of which run shows. In addition, there is The Central Bernese Mountain Dog Club which does not run shows because it is, as yet, not recognised by the KC.

In addition to classification into all-breed/group and breed (speciality) shows there is a division into Open and Championship events. There are other classifications, sufficiently minor to be ignored. The basic difference between Open and Championship shows is that, at the latter, a Challenge Certificate is on offer for the best of each sex within each breed. The Challenge Certificate or CC, as it is known, counts towards the title of Champion. For a Bernese to carry that coveted title it must win three CCs under three different judges. In some breeds, three CCs only brings the title Show Champion (Sh. Ch.) until the dog wins some working qualification to earn the full title of Champion (Ch.). This affects gundogs and Border Collies, but does not apply to the Bernese.

An Open show will have classes for various breeds, or for a single breed if it is a breed club event, and it will be run exactly as a Championship show except that the judges may not be as experienced as those at a

A typical scene at a British Open Show (Cheshire 1987). The judge, Helen Davenport, is going to congratulate her BOB winner Coliburn Truce (Tirass v Waldacker – Coliburn Pandora). He was ten months at the time, and went on to win one CC and five Reserve CCs.

Championship show and there is no award beyond the Best of Sex and the Best of Breed.

At both shows, the Best male and the Best female compete for Best of Breed (BOB) and the normal procedure is that the Best of Breeds then go into the Group (in the case of the Bernese, the Working Group) and compete for Best in Group. The six Group winners at an all-breed show will then compete for Best in Show (BIS). At some all-breed shows the group system is not used and all BOBs go to compete for BIS but, at Championships (called general championship shows), it is always employed. Of course, at a single-breed show, the top award is BOB since there is no other breed to compete with.

Some large all-breed Championship shows run over two, three or even four days, scheduling different groups on different days. If you are going to enter a show, you need to

contact the show secretary for a schedule on which you make your entries. Usually, these are printed several weeks before the show and you have to send your entries (and your cheque) well in advance of the show. There is a given date beyond which entries cannot be accepted.

At shows (breed/all-breed / Open / Championship) there are different classes. Sometimes these may be mixed breeds (at all-breed shows), but most serious breeders enter classes that are for their breed and no others. In Britain, classes are a mixture of age and award classes. That is to say, some classes cater for specific ages of dog while other classes are for dogs which have won certain awards. Open and Championship shows run similar classes but qualification for entry may depend upon wins at Open or Championship level. A typical British classification is shown in Table 5.1. Classes would be available for each sex, so that dogs only compete with

Table 5.1 Typical classes for a BMD show, each sex (UK)

Name of class	Qualification for entry
Veteran	Dogs over seven years of age
Minor Puppy	Dogs aged 6-9 months
Puppy	Dogs aged 6-12 months
Junior	Dogs aged 6-18 months
Special Yearling	Dogs aged 18-24 months
Maiden	Dogs that have not won a first prize (Ch./Open) excluding puppy classes
Novice	Dogs with no more than 2 first prizes (Ch./Open) excluding puppy classes
Undergraduate	As Novice above but Ch. shows only
Graduate	Dogs with no more than 3 first prizes (Ch. shows) excluding the previous classes
Post Graduate	Dogs with no more than 4 first prizes (Ch. shows) excluding the previous classes.
Limit	Dogs that are not Champions and not more than 6 firsts in Limit/Open classes (Ch. shows)
Open	Any dog over 6 months of age

dogs and bitches with bitches, but sometimes the Veteran Class is for mixed sexes. At most shows catering for Bernese Mountain Dogs there is only one judge who judges the dog classes and then proceeds to the bitch classes. However, at breed club shows many clubs have two judges, one for each sex. In that event, the BOB is judged jointly from the Best Dog and Best Bitch.

In all the classes from Maiden to Post Graduate inclusive any dog which has won a CC is ineligible and would have to go into Limit (if it has won one or two CCs) or Open.

These are the principal, but not the only, classes and, at any show, not all will be scheduled. The first five classes are age-restricted and the next six depend upon previous wins, with the last class being the Open class. The qualifications given are worded less exactly than the KC version. Few shows would give all these 12 classes for a breed, and a proliferation of classes can adversely affect entries which are divided by the large number of classes. Most Championship events would have eight or nine classes per sex for the major breeds. The shows would be better exhibitions if classes were by age without overlaps e.g. 6-9, 9-12, 12-18 and 18-24 months, with perhaps one or two other classes. However, sadly, this is not the popular wish in Britain in most breeds.

Although you could enter any dog in Open and it is feasible to enter a dog in several classes, this is not what an experienced exhibitor would advise. You should only enter one class with any specific dog because, if it wins, you have a chance, however remote, of winning Best of Sex and, at a Championship show, the CC. Enter classes for which your animal is the right age; thus,

enter a seven-month puppy in Minor Puppy and avoid Puppy even though your youngster is eligible. Enter an 11-month puppy in Puppy and not Junior, etc. Because Maiden and Novice classes attract dogs with few wins, they tend to attract poorer-quality animals and, with a good dog, you would do best to avoid them. A sensible breeder would enter age classes where possible, and next, probably, Post Graduate and, after some wins, Limit, and then, with a successful winning adult, the Open class. At most Bernese shows the 'toughest' class, in terms of entry and competition, would be the Limit class. If you are showing more than one dog, do not enter them in the same class!

The judge will deal with each class in turn, probably selecting only those animals for which he or she has a prize card. Thus, if cards go down to fifth place, the judge will probably pick out only five animals and discard the rest. This is discussed later under judging. When all the male classes have been judged, the winners of each class will be called in, provided that they have not been beaten (this can happen if a dog enters two classes and, for example, wins Junior but is beaten in Special Yearling). The unbeaten dogs are usually lined up from the senior class backwards and it is the judge's task to

Ch. Bernfold Winter Breeze (Windlenell Warlord – Kernow Summer Love) and, Ch. Majanco Loretta of Duntiblae (Basgal v Trubergluck – Kylebern Night Mystique).

Ch. Carlacot Fido winning the Working Group at Blackpool 1990. The judge is Tom Horner.

to prevent other dogs making their titles. This makes titles hard to achieve, especially if there is a top winning dog being exhibited at many shows. In most countries, Champions, once made up, do not compete for further CC (or equivalent) awards, though they do for BOB. Although Champions can compete at Open shows, it is normal courtesy not to do so but to keep them for Championship events. Again, it is not the norm to show under a judge who has already given the dog a CC, although an exception might be Crufts or a major breed show.

In Britain, first-prize rosettes or cards are red, with blue for second, green for third and yellow for fourth (which is called Reserve).

SHOWING IN AMERICA

American shows are simpler than those in Britain. There are all-breed and breed club (specialty) events but no division into Championship and Open. All shows are able to contribute towards the title Champion depending upon the 'points' available. These are one, two, three, four or five points for what is termed the Winners male (or female). The number of points will depend upon the number of dogs entered and present, the breed involved and the area where the show is taking place. Tables are drawn up by the AKC for each breed and region so that each club knows what is

select the best one as Best Dog. If this is a Championship show, that dog will usually win the CC (though the judge can withhold if, in his or her opinion, no dog is considered worthy of the title Champion). The second best male at a Championship show would gain a Reserve Challenge Certificate (Res. CC). This is prestigious, but does not count towards a title. However, if the CC winner was disqualified later for some infringment of rules, then the Res. CC animal can be upgraded by the KC to the CC award. Judges thus have to sign CC and Res. CC cards to say that the winner is worthy of the title Champion.

Professional handlers abound in some breeds but, in Bernese, most exhibitors handle their own dogs in the ring or they are handled in an amateur capacity by friends. At Championship shows, Champions must enter the Open class unless they are still eligible (unlikely) for an age class. This means that a Champion can continue to win CCs over and above the minimum three and that Champions, by winning more CCs, help

Am. Ch. Heartlights Baby Grand (Shersan Chip Off The Ol' Block – Heartlights Autograph): BOB 1990 BMDCA Specialty.

Am. Ch. Duntiblae Dark Watchman (Ch. Clashaidy Nordic Fire – Duntiblae Dark Rahni) winning a Group 4th in 1989. He was a British export to the USA. Photo: Booth.

needed for the points they seek. Thus, in one breed in one area, the points may be four but, in another area, the same entry might only be worth three points. Shows that have too small an entry to gather points are very minor and, in most major breeds, a specialty show is likely to be worth five points for each sex. Points are allocated to the sex so, at the same show, one sex may be higher pointed than the other. Shows which gain three or more points for the sex are termed 'majors'.

For example, at the BMDCA Club Specialty in Rhode Island in 1998, the number of males needed for points in that area at that time was two for one point, four for two points, six for three points eight for four points and 12 for five points. The corresponding numbers needed for females were two, five, seven, 12 and 19. The show actually had several hundred Bernese present but the number of dogs needed to make a show a major is clearly very small. Over the period 1993-97 there were, in the USA, an average of 1,042 shows per year at which Bernese Mountain Dogs were exhibited, with an average of 8.78 dogs per show. This is extremely small in terms of the mean number of Bernese on show and compares very unfavourably with Europe, even though in recent years the BMDCA Specialty has been the largest Bernese show in the world.

To become an American Champion a dog must gain 15 points under at least three different judges, with at at least two of the shows being majors awarded by two different judges. Thus, the fastest way to gain a title would be to 'win' three five-point-majors and the slowest would be to win three three-point majors plus nine one-point events. The classes at AKC shows are given in Table 5.2.

Table 5.2 Typical classes for a BMD show, each sex (USA)

Name of Class	Qualification for entry
Puppy 6-9	Dogs aged 6-9 months
Puppy 9-12	Dogs aged 9-12 months
Junior 12-18	Dogs aged 12-18 months
Novice	Dogs without a class win as an adult at a pointed show.
Bred by exhibitor	Any dog other than a Champion to be handled by a family member
American-bred	Any USA-bred dog other than Champions
Open	Any dog over 6 months (traditionally Am. Chs. do not enter but foreign Champions can)
Best of Breed[1]	American Champions (both sexes combined)

[1] Sometimes called the Specials class.

Classes are judged much as they are in Britain and, at the end of the open class, all winners compete for what is termed 'Winners' Dog. This animal receives whatever points are available for that sex. At this stage bitches are judged and the same procedure leads to 'Winners' bitch. The two winners then compete for Best of Winners. If the dog had three points but the bitch four and the dog beats the bitch for Best of Winners, then he would also get four points but the bitch would not lose hers. At this stage, the Specials class is judged and the Specials winner competes with Best of Winners for Best of Breed. Whichever sex wins BOB (termed BB in USA), there is also a Best Opposite Sex award.

The American show system means that a Champion does not compete to prevent non-Champions getting their points but does have the chance to gain BOB. At an all-breed event, the BOB then competes in its Group and, if successful, for BIS. This means that BOB, Group and BIS awards are prestigious. It does, however, also mean that Champion is a somewhat easier title to win than it would be in Britain, where Champions still compete for the CC.

In most breeds the so-called parent club can hold an annual specialty at which the top animal may receive some sort of title such as Grand Victor/Victrix, but the ultimate honour is still considered to be a BIS win at an all-breed event. According to Chesnutt Smith (1995) only 13 Bernese Mountain Dogs had achieved this by 1994. However, one of these, Am. Ch. Shersan Chang O'Pace v Halidom had won 20 BIS. In Britain, several Bernese have had group wins but only Ch. Hildrek Jonquil has won a BIS at an all-breed Championship event. In America there are seven groups and Bernese are in the Working Group.

Frau Gasser of the Waldacker kennels with Arthos v Waldacker (Int. Ch. Hondo v Bernetta – Mirabella auf der Steini) and Herr Krauchi of the Nesselacker kennels.

SHOWING IN EUROPE

As in other parts of Europe under FCI control, Denmark has breed and all-breed events but it has many fewer classes than in Britain and there is a greater use of age classes. The Danish example is used to illustrate the situation but there are minor differences in different countries.

Unlike in the UK and America, if there is only one judge then he or she would judge a male class followed by the corresponding female class. If there are several judges, as might be the situation at, say, the Swiss National Klub show, then judging may be going on simultaneously. At most events, a CAC is available to the best of each sex, excluding the Champions. The CAC (Certificat d'Aptitude au Championnat) is the equivalent of a British CC and winning

Table 5.3 Classes in Denmark (titles translated) for each sex

Name of Class (translated)	Qualification
Baby	Dogs of 4-6 months
Puppy	Dogs of 6-9 months
Champion	Dogs that are title-holders
Junior	Dogs of 9-18 months
Intermediate	Dogs of 15-24 months
Open	Any dog over 6 months
Veteran	Dogs over 7 years

European Sieger 1997, Klub Sieger, and Danish Ch. Sennettas Sixten (Dajan vd Hausmatt – Danish Ch. Sennettas Noa-Noa), born 1995, handled by Lizbet Ramsing. The author made this dog Excellent and BOB at the Danish Club Show in June 1998. The following week he became World Sieger in Helsinki.

Danettas Laro: An important dog of the 1970s, bred in Denmark. Photo: Ramsing.

three of these, under no less than two different judges, brings the title of Champion for the particular country, e.g. 'Champion Suisse de Beauté' in Switzerland. In some countries the requirement is four CACs.

When the judge has finished all the classes, the best male can be awarded the CAC but the Champions do not compete, though they do compete with the CAC winner for Best of Sex. The winner of this can then compete with the Best Bitch for BOB but that may not take place at a specialist breed show. As

Table 5.4 European Grades

Grade	Qualification
V: Vorzuglich (Excellent)	An outstanding specimen with no major failings. An irregular bite may be accepted.
SG: Sehr gut (Very Good)	An outstanding animal with minor defects. An odd missing PM may be ignored.
G: Gut (Good)	An average animal, minor dental faults tolerated.
Gen: Genugend (Sufficient)	A tolerable animal, basically below average or average. Certain dental faults allowed.
Ungen: Ungenugend (Insufficient)	A poor-quality animal or one with a serious character failing or a specific serious defect.

in America, once a dog has won its three (or four) CACs, it does not compete for any more nor does it prevent other dogs making their titles.

At certain shows a CACIB may be on offer. This is similar to a CAC but is an international award and can be made to the Best of Sex, including the Champions. If a dog wins four of these in three different countries, including one in its own country, it carries the title of International Champion (Int. Ch.). Few dogs gain this award.

In most of Europe dogs are graded, and the grades are shown in table 5.4 with German and English titles.

In some breeds V cannot be given to a dog under 24 months of age but, in others, V may be given to yearling animals. Puppies are usually graded as Promising or Very Promising, Sufficient or Insufficient. In countries under FCI control, the Bernese is classified in a group that relates to Swiss cattle dogs. Where grading is used, only V and SG grades are really breedable animals.

SHOW GROOMING

Any breed that has white markings needs pristine whiteness at a show, and I would expect to bath a dog prior to the event. Some breeders bath the dog a few days before the show, others the previous day, but some bathing is essential. Before bathing, the dog should be thoroughly groomed and combed to remove dead hair. This makes the

coat easier to shampoo and to subsequently blow dry. There are many acceptable canine shampoos and we have used them successfully, but we now use a baby shampoo with added conditioner which is mild and effective. Using a sponge to get the shampoo into the coat will make the job easier. You are, after all, trying to introduce water to a weatherproof coat.

For drying, we use a professional dog-drying machine which blows hot air over the coat. In broad terms, a shampoo and a good brush and comb is the basis of preparing a Bernese Mountain Dog for the show ring. However, it is desirable to pull out 'streamers' around the ears which can be done with a metal comb or with your fingers. Failure to do so detracts from overall smartness and from the smooth outline of head and neck. As a judge, I do not penalise streamers in the ring though I do not find them appealing. Some trimming of the feet with a pair of scissors makes for neatness, as does some trimming of the rear pasterns. Bernese are not, or should not be, very lippy, so they do not generally salivate and should not require bibs before the event such as those seen on Newfoundlands.

Many Bernese have excellent feet which usually means that nails are worn down naturally, but sometimes they do need cutting in certain dogs and care has to be taken to avoid the quick (which contains the blood supply). If you are going to cut toenails, have a blood coagulant preparation available in case you do cut too far into the quick and make the nail bleed. Clipping nails should, however, be done regularly, not just before a show. That way, nails are kept at the right length and may well grow more slowly or at least have minimal quick.

In America, grooming has become a major

Dajan vd Hausmatt, the sire of Sennettas Sixten.
Photo: Ramsing.

feature of shows and many dogs are clipped along the back as well as groomed almost to excess. While the net impression is largely one of great neatness, the effect is that a judge must handle every exhibit to determine whether the bone is really as good as it looks and whether the backline is real or imagined. In general, American owners use grooming to excess and this does detract from the pleasure of showing dogs as well as giving a mistaken impression of many dogs.

JUDGING

If you have been active in a breed for some time and if you have had some success in the show ring, you may be asked to judge. In most countries, there is a judging training scheme which aspiring judges must attend and pass. This was never the case in Britain but, even there, the KC is moving down the road of insisting that new judges pass either the KC's scheme or ones set up by the Breed Council or by breed clubs.

At non-Championship events in Britain there have been no rules about who judges Open shows, whether breed or all-breed. However, to judge a Championship event the judge has to be approved by the KC, which is the policy in most breeds in most countries. In some countries, the control of judging is in the hands of the breed club and is then rubber-stamped by the national Kennel Club concerned. In most countries, there is more control than in Britain, but usually there is also reciprocity, in that judges approved by one KC will be approved by others.

Judges are usually of two kinds; either all-rounders (multi-breed in the USA) or specialists. In some countries, notably Britain and America, many judges exist who are approved to judge a multitude of breeds and

The line-up of the BMD Club of GB at the 1991 Festival. BIS was Ch. Katelyn Wake Of The Storm with handler J. Silman; Mrs B. Griffiths and Mrs J. Cochrane, judges; Maurice Johnson, patron; John James , show manager; E. Wrighton with Pownall Prima Donna Of Temeraire BOS.

it is my view that one cannot possibly know enough about such a number of breeds to be truly expert. Clearly, there is a need at small shows to have multi-breed judges since such shows cannot afford a specialist for every breed but, at speciality shows and major events with big entries, specialist judges should be used.

Both my wife and myself judge at Championship level. I judge German Shepherd Dogs as well as Bernese and my wife judges Bernese. We have both judged abroad under systems different from those of the KC. Both of us consider that we are still learning, even after my 45 years in German Shepherds, and that should be true of any judge. The day you feel that you know it all and have nothing more to learn is the day you should stop judging.

If you are a Bernese enthusiast and actively breed and exhibit, the time may come when you wish to judge the breed. Of course you need to be asked, and touting for appointments is considered bad form and rightly frowned upon. You will therefore have to wait to be invited but, in the meantime, you should attend breed seminars about the breed in general and especially those concerned with judging. You should seek to attend the appropriate judging courses and only if you pass can you expect to proceed further.

PRACTICAL TIPS ON JUDGING

If you do get asked to judge, then you should confirm invitations in writing and have it all confirmed by the club. You can normally expect to get your travelling expenses paid but are unlikely to get a fee, nor in my view, should you seek one. Of course, you need to look reasonably smart in appropriate gear, which means that women judges should not wear low-cut dresses or ultra-short skirts and men ought to be in jacket and tie, not in Bermuda shorts. Neither sex should judge in jeans! You will need a notebook and pens or pencils (pencils work better if it rains), and you will be given a judging book by the club. You can take a measuring stick if you have one. You might expect a club to have one available, though that is improbable at most British Bernese shows (except for the NBMDC), and most owners and their dogs would not recognise a measuring stick.

Most of all you need knowledge, ring presence and the honesty not to show fear or favour. If your best friends have the best dog in the class, put it first. If they have the worst dog, put it last. The first course of action may bring ringside comment that you are 'bent' (crooked), and the latter might lose you a friend. However, if that is what the dogs deserve, that is what you should do. Do not prejudge or bring into account things you saw at other shows. If you have seen a dog back away in fear at a previous show but the same dog is under you today, then judge it on the day, not in the light of what it did previously. Do not try to identify dogs, especially not by their handlers. The dog may not be the one you think it is and, in any event, you should be working from first principles. If the dog looks poor, then judge it accordingly. If you think it is a big winner but it still looks poor, then judge on what you see, not on past reputations. The other judges may be the ones out of step, not you. Then again, it may not be the dog that you thought it was. You should find out what the rules are in the location you are judging. If you are judging in your own country, then you should know the rules. If judging abroad, determine what it is that they want you to do and work by their rules.

There are different sets of criteria in terms of objectives. In Britain and America, the principal aim is to determine the prize-winners, so that winning the first prize is the object of the exercise. While it is your task to find the best animal to receive the first prize, it does not follow that the animal is a good one. When it comes to giving out the CC (or equivalent), you may have to sign to the effect that the dog is worthy of the title Champion, so the dog ought to be an excellent animal. However, in some classes, you may have had a poor group of dogs and have placed them in the right order but not have been impressed with any of them. In

Pictured (left to right): Ch. Carlacot Heather b 1987 (Tirass von Waldacker At Coliburn – Carlacot Ebony) and Ch. Carlacot Flame b 1985 (Carlacot Candyman – Glanzbergs Kirsch Of Carlacot).

Ch. Temeraire Penny Black Of Crensa b 1980 (Ch. Tarncred Tarquin Of Temeraire – Temeraire Tranquility): Winner of 13 CCs and eight Reserve CCs, shown as a youngster (inset) and as an adult. Photo: Russell Fine Art.

other words, the winner was the best of a bad lot. The winner's owner may never know that, and may not care as long as he or she has the first prize.

In many other countries, dogs have to be placed in order but you may also be asked to grade along the lines given in Table 5.4. Thus you might give an adult first prize but only grade it Very Good. Most owners in such locations would be happier getting an Excellent grading, even if they did not win the class. I grade animals when judging. In Britain, the KC does not allow grading cards to be distributed but nevertheless individual methods of judging may involve grading each dog. If you are going to use grades (as you will have to in Europe), then you must know the criteria which determine the grade you can give.

It is a sound policy (obligatory in some countries) to have all the dogs in a class line up in numerical order. Each handler will have the number on a sleeve or, better still, wear pull-over jackets bearing numbers. Ask for the dogs to trot around the ring once or twice to give you an idea of what catches your eye, then take each dog in numerical order. Ask for them to come towards you on a loose lead. A dog that is nervous may baulk at this, so the exercise helps to identify character failings. Ask the age, check the teeth and testicles (in males!) and then ask for the dog to be posed. At this point, you should ideally take notes on the dog. Some judges never take a note but, that way, they miss things and, however good your memory, it is fallible in a large class and can lead to gross errors of judgement. In some countries you may have to give a critique of the dog there and then, and give it a grading. Your critique will be given to exhibitors and may be published in the appropriate breed magazine. In Britain, you will be asked to present a report for the two weekly dog papers (*Our Dogs* and *Dog World*), but only on the first two animals. Because of this many, judges argue that notes on anything else are pointless and, certainly, your notes may never see the light of day. However, the Northern BMD Club in Britain does publish a report on every dog as far as their own shows are concerned, and they have a club magazine in which to publish them. The club insists on such reports from its judges as a condition of the appointment. Published or not, the notes are for your own benefit, to make sure that you can evaluate each dog. Here are some suggestions on the sort of report you might produce on the hypothetical Bernese presented to you for judging.

Ideally, start with an overall impression of the dog: is he well-proportioned, medium-sized, of medium strength? Comments about dentition and character can be made on each dog, or you may choose to comment overall and only comment on those dogs which have a failing in dentition or character. You could, in the first case, have an overall comment to the effect that all dogs had correct dentition and satisfactory characters unless otherwise stated. Otherwise, each dog requires some comment in these areas, such as "correct bite, full dentition, good temperament".

Now look at the head and work your way down the dog and write down what you see: "Well marked with good pigment; slight white spot at nape; good ear placement and carriage; correct head with good expression; slightly forward-placed shoulder; long upper arm; level back with good croup; good width of thigh and long second thigh; rather long in rear pasterns; tail bushy but slightly short."

Next, ask for the dog to be gaited away from you and back towards you, then ask for him to trot around the ring at a gait (not pacing) and make further comments on gait: "Good hind thrust; slight tendency to drop on the forehand; parallel rear pasterns; throws left forefoot outwards." And so on.

We have written the above report on a fictitious dog as though it were for publication. In reality, you may use

abbreviations or shorthand – the real thing or your own – or you may use a tape recorder. At all events, you have a record of that dog and can then grade him accordingly. Even if you are not being asked to grade, it will help your judging to do so. I would use a sheet of paper for each class, with columns headed by the grade, and would put each dog's number under the appropriate column so that the final result in a class of ten might look like Figure 5.1, where the numbers represent the dog's catalogue number.

Excellent	Very Good	Good	Sufficient	In-sufficient
1013	1011	1010	1016	1012temp
1014	1015			
1017	1019			
1018				

Figure 5.1
Judging notes showing gradings for each dog

As you can see, you have four Ex dogs, three VG, and one each in the Good, Sufficient and Insufficient grades. Number 1012 is obviously last because it has a character failing and, by the same token, 1016 is ninth and 1010 is eighth. However, you have still to place the four Excellent dogs in order and the three VG dogs in order behind them. I would suggest pulling out the four Ex dogs and reorganising them in merit order e.g. 1017, 1013, 1018, 1014 and then add on the three VG dogs 1019, 1011, and 1015, followed by 1010, 1016 and finally 1012. In this order, I would suggest running the dogs around the ring to see how they perform. Work from the back because, that way, a dog can go forward even if, in a small ring, you split the class into two.

Obviously, in this theoretical example, the final three dogs are more or less fixed by their grades, but the first four and those in places 5-7 could change within their grading group. On side gait, you can assess dogs against their nearest rival because they are placed beside one another. You can run adjacent dogs across the ring to assess front and rear action in both dogs simultaneously and quickly arrange the line-up. Your final order might be:1017, 1018, 1013, 1014, 1019, 1015, 1011, 1010, 1016 and 1012 based upon movement. Note that your initial line-up should be based on construction, so that 1017 is picked out as the best of the ten. He should only be moved down the order if his performance when moving is imperfect and, even then, he could only (at the very worst) go from first of the Excellents to fourth and last of the Excellents. In this example, 1018 started behind 1013 and they changed places. It is imperative that 1013 is better in construction and merit than 1018 (however small the difference), because 1013 started ahead of 1018. Only by better or sounder movement should 1018 go above 1013, not on construction. If 1018 were the better constructed he should have started in second place.

Most British all-rounders and many specialists simply pick out five dogs (if there are five prizes), line them up and that is the end of judging. It may be fast but it is grossly inefficient, since the only occasion that the adjacent places get alongside one another is when the class is finished. The system described above is potentially far superior to the slapdash British method, which has been developed by all-rounders and those who somehow feel that speed is more important than accuracy. Of course,

many British judges are quite incapable of grading and of writing notes on lower order dogs. Indeed some judges never produce a critique. It is my opinion that, at Championship and breed shows, a critique should be obligatory and part of the judging contract.

In most countries, once the classes are finished, the class winners come together to let the judge select the best animal of that sex or the potential CAC winner or the Winners animal (in the USA). I suggest lining the winners up from the senior class backwards so that the older, more senior dogs are at the front and it is likely that the winner will come from among these. If grading has been undertaken, then the Best Dog will come from those graded Excellent. In Britain it can, in theory and in practice, come from any class – even the 6-9 month puppy. That may be feasible at a small all-breed Open show, where the puppy is outstanding and a future Champion in the making, but it is highly improbable that it should happen in a breed, Open or Championship event. Most serious judges would run the younger animals round once and then discard them, seeking the Best of Sex from among senior animals. If a Reserve Best of Sex or runner-up is needed, then the second animal in the class from which the Best of Sex was picked could come in to challenge for this spot if the judge requires this (mandatory in the US).

At your first show you may make some errors. Indeed, judges can make errors or have second thoughts even when highly experienced. The judge who has never made an error is, hopefully, no longer judging, since such arrogance is best outside and not inside the ring. If you learn from your mistakes, all is well. Ask an observer whose opinion you value to critically comment on

Table 5.5 Winners of BOB (BIS) at the BMDCA Specialty   1976-98

Year	Winner[1]	Sire / Dam
1976	Zyta v Nesselacke	Astor v Chaindon / Miggi v Nesselacker
1977/8	Alpenhorns Copyright of Echo*	Tryarr Alphorn Knight Echo / Tryarr Alphorn Brio
1979	Halidom Davos v Yodlerhof *	Grand Yodler of Teton Valley / Ginger v Senseboden
1980/2/3	Ashley v Bernerliebe*	Galan v Senseboden / Dault Daphne v Yodlerhof
1981	Marens Ajax*	Alphorns Copyright of Echo / Clara's Blass
1984	Broken Oaks Dieter v Arjana*	Wyemedes Luron Bruce / Broken Oaks Arjana
1985	Bigpaws Yoda*	Bari v Nydegghoger / Kala v Breiterweg
1986	Shersan Chang O'Pace v Halidom*	Halidom Davos v Yodlerhof / Halidom Kali v Muensterplatz
1987	Harlaquins Thor the Bear*	Valleyvu's Teddy Bear / Harlaquin Brit the Skywalker
1988	Deerpark Heartlight*	Ashley v Bernerliebe / Deerpark Daisy
1989	Alpenblicks Alpine Alpenweide*	Pikes Harpo J Andrew / Alpenweide's Alpha Heidi
1990	Heartlights Baby Grand*	Shersan Chip off the Ol' Block / Heartlight's Autograph
1991/3	Donar v Mutschen*	Hansi v Seewadel / Assi v Mutschen
1992/6	Swiss Stars Blue Baron*	Dallybecks Echo Jackson / Vombreiterwegs Swiss Lace
1994	De-Li's Foregone Conclusion*	De-Li's Original Score / De-Li's Foreign Intrigue
1995	De-Li's Standing Ovation*	De-Li's Foreign Touch / De-Li's Heart of Gold
1997	Nashcms Taylor Maid	De-Li's Standing Ovation / Nashems Becken v Woodmoor
1998	Schmucki Udo Anabelle	Udo v Gabiarzbinden / Zarte Eky

what you did. No two judges, however skilful, will agree on everything, but they should be agreed on the gradings of the dogs even if they had them placed in a different order. In the example given above, the four Excellent dogs could legitimately be placed by another judge in a different order, so long as they were in the first four places and not interspersed with the Very Good animals.

WINNERS AT MAJOR SHOWS

In most countries there is a major show which is held in greatest esteem. It is usually the parent breed club because, in most countries, there is either one club or one major club. Of course, any club can pick judges that are far from ideal, so the dog winning at the major event may not always

LEFT: Ch. Gillro Jack Flash Of Manadori b 1980 (Takawalk Kalamoun – Gillro Sabella): Winner of four CCs. He was BIS at the BMDC of GB in 1984 when this photo was taken with owner Dot Fry. Photo: Hartley.

be the best available, but, overall, there will be a tendency for the top winners at the premier event to be among the best dogs of the day.

Table 5.5 shows the BOB (BB) winners at the BMD Club of America Specialty, which is the largest Bernese show in the world with several hundred entries in conformation, quite apart from Obedience, Agility and Draft classes. The show is always a five-point major in both sexes and, aside from 1985 and 1998, the BOB winner was, or became, a Champion. Only five animals have won BOB more than once, but the BOB in 1997 had been BOS the previous year. The show is held in a different location each year and circulates around the country to local host clubs, though it is overseen by the BMDCA.

ABOVE: Ch. Bernalpen Welsche 1986-1987 (Ch. Transcontinental Boy Of Clenraw – Inchberry Snow Queen At Bernalpen). She won the bitch CC at Crufts in 1992 and ended up with 12 CCs and three Reserve CCs. She also has a Ch. daughter – Ch. Bernalpen Ketje – sired by Tawajah's Leopold.   Photo: Trafford.

Table 5.6 shows the winners of BOB at Crufts in Britain over the last twenty years. There are several breed clubs and, although the BMD Club of Great Britain is termed the parent club, no club has precedence over another. Crufts is world-famous and, nowadays, usually attracts a large Bernese entry in excess of 200, which is the equal of, or better than, many breed club entries. Accordingly, rather than list breed club events, the Crufts show has been chosen as the representative of Britain. The show was originally held in London and, in more recent years, has been staged in Birmingham. Only two animals won BOB at Crufts more than once but some dogs won the CC more than once. The first CC ever awarded in the breed was at Crufts 1977, to Meiklestane Dark Ace.

Ch. Arrowmeet Chieftain: BOB at Crufts 1993.

Table 5.6 Winners of BOB at Crufts, England.

Year	Animal[1]	Sire Dam
1977	Meiklestane Dark Ace *	Duntiblae Nalle Tarncred Tara
1978	Forgeman Fedora*+	Duntiblae Nalle Kisumu Belle Fleur of Forgeman
1979	Tarncred Puffin*	Duntiblae Nalle Tarncred Black Watch
1980	Folkdance at Forgeman	Tarncred Puffin Forgeman Folksong of Tarncred
1981	Millwire Double Blank of of Frebren*	Duntiblae Dark Fortune Millwire Ace of Diamonds
1982	Duntiblae Dark Avenger of Forgeman*	Duntiblae Nalle Duntiblae Eva
1983	Coliburn Ember+	Jumbo v Waldacker at Coliburn Rena v Lyssbach at Coliburn
1984	Gillro Jack Flash of Manadori*	Takawalk Kalamoun Gillro Sabella
1985	Forgeman Forrester*+	Mustang v Nesselacker of Glanzberg Folkdance of Forgeman
1986/88	Duntiblae Dark Protector*	Duntiblae Forgeman Fusilier Duntiblae Bernax Bardot
1987	Manadori's Star Dreamer+	Gillro Jack Flash of Manadori Glanzbergs Edelweiss of Manadori
1989	Clashaidy Nordic Fire*	Tarncred Bullfinch Tarncred Tattoo of Clashaidy
1990	Forgeman Fancy Free of Mixbury	Dingo de Froideville Duntiblae Forgeman Forgetmenot
1991	Duntiblae Dark Viking*	Choristma Monch of Vindissa Duntiblae Dark Pleasure
1992	Carlacot Genesis at Nellsbern*	Clashaidy Nordic Fire Carlacot Ebony
1993	Arrowmeet Chieftain*	Duntiblae Dark Dexter Korinti Belle of Arrowmeet
1994	Clenoja Fidos Prince*	Carlacot Fido Carlacot Gorse
1995/96	Hildrek Jonquil	Pascha v Nesselacker of Glanzberg Lady v Nesselacker of Hildrek
1997	Bernfold Dawn Chorus	Windlenell War Lord Kernow Summerlove at Bernfold
1998	Sitzendorf Scrumptious at Duntiblae+	Cotesbach Dexters Cassidy Bisbie Turquoise of Sitzendorf

[1] Animals marked * are males and others are females. All animals were or became Champions except those marked + but titles are omitted for ease of presentation. This also applies to parents.

6 *GENETIC PRINCIPLES*

A dog is made up of millions of cells, each of which contains a nucleus in which an electron microscope would show up thread-like structures. These structures are called chromosomes and the number of these is identical in every normal dog and is also the same in the wolf, coyote and golden jackal. There are, in fact, 78 chromosomes or, more accurately, 39 pairs, because there are 39 slightly differently shaped and sized chromosomes and each pair of identical ones is called a homologous pair. In some species, the chromosomes are markedly different, but in the dog this is less obvious, though they do range in size. Each species has a given number of chromosomes, which is found in all normal members of that species. Thus, there are, for example, 46 (23 pairs) in man, 60 (30 pairs) in cattle and 38 (19 pairs) in the cat.

One member of each homologous chromosome pair has come from the father and one member from the mother. If all dog cells carried 78 chromosomes then there would be complications in reproduction, but it is known that germ cells (sperm and ova) carry only one member of each pair. An individual sperm carries one of each of the 39 sets as does the egg (ovum). Thus, when the sperm unites with the egg, we are back to 78 individual, or 39 pairs, of chromosomes. In this way the species' chromosome number remains constant.

Abnormal chromosome numbers can occur, such as with Down's syndrome in man where there are three copies of chromosome number 21, but this type of anomaly is rare in dogs and, in most cases, abnormal chromosome number leads to foetal death.

The process by which a germ cell receives only one of each of the chromosomes is termed meiosis, and is a reduction division during which cells divide after first ensuring that each new cell carries one of each of the chromosomes. To a degree, there is an element of chance in that while each germ cell must contain one member of each of the 39 pairs, it is purely random as to which chromosome goes to which germ cell. One sperm may get Chromosome 1 that originated with the father and another will get Chromosome 1 that originated with the mother. On average, about half will have originated with each parent but individual germ cells could vary enormously from that pattern. With 39 chromosome pairs, the number of possible combinations is legion.

Not only is there considerable variation between cells in terms of which chromosomes they receive, but there is a further element of chance about which sperm meets up with which egg. There are millions of sperm in an ejaculate and innumerable combinations are possible. When sperm and egg unite, the new fertilised egg is back to 78 chromosomes (39 pairs) and half have come from each parent. Thus each puppy derives half its genetic material from father and half from mother. Just as it has 50 per cent of its genes in common with each of its parents, it has 50 per cent of its genes in common with its siblings (brothers and sisters).

The new fertilised cell has the capacity to duplicate itself by a process called mitosis. In this system, the chromosomes split down their length to form chromatids which are then drawn to opposite ends of the cell which, in turn, constricts between them so that we now have two cells, each with the same identical combination of chromosomes. It is a principle of normal growth that cells multiply, but without changing their genetic composition.

In simple terms, all the cells deriving from the original fertilised egg are the same. A particular chromosome will carry along its length a series of genes which are integral parts of the chromosome and are made up of deoxyribonucleic acid (DNA) which in turn is composed of sugar, phosphate and nitrogen bases called purines (adenine and guanine, or A and G) and pyramidines (thymine and cytosine, or T and C). The arrangement of these bases at a specific point of locus is the basis of a gene. The two original cells with their 39 individual chromosomes must contain all the instructions needed for that dog to function.

Instructions are needed to determine sex, details of the anatomy, the functioning of organs and the like. All the complexities of a living organism such as a dog have to be reproducible from the instructions in the original genetic material.

A specific gene is always found in the same location, i.e. on the same specific chromosome in a particular area of it. Because an animal has two versions of each chromosome (having got one from each parent), it has two places for the specific gene to occur. One is on the chromosome that came from father and one on the chromosome that came from mother. Genes can, of course, vary. If we look at coat colour in the dog, there are many different genes and at each gene locus there may be more than one alternative. Alternative versions of a gene are termed alleles. The difference between one allele and a contemporary may be quite simple and relate to one change in the arrangement of the bases. At the agouti series locus, for example, there are six alternative alleles: A gives solid colour, a^y golden sable, a^w wolf grey, a^s saddle marked, a^t black with tan points and a recessive black. If a breed had all of these genes then any dog within the breed could carry any two alleles. If it carried two the same, such as $a^y a^y$, then it would be homozygous for this allele and be golden sable. If it carried $a^y a^t$ then it would be heterozygous but it would still be sable because the a^y version is dominant to the a^t version. A dominant allele is one which imposes its set of instructions when present only once, while a recessive allele is one that must be present in duplicate for it to 'work'.

The agouti series is a locus with multiple (more than two) alleles, but a dog can only have two of them (the same or different) because it only has two places for the allele to be, i.e. on a specific chromosome at a specific locus, because the dog only has two of the same chromosome. The Bernese has the agouti series but is believed to carry only one allele, namely the a^t version, so all Bernese are a^ta^t. In contrast, the German Shepherd can have all except the A, and can thus appear in a variety of colours. Dominance in the agouti series is in the order given above so that a^w is dominant to a^t, but is recessive to A and to a^y. The normal system of nomenclature is to use a capital letter for a dominant allele and a lower-case letter for the recessive. With several alleles, suffix letters are used as in the agouti series.

At another locus we have the B series, which produces black or brown/red pigment. This locus has only two alternatives: black (B) which is dominant to red (b), so dogs can be either pure black (BB), black carrying red (Bb) or red (bb). Note that the BB and Bb individuals are identical in their appearance, i.e. they are both black in colour, but they are different in their genetic make-up. In this gene series we have only two versions that we can see, black or red, and we call this the phenotype. However, there are three different genetic combinations BB, Bb and bb, which we call genotypes. Because BB and Bb are equally black we cannot distinguish genotype from the phenotype, but if we bred from them we would get different results. The BB animal could only give rise to black offspring, but the Bb animal could produce reds if mated to another Bb or to a bb animal. If we only ever mated our Bb animal to BB mates then we would never know that it was Bb because its offspring would all be black. Note that B/b give rise to black and red pigment but this

does not mean that the animal is solid black. Almost all Bernese carry the BB combination, but they are not solid black because the a^ta^t combination determines the coat pattern of black with tan points. A Bernese carrying bb (very rare) would not be black and tan but red and tan. By the same token, a Samoyed carries B (hence its black nose), but it is all-white because a gene at another locus masks the black coat colour but does not affect the nose. All dogs with black noses must be carrying B at least once, even if they are not black in colour. Dogs with brown or liver noses carry bb in duplicate but they may not be brown (red) in coat colour because it will depend upon what other genes they carry.

In looking at dog breeding, we have to define the term 'trait'. We could describe a Bernese as having a blue eye, a steep lay of shoulder and a short tail. This is the phenotype of that animal, but the traits we have been describing are eye colour, shoulder placement and tail length. Blue eye is not a trait, merely a version of the trait of eye colour. The next dog we see might have a dark-brown eye, the third one a yellow eye and the fourth a black eye. The dark-brown eye may be the 'best' version but all four – blue, brown, yellow and black – are phenotypic variations of the trait eye colour. A dog with an aggressive temperament is demonstrating a version or phenotype of the trait 'temperament'.

Some of the traits we examine in the dog are relatively simple in their mode of inheritance, such as the B/b situation described above. In contrast others are more complex. As we shall see later, a Bernese may have a litter size that ranges from one to 16. There are not, however, sixteen different alleles giving from one to 16 puppies, but a complex combination of different genes and this feature will be discussed later.

Let us revert to the issue of coat colour and the B/b combination. Suppose we mate a pure breeding black Newfoundland male to a brown bitch. In this breed, the bb colour is termed brown, not red, but it is the same gene. The black dog is BB and the brown bitch has to be bb because, as a recessive allele, unless b is present in duplicate, the dog cannot be brown. What will result? Well, the black dog produces sperm that have only half of his chromosomes so, on the one carrying the B/b series, he only has B therefore all his sperm will be B. In contrast, the brown bitch produces ova that are all b. When sperm and ovum meet we are back to two of each chromosome and thus we have a Bb animal. All the litter will be of this type, so all the puppies will be Bb and appear black. They will, of course, be just as black as their father, but he was a pure breeding (BB) black and they are blacks carrying brown (Bb). If we were to mate two of these littermates together, what would result?

Now the parents are both black but they are black dogs carrying a brown allele (Bb) and, as a result, half their sperm/ova will carry B and half will carry b. The situation will be as in Figure 6.1.

		sperm B	sperm b
ovum	B	BB Black	Bb Black
ovum	b	bB Black	bb Brown

Figure 6.1 Mating of two Bb Newfoundlands

This is called a Punnett square, and shows a ratio of three blacks to one brown, or 3:1. In reality, the ratio is 1 purebreeding black, 2 carrier blacks and 1 brown or 1:2:1. This is a typical way in which a recessive trait appears or is hidden; it can be applied to any single gene situation and will work regardless of which parent was the original black. The 19th century work which pioneered this type of understanding was that of the monk Gregor Mendel and, as a result, such traits are often called Mendelian traits. A principle of Mendelian traits is that they are inherited as distinct entities; there is no blending and genes remain unchanged from generation to generation. Although we have used a Newfoundland example, the same would apply if we used black and red Bernese but that is a very rare event and most of us may never see a red Bernese.

Let us now complicate matters by adding a second gene. Still using Newfoundlands, let us take a black which carries brown (Bb) and take account of the white markings seen in some Newfoundlands, which come from the S series. This gene has four alternatives, S, s^i, s^P and s^w, of which the Bernese only has s^i. The Newfoundland has two of these alleles, namely S for solid colour and s^P for piebald spotting. Let us take two black dogs (one of each sex) of the type Bb, which do not exhibit white markings but which, unbeknown to us, carry piebald spotting recessively. Solid colour S is dominant to piebald spotting s^P. We are thus mating two animals that are both $BbSs^P$. Mating them will be as is shown in Figure 6.2.

In Figure 6.2 we have four alternative sperm and ova and, from two black animals, we have produced a situation of nine blacks, three browns, three Landseers and one brown and white. Of course, the mating

| | | Dam BbSsᵖ | | | |
| | | ova | | | |
		BS	bS	Bsᵖ	bsᵖ
	BS	BBSS Black	BbSS Black	BBSsᵖ Black	BbSsᵖ Black
Sire BbSsᵖ	bS	BbSS Black	bbSS Brown	BbSsp Black	bbSsᵖ Brown
sperm	Bsᵖ	BBSsᵖ Black	BbSsᵖ Black	Bbsᵖsᵖ Landseer	Bbsᵖsᵖ Landseer
	bsᵖ	BbSsᵖ Black	bbSsᵖ Brown	Bbsᵖsᵖ Landseer	bbsᵖsᵖ Brown/white

Figure 6.2 Mating Newfoundlands with two genes involved

would probably not give rise to 16 offspring so the numbers would only apply over a large number of matings though the ratios would be accurate. Note that brown and white would be an undesirable colour in this breed although there is nothing biologically wrong with the animal. Note also that, although we mated two solid black animals, from their progeny we can asccertain that both parents must have carried b (brown) and sᵖ (Landseer) because both these recessive colours cropped up in the progeny and could only do so if both parents carried the necessary alleles.

Clearly, there are all kinds of combinations one can make, not only with black/brown and Landseer, but also with other gene combinations and with more than two loci. If you know the genotype of the parents, you can work out which sperm/ova will be present and calculate, using a Punnett square, the type of progeny that will result.

EPISTASIS
Thus far we have mainly assumed that each gene acts in isolation from others and that is, to a degree, true. However, sometimes a gene at one locus can influence the expression of a different gene at a different locus, as in the case of the Samoyed referred to earlier. This is a phenomenon called epistasis. It can best be explained by coat colour in the Dobermann. This breed carries the aᵗaᵗ pattern found in the Bernese, which gives rise to black with tan points, but it does not carry the white markings (sⁱsⁱ). It also carries the B/b allele, giving rise to black (BB/Bb) or brown (bb) but called red in this breed. The Dobermann also carries the D gene, as does the Bernese, which allows the pigment to express itself. However, all Bernese appear to be DD but the Dobermann has the other alternative d. The allele d is recessive to D but, when present in duplicate (dd), it causes black pigment to be changed to blue and red pigment to change to fawn. This change will be already obvious at birth. The DD and Dd combinations do not alter the basic pigment pattern.

Dobermanns that carry BB or Bb are black while those that carry bb are red, but this gene only affects black pigment not tan markings so that basic pattern of the aᵗaᵗ combination is unchanged but dogs are either black with tan points or red with tan points. The bb combination also affects the nose pigment which turns liver or brown. Of course each dog requires the D/d gene. If a dog has the DD or Dd combination, then it will be unaffected and be black or red as the case may be. However, dogs which carry dd will be blue and tan (if they also carry BB or Bb) or fawn and tan (if they are bb). There are nine different genotypes but only four phenotypes, which are shown in Table 6.1.

Table 6.1
Colour combinations in the Dobermann

Phenotype	Genotypes[1]
Black	(1)BBDD(2) BBDd(3) BbDD(4) BbDd
Red	(5) bbDD(6) bbDd
Blue	(7) BBdd(8) Bbdd
Fawn	(9) bbdd

[1] Note that all 9 genotypes also carry $a^t a^t$ so all have tan markings

The only colour that can have the genotype identified from the phenotype is number 9, the Fawn (called Isabella) which carries the double recessive bb and dd. All the others have alternatives and there are four kinds of black. The type (1) animal will only ever give rise to black offspring, but the type (4) can give rise to all possible colours depending upon what it is mated to. Using Punnett square techniques, it is possible to take any two of the nine combinations given in Table 6.1 and work out what sort of progeny will result. Thus mating (4) to (4) will give rise to a ratio of 9 Black, 3 Blue, 3 Red and 1 Fawn – given enough matings. In contrast (9) to (9) will given rise to 100 per cent Fawns (all bbdd).

LETHAL GENES

Some genes are lethal in certain combinations. For example, the blood disease Von Willebrands is thought to be a dominant condition in many breeds in which the homozygous dominant version (VWD,VWD) leads to early death, the heterozygote (VWD,vwd) is affected by the blood disease at varying levels and the homozygous recessive (vwd,vwd) is normal. In some breeds this disease is recessive and operates differently.

Similarly all merle dogs are Mm, as opposed to non-merles which are mm, because dogs that carry the merle gene in duplicate (MM) are all-white and likely to have impaired hearing and sight. Note that both these are examples of what might be termed partial dominant action or incomplete dominance. If VWD and M were fully dominant, then the combination VWDvwd would have the same effect as VWDVWD and Mm would be identical to MM. In those circumstances, the VWDvwd and Mm combinations would be as badly affected as the double dominant alternatives.

It must be understood that dominant genes are not always 'good' and recessives 'bad'. Obviously, lethal/semi-lethal genes are undesirable, whether dominant or recessive, but most deleterious versions tend to be recessive on the grounds that, if a dominant gene is deleterious, then the animal which has the gene exhibits the problem and is consequently culled from breeding. Over time, most dominantly inherited defects tend to be lost from the population. Deleterious genes with a late onset are harder to cull than those which are seen early in life. Progressive Retinal Atrophy (PRA) is a recessive trait but it tends to be obvious only when a dog is two to four years of age (possibly one to two years in the Bernese Mountain Dog) and, by this time, the animal may have been bred from without the breeder knowing that it was an affected case.

SEX INHERITANCE

Earlier it was stated that each dog carries 39 pairs of chromosomes, each member of a pair matching its partner. We must now make a slight alteration to that rule. Females possess one relatively large pair of chromosomes, but males carry only one of these and its partner is a small chromosome. Traditionally the large chromosome is termed X and the small one is Y, and they are known as sex chromosomes while all the others are termed autosomes. The dog, as a species, thus has two sex chromosomes and 76 autosomes. The term autosomal recessive refers to a recessive allele carried on an autosome. All the conditions discussed thus far have been autosomal.

All females are XX and all males are XY. As a consequence, all ova carry one X and sperm carry either an X or a Y. If X-bearing sperm reach the ovum first, the resultant foetus will be XX and female and if Y-bearing sperm get there first, the foetus will be XY and male. One ought to expect equal numbers of males and females but, in most cases, the Y-bearing sperm either move faster or the ovum has a predeliction for Y-bearing sperm, such that more males are conceived than females. Generally, in most mammalian species, there are slightly more males conceived and born than females so that the sex ratio is about 103-106 males per 100 females.

Obviously, anything carried on the Y chromosome can only pass from father to son, whereas anything on the X chromosome can occur in either sex. It is believed that little of any importance is carried on the Y chromosome, which exists only to determine maleness. The X chromosome carries several features such as haemophilia A and haemophilia B, the first of which can occur in any breed of dog though it is not reported in many. Haemophilia B is rare and known in only a few breeds. A disease similar to Duchenne's muscular dystrophy is also carried on the X chromosome and seen in Labrador Retrievers. In man, there are over 60 X-linked diseases, though many are rare.

Most sex-linked diseases, the term given to those carried on the sex-chromosomes, are recessive. If we use haemophilia A as an example, the allele which causes blood to have impaired clotting ability is recessive to the normal allele. We could label the normal allele H and the haemophiliac allele h. We thus have three kinds of female and two kinds of male. These are shown below:

$X^H X^H$ (normal) $X^H X^h$ (carrier) $X^h X^h$ (haemophiliac) are females and

$X^H Y$ (normal) $X^h Y$ (haemophliac) are males.

Note that males are affected or normal and never carriers. They are affected even though they have just a single dose of the gene because the Y chromosome is almost inert and cannot countermand the h allele. In contrast, females have to carry hh in duplicate to be affected. Blood tests can determine if the male is haemophiliac or not, but are currently less effective at identifying 'carrier' females.

The commonest way of obtaining an affected male is by mating a normal male to a carrier female. This gives rise to males that are either normal (50 per cent) or affected (50 per cent), while the females are either clear (50 per cent) or carriers (50 per cent) though the females are hard to distinguish between. Some males with haemophilia die young, but others live to reproduce and they will produce perfectly normal sons (because these inherit their father's Y chromosome). However *all* the daughters of a haemophiliac get their father's h allele and are thus carriers. These, in turn, can mate a normal male and the cycle starts again. Although affected females can be produced, they have to involve affected males and either carrier or affected females. Mating a carrier female to an affected male is so rare an event that haemophiliac females are hardly ever seen.

SEX-LIMITED AND SEX-CONTROLLED TRAITS

Genes carried on the X/Y chromosomes are termed sex-linked and there are two other terms which need explanation. A sex-limited trait only appears in one sex, though the genes which produce it may be carried by both sexes. An obvious example is milk production in any species which is only measurable in females, while a male example is cryptorchidism which is demonstrated only in males but can be produced by genes derived from females. Sex-limited traits operate like other autosomal traits, but prediction is harder because only one sex demonstrates the feature.

Sex-controlled, sometimes called sex-influenced, traits are carried autosomally and can appear in either sex but they are more likely to be seen in one sex. Thus spina bifida in man is seen in both sexes but is more common in female children. Similarly, hip dysplasia in man is more commonly seen in females and it is noteworthy that, in some breeds of dog, the hip status of females tends to be worse than that of males.

REDUCING THE INCIDENCE OF SIMPLE GENE DEFECTS

If one is seeking to reduce the incidence of a simple Mendelian defect or gene, then not using affected animals will obviously help. If Landseer sPsP Newfoundlands were not bred from, the incidence of the sP allele would reduce and that of its counterpart S would increase. Of course, dogs that were SsP would slip through the net because they would be solid-coloured. As the incidence of sPsP declined then an increasing number of the sP alleles would be hidden in the SsP combination. Elimination of the Landseer allele would require that all carriers were identified and discarded from breeding. Clearly, that would require test mating or a recording scheme which noted every self-coloured animal producing spotted progeny. This would be a lengthy and costly business and, of course, need not be undertaken because Landseer is an acceptable version of the trait and we have merely used it as an example. However, reduction of PRA would be desirable but would be even more difficult because it is late in onset. Gene mapping makes the task easy, but thus far only Irish Setter PRA is assessable in this form.

With simple genes, once the animal's genotype is known there is nothing to be gained from pedigree analysis. If a dog called Alfie has given rise to hypomyelinogenesis (trembler) puppies, then Alfie, who is clearly normal to look at, has to be a carrier. If trembler were to be depicted by the allele t^+, then Alfie must be of the formula Tt^+ and it does not matter where he derived the defective allele from, only that he must carry it. The problem arises when looking at his offspring. They have an equal chance of getting T or t^+ and, if Alfie is mated to normal TT bitches, the offspring will all be normal but half will be TT and half Tt$^+$ with no means of knowing (at present) which is which. If Billie is a son of Alfie and appears normal then he has a 50 per cent chance of being TT and a 50 per cent chance of being Tt$^+$. However, if Billie has produced offspring without any trembler puppies occurring, then the chances that Billie is clear (TT) increases, especially if he is mated to some 'suspect' lines or is widely used. Now let us consider an animal, Chuck, who is a grandson of Alfie. Provided the intervening generation is clear or unknown (in trembler terms), Chuck has 0.5 x 0.5 = 0.25 or a 25 per cent chance of being a carrier and a 75 per cent chance of being free. Thus the further animals are removed from Alfie in generation terms, the less the risk, because each generation the risk is halved. It thus becomes an issue of risk taken. Should we use a great-grandson with a 0.5 x 0.5 x 0.5 = 0.125 (or 12.5 per cent) chance that he carries t$^+$ and a 87.5 per cent chance that he is free, or do we avoid the line completely?

This clearly has to depend upon the nature of the defect we are looking at and the relative risks. It also has to depend upon the quality of the animal we are thinking of using. If the dog under discussion is merely, say, a Very Good animal then we may decide not take the risk. In contrast, if the dog is an Excellent animal with much to offer, the risk may be worth taking. All dog breeding involves some risk and the failure to take risks at all probably means that you have given up breeding!

GENE MAPPING

At present, a great deal of research is going on in many universities and laboratories worldwide to map canine and other animal genomes. A popular version of what gene mapping entails was produced by Archibald and Haley (1993). Much of the research in canine mapping is stimulated by human medicine funding on the grounds that many canine diseases are similar to those in man. Gene mapping allows the actual genes to be identified from a sample of blood or hair or other body tissue, and it would enable an animal to have its genotype identified even in the case of recessive traits. Thus PRA in the Irish Setter has been identified as rod cone dysplasia type 1 (rcd1) and its location mapped. For that disease we can now determine and distinguish between PP(normal), Pp (carrier) and pp (affected) animals. This has a tremendous bearing upon genetic selection because it means that pp animals can be identified early in life before they suffer from the disease and Pp animals can also be identified without the need for test mating. A pp animal may need to be culled because, eventually, it will go blind, but a Pp animal will be quite safe since it will never exhibit the problem, though it is best not bred from. However, even in this case, care has to be taken. If one is dealing with a Pp animal with a great deal of virtues to be had, then there may be a case for using the animal on normal mates and following up progeny. This is very feasible if gene mapping itself becomes feasible.

As more diseases become identified in this way, it will be possible to reduce and even eliminate such genetic disease very rapidly, and several other diseases are well on the way to discovery or have been identified. In an essay on the subject Holmes (1998) used the title *Canine genetic disease: the beginning of the end?* While we would like to think that this is true we are not even sure that, at present, we have reached the end of the beginning. There are still numerous Mendelian diseases to be identified and, of course, some of the major diseases like hip dysplasia, elbow arthrosis and epilepsy, to name but three, are known to be, or are likely to be, polygenic traits, in which area gene mapping is much less advanced, though it is going on. No one would be happier than me to be able to genetically assess our dogs by a simple blood test, but that is a long way away for many diseases and even further for polygenic traits. Even the excellent work on identification of PRA in Irish Setters (Farber et al., 1992) has not been applicable to other breeds, because Irish setter PRA (rcd 1) is not like that in other breeds where the gene(s) appear at another locus, not yet discovered. Within the next five years an increasing number of Mendelian traits will be identified and steps taken to eradicate them, but not all genes. Polygenic traits may still be here in ten, perhaps twenty, years from now. At the risk of sounding Luddite, the practical nature of selecting dogs and planning matings may change very little. One thing is certain, all the genetic mapping in the world will be of little help if kennel clubs and other ruling bodies do not insist upon application of the science to dogdom. I would like to feel that breeders will do things because of their concern for the breed, but many breeders are far from altruistic and we cannot rely on them doing things for 'the good of the breed'. Most breeders will do the right thing because it is right and because they will benefit in the long term by doing so, but a small number may have to be compelled to conform once the genetics and the way to combat the problem are established. In the meantime, DNA fingerprinting, as it is popularly called, is proving invaluable for paternity testing (Binns et al., 1995) and can be applied to

defect elimination once mapping is done.

Gradually, as more genes become identified and mapped, DNA testing will indicate carrier animals and allow breeders to take the right decisions. In Bernese, the removal from breeding in the mid-1980s of many of the sires known to carry hypomyelinogenesis helped to reduce the frequency of the allele, but some carriers remained in the population and the defect, though rare, is not unknown. Of course, it also removed some of the very best dogs, and the fear which people had about using offspring of known carriers reduced the use of some dogs with much to give. DNA testing would allow the use of known carriers in certain circumstances because their offspring could be DNA-tested from the start and carriers not used for breeding. Thus a valuable animal could be bred from to pass on its virtues without the transmission to the breeding population of the defect.

If a recessive gene (a) is lethal in the homozygous state then its incidence will reduce in a randomly mated population because all the animals that are aa die and do not reproduce. In effect, natural selection works against the spread of the disease. The gene still continues through Aa animals but would decline slowly if there was no conscious effort to select for it. In broad terms, breeds do not change if there is no attempt to change them but, of course, breeding is rarely random though much of it may be inadequately thought about.

POLYGENIC (QUANTITATIVE) TRAITS
Although, in dogs, many simple Mendelian traits are considered important, especially those creating disease (see Chapter Ten) or those concerned with features like coat colour, the most important features are not

inherited in this way. Pedigree dog breeders sell the majority of their puppies as companion animals. Breeders therefore have a requirement to produce acceptable temperaments of the kind the pet owner wants and needs. Any sensible breeder, regardless of breed, will place a great emphasis upon temperament and character. Simultaneously, a breeder will be seeking to produce dogs that conform to the Breed Standard and will thus be selecting for various physical attributes. These traits do not fit into simple distinct boxes in the way that coat colours do. For example, wither height in the Bernese will range from less than 57 cms (22½ins) through to more than 28ins cms depending upon sex. The smallest bitch should be 58 cms (23ins) and the tallest dog 70 cms (27½ins), but animals below or above the extremes will occur. Measurement is usually to the nearest centimetre, but animals vary by very tiny amounts. In addition, if the sexes are examined separately, it will be seen that each population shows a curve similar to that shown in Figure 6.3. In other words, most animals are around the mean and there is a decline in numbers as one moves towards the extremes. This is called a Normal curve or a Normal distribution.

The pattern shown in Figure 6.3 is typical of many features that are important in the dog. Litter size, for example, would, if given enough numbers of litters, follow the same trend. If one examined a specific conformational feature such as shoulder placement or body weight, a similar pattern would be seen. Such a pattern can be shown to derive from the fact that such traits are influenced by a number of different genes, each of which may have various alternatives or alleles. Each gene may have a small effect,

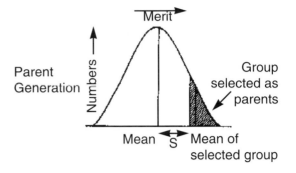

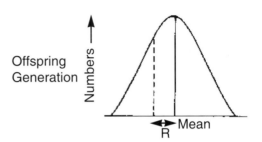

Figure 6.3 Illustration of selection differentials (S) and response to selection (R)

but collectively they have a marked effect. Such traits are polygenic traits. Moreover, whereas coat colour is not influenced at all by the way a dog is fed or managed and is thus entirely a genetic feature, traits such as wither height, body weight, shoulder placement, temperament or litter size are all influenced, in part, by the way we feed, rear and/or socialise our animals.

Traits of this kind are often called quantitative traits to distinguish them from traits like coat colour which are termed qualitative traits. Qualitative traits fit into distinct and clearly defined groups, whereas quantitative traits show what is called continuous variation. When we examine a trait of this kind, let us suggest wither height–we find that the height we can see and measure is made up of several features. What we see is called the phenotype, a feature we have already discussed, but it is made up of a genetic and an environmental component. The actual height of a dog will be determined by his breed mean, to which will be added or subtracted his genetic potential and the effect of the environment that the dog has received.

If we call the phenotype P, the genetic value G, the environmental value E and the breed mean M, then the feature can be expressed as:

$$P = M + G + E$$

Sometimes the formula is expressed as P = G + E, but it seems appropriate to include a breed mean value so that breeders realise that in selecting for any polygenic trait they are working in deviations from a mean, not in abstract isolation. The Newfoundland breeder working with BVA/KC hip scores is operating in a breed that averages about 30, while the Bernese breeder is using a mean of around 16. A score of 30 might well be discarded by a Bernese breeder seeking to enhance hip status, but would probably be used in Newfoundlands. For this reason, breed mean must always be borne in mind.

Let us examine three male Bernese (A/B/C), of the same age, whose wither heights are: A = 64, B = 68 and C = 70 cms (25¼, 26¾ and 27½ins)

These heights represent the phenotypic value of each dog and we can express them as deviations from the mean value for the breed, which we can say is 66 cms (26ins). Expressed as deviations (cms) from breed average A = –2, B = +2 and C = +4. That much is straightforward, but suppose we could determine their genetic value as being A = –1cm (-0.4ins), B = +1cm (+0.4ins and C = +2 cms (+0.8ins).

We can now say that measurements, taking account of genetic merit, should have been:

A (66 –1) = 65 (25½ins)
B (66 + 1) = 67 (26½ins)
C (66 + 2) = 68 (26¾ ins)

Actual measurements were 64, 68 and 70 cms, (25¼, 26¾ and 27½ ins) so environmental influences were –1, +1 and +2 for A, B and C respectively. Thus, in addition to being genetically less good, A was environmentally disadvantaged and B and C had helpful environments, but C more so than B. The most likely influence upon height, from an environmental point of view, would be nutrition, so we might conclude that A had not been well reared whereas B and C had, particularly C.

When we assess the wither height of a dog we are assessing the phenotype and we will not know the genetic and environmental influences, but we can say with certainty that what we see (the phenotype) is the result of genetic and environmental influences taking that dog away from the breed mean in either an upward or a downward direction.

Genetic influences can principally be of two kinds: either due to specific combinations of genes or due to what are called additive effects. If a dog has a favourable combination of genes, it cannot transmit this to its progeny because genes are transmitted as samples and in so doing the favourable combination is broken up. However, additive effects can be passed on.

If a trait was controlled by three genes, each with the alternative of + or 0, then an animal which carried + + + + + + would pass on + + + to its progeny, whereas an animal that carried + 0 + 0 0 0 would pass on anything from + + 0 through to 0 0 0 but, on average, would tend to pass on half of its + alleles, namely + 0 0. If we can assess the additive component, we can predict the breeding value of animals. In general terms, an animal passes on half of its genetic value to the next generation.

If we can measure progeny performance we can go some way to predicting the breeding value of an animal. However, the minute we start to look at progeny we have to be certain that we do not bias the figures. If we mate a sire to very large bitches then the wither height of his progeny will depend, not only on the sire's breeding value, but also on the bias given him because the bitches were not random but were actually large. In contrast, if the sire is mated to a more or less random sample of bitches, then his breeding value can be defined more accurately. This does not mean that he must mate average-sized bitches. He can mate bitches of any size but, overall, they should average about 62 cms (24½ins), the breed female average height.

Suppose the mean wither height of males is 66 cms (26ins) and we use a sire whose progeny (at least 10 and preferably more) out of a random sample of bitches (as far as wither height is concerned) measure 67 cms (26½ins). The mean height of progeny is 1 cm above breed mean and, since a sire passes on half of his superiority, we can conclude that the breeding value of the sire in question is +2 cms for wither height. Breeding value can be defined as twice the deviation of the progeny mean from the population mean. A sire whose progeny averaged 64 cms (25¼ins) would have a breeding value of 2 x (64–66 [25¼–26ins]) = 4 cms (1½ins).

Of course we are working with limited numbers, we may not be certain that the mates were actually a random sample and, in any specific instance, a sire can pass on a sample of genes that is far from typical of what he might be expected to do. He could pass on a very good or a very bad sample but, the greater the number of progeny and the more random his mates, the more precise will be our estimate. However, we would be wiser to call the feature we have been discussing the Estimated Breeding Value (EBV). Suppose the EBV for wither height of a sire was +2 cms (¾in), and that of the bitch to which he was mated was +1cm, then the EBV of their offspring would be :

$$\frac{2 + 1}{2} = +1.5 \text{ cms (½in).}$$

In other words, the *predicted BV* of the offspring is half that of its parents. Of course, we use animals before there is any information available on progeny. If we wanted to increase wither height in the Bernese, one way to achieve this would be to select the tallest animals and breed them together. If we bred only from dogs in excess of, say, 68 cms (26¾ins) and bitches in excess of 65 cms (25½ins), then gradually the mean height of males (66 cms [26ins]) and that of females (62 cms [24½ins]) would increase. Wither height would increase quite rapidly, because the height of an animal is a good clue to its Breeding Value.

Suppose we wanted to increase litter size from the present mean of, say, 7.4 pups per litter. One way might be to breed only from those animals which came from large litters. We could say that we will only breed from dogs and bitches that came from large litters of 12 or more. If we did this we would make very little progress, though some improvement might occur, but it would certainly not be as effective or as rapid as in the wither height situation. It is easier to raise height in the breed than to increase litter size, even if we breed from the very extremes of litter size.

HERITABILITY
The above fact about litter size compared to wither height is because the heritability of litter size is much less than the heritability of

wither height. What is heritability (symbol h^2)? It can be defined as the extent to which superiority of the parents is transmitted to their offspring, or as the reliability of the relationship between performance values and breeding values.

If a trait is highly heritable then the performance of an animal gives a good guide to its breeding value. If the trait has low heritability then animal performance is a poor guide to offspring performance. Heritabilities range from 0 to 1 or from 0 to 100 per cent. Wither height has a heritability of about 65 per cent, whereas litter size has a heritability than may be as low as 10 per cent. The difference explains why selection for wither height will be effective and selection for litter size will not. This does not mean that litter size is not under genetic control, far from it. Litter size is very much under genetic control, but it is largely a result of combinations of genes (called non-additive factors) which cannot be transmitted. A prolific bitch producing a large litter, say twelve, will very likely continue to have large litters all her life, certainly until old age, but her daughters may have large or small litters because most of that bitch's superiority was due to a favourable combination of genes which she could not pass to her daughters. In contrast, if a bitch is tall (say 65 cms [25½ins]), she carries additive genes to this effect and will pass them on to her progeny. Her progeny will, of course, vary in height because some will get a better sample of her genes than others, but, overall, she will produce larger than average offspring because she is about 3 cms (1¼ins) taller than the breed average of 62 cms (24½ins) and the trait is highly heritable.

Heritability is always used of a trait and a population. Thus the heritability of wither height in German Shepherd Dogs is 65 per cent, or the heritability of fear in Labradors is 50 per cent. This tells us that heritability relates to a specific population for a specific trait and, it could be said, even to a set point in time. It is a population measure, not a feature of an individual animal. Because fear is 50 per cent heritable in Labradors, it does not follow that the same applies to another breed, or to Labradors in a country other than Australia, where the calculation was made. However, heritability studies in dogs are rare and thus we have to use estimates until new figures can be produced.

The term 'heritable' is often confused with 'heritability'. For a trait to have a heritability and to be heritable there must be variation. The trait 'ears in the dog' is not heritable, because all dogs have two ears and differences do not exist. We cannot select for the trait 'ear number'. Ear number is under genetic control, in that, somewhere, there is a DNA instruction to this effect but the instruction is identical in all dogs. In contrast, ear length or ear shape are heritable traits and will have a heritability, though they may not yet have been calculated.

When traits are heritable, then relatives will resemble one another. The higher the heritability and the closer the relationship, the greater the resemblance. Tall dogs will tend to have tall progeny; long dogs long progeny. Parents and offspring and brothers and sisters (full siblings) will have 50 per cent of their genes in common and thus resemble each other. Calculation of heritabilities relies on the relationship, in that the commonest way of assessment is the correlation among half 'sibs' (usually animals with the same father). The correlation is multiplied by 4 to give the heritability. Another way is to assess the regression of offspring on sire, and this is multiplied by 2 to give the heritability.

Table 6.2 gives some heritabilities of canine traits. Where possible, Bernese values have been used but other breeds are included as being a better guide than no information at all. The paper of Verryn and Geerthsen (1987) gives more values than have been cited here, but the principal ones are listed.

Knowing the heritability of a trait is vital in the business of selection. If a trait has a low heritability, it means that an individual's perfomance is not a good guide to its breeding worth. The whole purpose of selection is to identify the best and then use them, but, if the best in phenotypic terms is not the best producer, such a policy is not going to work. Such evidence as we have does suggest that many conformational traits may be moderately-to-highly heritable and, thus, the animal's performance is a fair guide to what it will produce. Heritabilities of reproductive traits tend to be low, suggesting that improvement in this area is best achieved by other methods such as crossbreeding. However, that is, by definition, unavailable to purebred breeders.

Accuracy of measurement can enhance heritabilities. This applies not only to getting something like wither height accurately measured, but also to ensuring that sex effects are taken account of and that, if animals are assessed at different ages, then adjustment for age must be made. Age corrections may not apply to wither heights measured as adults, but sex effects would obviously apply. Age and sex would apply to things such as body weight and chest girth. Similarly, features like litter size may be affected by parity of the dam. Hip score and elbow score may both be influenced by sex and, if so, analyses would need to be undertaken for each sex, or correction factors to be used to adjust, say, females to what they might have scored if they had been males. In making any analyses it is crucial that environmental factors (age / sex / parity / etc. are all environmental features in this context) are corrected for in some way. If we are measuring wither height, for example, there would be no point in measuring some dogs at six months of age and others at over two years of age because the first would not be comparable and would be inaccurate as a guide to the dogs' true height.

Table 6.2 Heritabilities (percentages) for some canine traits

Trait	h^2	Breed	Source
Back length	44[4]	GSD	Verryn and Geerthsen(1987)
Body weight	41[4]	GSD	Verryn and Geerthsen (1987)
Chest depth	54[4]	GSD	Verryn and Geerthsen (1987)
Elbow arthrosis	34[1]	BMD	Swenson et al. (1997b)
Elbow arthrosis	28[2]	BMD	Swenson et al. (1997b)
Fear	50	Labrador	Goddard and Beilharz(1982)
Hip grade	34[2]	BMD	Swenson et al. (1997a)
Hip score	40[3]	BMD	Willis (1997)
Rear Pastern length	51[4]	GSD	Verryn and Geerthsen (1987)
Wither height	65[4]	GSD	Verryn and Geerthsen (1987)

[1]regression of sons on sires [2]regression of daughters on dams.
[3]paternal half sibs [4]combined figures : half sib and offspring parent.

SELECTION

All dog breeders, unless they are what is commonly called puppy farmers, are in the business of selection. Each breeder may be selecting for slightly different objectives, but most are seeking to produce animals which conform as closely as possible to the Breed Standard blueprint. In doing so, they will be seeking some measure of character such that their animals are acceptable, not only in respect of the Standard, but also as companion animals. Some breeders may be seeking specific features such as working ability or tracking prowess or, in the case of police or guide dog organisations, animals which will be suitable for those purposes.

Every breeder has to decide what to retain from their litters and which stud dogs to use; whether to use well proven sires or new up-and-coming ones; whether to keep a stud dog or use someone else's. Breeders also have to determine whether to base selection upon the dog itself, or to look also at relatives and how much attention to give to pedigree.

In selecting one dog and rejecting another, a breeder is directly influencing the gene frequencies that will be found in the next generation. Keeping big animals involves a move towards the genes that influence increases, as opposed to reductions, in height. By selecting undermarked Bernese, a breeder would be seeking to reduce the genes influencing the extension of white. By setting a limit on what hip or elbow score/grade will be used, the breeder is seeking to move towards genes for lower rather than higher scores or grades.

In any selection programme there is a standard formula which might be said to be the key indicator of progress. This has three components: the heritability (h^2), the selection differential (S) and the generation interval (t). Where R equals the response to selection the formula reads:

$$R = \frac{h^2 \times S}{t}$$

Selection differential is defined as the superiority of those animals selected to be the parents, compared with the mean of the population from which they came. If the wither height of male Bernese averages 66 cms (26ins) and we selected for breeding only dogs that average 68 cms (26¾ins), then the selection differential for wither height is 68 – 66 = +2 cms (26¾ – 26ins = ¾in).

Of course, this is the selection differential of males. There are, in fact, four routes:

Males to breed Males

Females to breed Males

Males to breed Females

Females to breed Females.

Because we need fewer males than females we can afford to be more selective about which males are worth breeding from than we can be about females. Many breeders may not select very strongly on the female side but will do so on the male side. In broad terms, the better the parents are, relative to the mean of the population from which they came, then the greater the value of S.

The progress made from generation to generation will depend upon the heritability multiplied by the selection differential. If, for example, we select parents that exceed the wither height of the breed by an average of 3 cms (1¼ins) then, if the heritability of wither height is 65 per cent, the progeny should have a mean wither height of 3 x 65/100 = +1.95 cms (¾in). In other words, the next generation should be 1.95 cms (¾in) taller on average.

Table 6.3 Generation interval (months) in four breeds in Norway

Breed	Route used				
	Father to son	Father to daughter	Mother to son	Mother to daughter	Overall
Bernese	54	53	47	42	50
GSD	65	59	51	56	58
Newfoundland	43	51	46	55	47
St Bernard	48	44	33	37	42

(after Lingaas, 1989)

Clearly, the degree of precision of measurement will be important but, in general terms, the more superior the parents are and the higher the heritability, the greater the potential progress. Thus far we have talked about progress per generation and, clearly, generations vary with species. In man, one can legally reproduce from the age of 16, but a generation interval is more like 25 years. This is the average age of parents when their progeny are born. While one can have a litter from a Bernese bitch of less than two years, the mean generation interval is over four years.

Lingaas (1989) calculated generation intervals in eight breeds in Norway, which included the Bernese, and his data are shown in Table 6.3 for three breeds plus the Bernese. Lingaas gave his data in years and these have been converted to the nearest month. The overall generation interval for all eight breeds was 4.21 years or 51 months. The route for father to sons averaged 52 months and that for father to daughters 51 months. The corresponding routes for mothers to sons and to daughters were 47 and 51 months respectively. Of the four breeds listed in Table 6.3, the German Shepherd Dog had the longest interval, with Bernese some eight months shorter. In general, routes via fathers were longer than those via mothers. This suggests that males are used to an older age, which is to be expected. In Britain, for example, the KC will not normally register puppies from bitches aged in excess of eight years, but a sire may be used as long as he is able to service bitches.

Going back to the response formula and using the wither height example: we used parents that were 3 cms (1¼ins) taller and assumed a heritability of 65 per cent or 0.65. We can now use a generation interval of 50 months, so that progress would be:

$$\text{Response} = \frac{3 \times 0.65}{50} = +0.039 \text{ per}$$

month or +0.468 per year

At less that half a centimetre (¼in) per year this may not seem a great deal, but it illustrates that progress, even for a highly heritable trait like with wither height, is not always rapid. Technically, one should assess each route separately, dividing the superiority of each by the appropriate generation interval. The older the parents that one uses, the longer the generation interval will become. However, breeders should not sacrifice quality for age. If a sire is very outstanding (and suitable for your lines), then use him even if he is aged, assuming he is still fertile.

In farm livestock, we can talk about selection of new stock to replace older animals. For example, if the bull a farmer is using is very superior to the cows he is used on, it would pay to retain more daughters than if the sire was only marginally superior to the cows. However, this is somewhat unrealistic in dogs, where breeders have emotional ties to animals and do not discard older bitches but keep them on as pensioners when their breeding life is over. This may prevent breeders bringing in younger animals because of space restrictions.

In dog breeding terms, you should seek to amass as much information as possible on your breeding animals. This can be factual data like heights, weights, hip and elbow score etc., or subjective material such as shoulder placement and hind angulation. Groups like Berner-Garde in the USA are set up to do just this with factual data. Similarly, breed surveys are invaluable as sources of subjective information which, by their very nature and by their accumulation, can serve in an objective way.

All breeders should keep records, not only on pedigrees, but on everything else they can record, relevant to their stock. For example, any intelligent breeder will obviously hip and elbow score the breeding stock, but it would be valuable to encourage the buyers of your stock to do the same if they will. Even if these animals are not intended as breeding stock, the accumulation of data helps to provide sibling and progeny data that aids the breeder.

In simple terms, breeding for polygenic traits is all about breeding from the best. The difficulty comes in deciding what is 'best' and who is making that decision. The pet owner whose Bernese is a joy to live with may well regard him as the 'best' but, as a specimen, the animal may have little to contribute beyond his character and is thus unlikely to advance the breed. Ideally, breeders will be selecting those dogs which have acceptable hips and elbows and good characters but which also conform most closely to the Standard. In some countries, rigid rules exist about hip/elbow grades so breeders have to conform to them. In most English-speaking countries you are free to do as you please, but this is all the more reason for breeders to adhere to Standards and to understand what they are doing.

Many breeders buy their first dog, live with him and love him and then use him as the prototype of their future breeding. If their first dog happens to be a very high-quality animal they will be fortunate but, if not, they may spend the next ten years going down the wrong path. Loving your dog is no reason to make him or her a breeding animal, still less the prototype you are seeking to emulate.

MULTIPLE TRAIT SELECTION

Breeders are not working simply to improve one trait; rather, they are seeking to enhance their dogs in several different ways, often in too many ways. Sometimes the traits that we are seeking are positively correlated. That is to say, the genes that influence one trait also influence another in a positive way. Thus, if we select for increased wither height, we would, almost certainly, increase body weight because some of the genes affecting one affect the other. When the relationship is positive, both 'improve' together but, if the relationship is negative, then the task becomes harder.

Selecting for increased wither height may very well reduce the curve of second thigh and accentuate the length of the rear pastern.

We have no scientific proof that this is the case, but neither do we have data to disprove it. By the same token, some breeders argue that dogs with extra rear toes have better bone. Again, one cannot prove this but, if true, there is a problem, since heavier bone may be desirable but additional digits are clearly not.

The more traits that you seek, the harder it is to achieve success. No animal has everything right and so a breeder seeking forty different things may well stagnate in a morass of selection dilemmas. There are ways of selecting for multiple objectives but most require data that, at present, is not generally available to dog breeders. One technique that breeders may use (though it is unlikely that breeders call it by its correct name) is Independent Culling Levels.

Under this technique, the traits needed by the breeder are determined and a minimum standard is set for each one. Then the animals are assessed/measured for the traits desired and each is evaluated against the standard set. A simple example is given below in table 6.4.

Animal D can be discarded as failing on several features, including character. Animal A also fails on several counts. Sire B has a structural failing in the shoulder, but C, E and F are promising. Animal C has too much white but is otherwise okay. Sire E has everything right, except that his elbow score is 1/1 and he is 69 cms (27¼ins) to the wither. Animal F is fine on every count, but his hip score is at the top of the limit. The fact that every animal fails on something is typical of real life – and bear in mind that we have only considered a few of the features that we would be seeking. In fact, we would take E or F as being the best bet. At this point, checking up on progeny of these two sires would be useful, assuming that they have progeny in the ring or which can be seen. Generally, use a sire that has progeny available rather than one that has none, assuming the progeny are suitable.

Breeders need to assess dogs in this sort of way and the more that we can learn about genetics, the better. For example, it would not be very sensible to include a requirement for the sire to have come from a big litter, because litter sizes that he will produce will have nothing to do with him but rather his mate, assuming he has normal fertility. If a trait has a low heritability, then the animal's own performance will have minimal effect and we can take a chance; if it is a high heritability, the sire will tend to reproduce his own qualities (and defects) in his progeny.

Table 6.4 Independent culling level selection[1]

Trait	Requirement	Sires					
		A	B	C	D	E	F
Markings	Minimal	+	+	lot	uneven	+	+
Height	66-68cm	65	66	67	66	69	68
Character	B or better	B	B-	B	D	B+	B+
Hips	<15 score	6/6	3/3	5/5	0/0	5/5	8/7
Elbows	0/0	0/0	1/0	0/0	0/0	1/1	0/0
Substance	Substantial	light	+	+	+	+	+
Head	V. masculine	s. weak	+	+	weak	+	+
Front assembly	good	+	fp	+	fp	+	+

[1]A + sign indicates animal conforms to requirement. fp = forward placed.

THRESHOLD TRAITS

Some traits are inherited in a polygenic manner, i.e. they are controlled by many genes, yet do not appear in a Normal curve pattern. For example, cryptorchidism not only has the complication that it appears only in males, but it is what might be termed an all-or-nothing trait, in that a dog either is or is not showing testicular retention. Similarly, survival of puppies is equally an all-or-nothing trait, in that they live or die and there are no grades. Such traits are termed 'threshold' traits, which means that there is a given number of genes which influence them for good or ill and, when an animal has a set number of these, the feature is seen. Many heart conditions are of this kind of inheritance, as is twinning in man. Polydactyly is another trait that appears to be a threshold feature and is applicable to the Bernese Mountain Dog.

If cryptorchidism was influenced by six genes, each with two alternatives (0/+) with + versions tending to induce the problem, then dogs could range from 12 zeros to 12 + genes. Suppose that it required 7 + alleles to induce cryptochidism, then all dogs with 7 or more + alleles would be cryptorchids and they could be discarded from a breeding programme. However, all those with 6 or fewer would be normal. The problem is that a dog with 12 zeros would appear just as normal as a dog with 6 zeros and 6 pluses. However, the 12 zero dog is not going to produce the problem, while the animal with six pluses could very well give rise to the cryptorchid problem in its progeny. Threshold traits are difficult to control because the seemingly normal animals are not equally normal. Breeders need to build up pedigree pictures of which threshold defects occur within the pedigree. In assessing potential risk, a normal dog with seemingly no abnormal siblings or close relatives may be a safer bet than a dog who is perfectly normal but who had siblings or a parent who showed the threshold trait being examined. In threshold situations, the closer a dog is to relatives with the problem under study, the greater the potential risk.

BREEDING SYSTEMS

Dog breeders cannot, by the very nature of their operation, avail themselves of crossbreeding, though it does take place and the prominence of Pluto v Erlengut in Bernese is testimony to that. There are certain advantages from crossbreeding but, since we are concerned with mating Bernese to Bernese, we will not waste time discussing them. As pedigree, or, more correctly, purebred breeders, we have access to random mating or to assortative mating, as well as to inbreeding or outbreeding. These will be discussed in turn.

RANDOM AND ASSORTATIVE MATING

Random mating is when any dog can mate any bitch. One sometimes feels that some breeders do operate using what seems like a purely random method. Random mating does not imply the absence of selection, since one can select a group of females very highly and then mate them randomly to some selected sires. This is, however, much more likely to occur in cattle or sheep than in dogs. Most dog breeders want to go to the trouble of choosing mates on the basis of information about both parents, though some seem content to mate to the nearest, most convenient or cheapest stud dog, without regard to merit. Let us therefore assume that random mating is a non-starter.

That leaves negative or positive assortative mating. Assortative mating is the mating of similar (positive) or dissimilar (negative) animals. Similar can be described as like to like, and dissimilar can be defined as unlike to unlike or compensatory mating. Positive assortative mating takes place if you mate the tallest sires to the tallest dams or the best hips to the best hips. Negative assortative mating occurs when you mate dogs with moderate hips to dogs with good hips (on the assumption that no-one knowingly uses poor hips in a breeding programme).

Positive assortative mating increases variation if, in addition to mating tall to tall you also mate small to small. If the Bernese Mountain Dog population is small in stature then breeding the tallest to the tallest may be desirable, but, if the breed is well distributed about the mean, then that policy will move the breed away from this middle position. Breeding extremes is not desirable when you want to retain a middle position. If we want Bernese to stay with mean heights of 66 and 62 cms (26 and 24½ins) for males and females respectively, then mating 70-cm (27½ins) dogs to 66-cm (26ins) bitches would be counter-productive, though it might be applicable in an individual case. Most breeders will be using both types of assortative mating at some stage of their breeding career, but it could be possible to mate two animals positively for one trait and negatively for another trait. Thus you might mate a poor shoulder to a good one, good hips to good hips and a moderate elbow to a good one, resulting in two examples of negative and one of positive assortative mating in the same mating decision.

Int. & Nordic Ch. Eros v Gehrimoos (Int. Ch. Beny v Dursrutti – Diana vd Holzmuhle): The dog on whom Duniblae Nalle was inbred.

INBREEDING AND OUTBREEDING

Inbreeding is the mating of related animals and outbreeding the mating of unrelated animals. In reality, all Bernese are, to a degree, related. They all go back to Pluto v Erlengut and a small group of animals, and they do so through numerous lines, but all of these animals are well back in the pedigree. A modern breeder with a five-generation pedigree will have no idea where Pluto is in that pedigree because he will have long ago 'dropped off the end'. The breeder is thus only looking at the immediate generations and, if the two animals have got ancestors in common within those four or five generations, the breeder is making a conscious decision about whether to inbreed or not.

Inbreeding involves having an ancestor (or more than one) appearing on both sides of the pedigree. That is to say, the ancestor must appear in the father's and in the mother's pedigree. The closer up in the pedigree the favoured ancestor appears, the higher the level of inbreeding. If, for example, a father is mated to his daughter (see Osi v Allenluften in Figure 1.1), then the father is in the first generation (parental) on one side of the pedigree and the second

Beny v Dursrutti

Eros v Gehrimoos

Soderkullas Vivo

Diana vd Holzmuhle
Soderkullas Chang

Soderkullas Mitzy

Soderkullas Arise
Carlo vd Grandfeybrucke

Duntiblae Nalle

Junker v Rappenfluh

Coletter v Leuenbuhl

Soderkullas Orli

Eros v Gehrimoos

Soderkullas Tatiana

Soderkullas Yrsa

Figure 6.4 Pedigree of Duntiblae Nalle born 9.11.1972

generation (grandparental) on the other). The inbreeding in such a mating would be 25 per cent. In contrast, if a mating involved having the same grandfather on both sides of the pedigree, it would be the equivalent of 12.5 per cent inbreeding. In man, the closest one can marry is first cousin and the offspring of a first-cousin marriage would be 6.25 per cent inbred. Figure 6.4 shows a three-generation pedigree of Duntiblae Nalle who was imported to Britain from Sweden in the early 1970s.

In Nalle's pedigree one ancestor, Eros v Gehrimoos, has been highlighted because Nalle was inbred to him. If we call the parent generation 1, grandparents 2, and so on, then Nalle was inbred on Eros 2:3, i.e. Eros was in the second generation on the father's side and in the third on the mother's. This is an inbreeding coefficient of 6.25 per cent. Full details of working out an inbreeding coefficient are given in Willis (1989, 1992).

Inbreeding increases the chance of getting genes from the favoured ancestor (in this case Eros), and also of getting the same gene in duplicate. Thus inbreeding increases homozygosity, i.e. it makes for dogs that are genetically AABBCCDD (or aabbccdd), as opposed to being AaBbCcDd or

heterozygous. Of course, there are thousands of genes in a dog and 6.25 per cent inbreeding would affect some, but not all. A dog that is 6.25 per cent inbred (called the Coefficient of Inbreeding) would be 6.25 per cent more homozygous than a dog of the same breed that was 0 per cent inbred. But even a non-inbred dog is homozygous for many genes: thus all Bernese Mountain Dogs are $a^t a^t$ even if they are outbred.

Let us now look at another pedigree, that of the British bitch, Ch. Folkdance at Forgeman. Her three-generation pedigree (Figure 6.5) illustrates inbreeding of a higher level than Nalle had, but it also illustrates inbreeding to two different ancestors, as well as showing how early British breeders of the 1970s made use of Duntiblae Nalle and Fox v Grunenmatt, a Swiss import born in 1971.

The pedigree of Ch. Folkdance shows inbreeding 2:2 on Duntiblae Nalle plus 3:3 on Fox v Grunenmatt, which amounts to 12.5 per cent plus 3.13 per cent, a total of 15.63 per cent (or 16.4 per cent after adjustments). This is moderately high. Fox was a very beautifully headed dog, rather lacking in stature, who subsequently proved to be a relatively poor hip producer. Nalle, in contrast, had stature and excellent character

		Soderkullas Vivo
Duntiblae Nalle		
Ch. Tarncred Puffin		Soderkullas Orli
		Fox v Grunenmatt
	Tarncred Black Watch	
Ch. Folkdance at Forgeman		Black Velvet of Nappa
		Soderkullas Vivo
Duntiblae Nalle		
Ch. Forgeman		Soderkullas Orli
Folksong of Tarncred		**Fox v Grunenmatt**
	Ch. Kisumu Belle Fleur	
		Kisumu Aphrodite

Figure 6.5
Pedigree of Ch. Folkdance at Forgeman, born 11.10.1977

as well as hardness, though he was a somewhat rangy type of dog. He also proved to be a very good hip producer. Mating Fox daughters to Nalle was very successful, in that Ch. Tarncred Puffin and Ch. Folksong are both bred in this way as can be seen in Figure 6.5. Some Fox offspring scored poorly for hips (in the 30s), though it was not known at the time, but the matings to Nalle vastly improved hip status in Fox grandchildren. In effect, the Nalle/Fox combination was successful.

Although Fox daughters to Nalle was successful, breeders need to beware of a policy whereby they mate progeny of imports in a sort of stereotyped fashion. Mating the daughters of Import A to Import B and those daughters to Import C and those, in turn, to Import D is not necessarily an intelligent policy, unless the succession of

imports actually compensate one another and gel, as they did in the Fox/Nalle combination. Not all imports are equally valuable. Some have been moderate-to-poor hip producers and mating a succession of poor hip producers has nothing to recommend it and would be better avoided.

Because many deleterious genes are recessive, inbreeding can bring about an increase in deleterious conditions. For example, it could increase the risk of hypomyelinogenesis or of PRA, but this is only feasible if the bloodlines carry the gene. Inbreeding does not create the problem; it merely brings it to the surface. If your stock are known to be free from a certain defect, inbreeding will not give rise to that defect, however intensely it is undertaken.

Let us assume (and this is assumption not fact) that the frequency of the

Table 6.5 Comparing random, inbred and non-inbred matings

Mating	Sire		Dam		Progeny		
	T	t+	T	t+	TT	Tt+	t+t+
Random	95	5	95	5	90.25	9.5	0.25
Random[1]	50	50	95	5	47.50	50.0	2.50
Daughters	50	50	75	25	37.50	50.0	12.50

[1]using known carrier sire

hypomyelinogenesis allele (call it t^+) in the Bernese is 5 per cent and that the normal allele (T) has a frequency of 95 per cent. Suppose also that we have three situations:
a) random mating within the population
b) mating a known carrier randomly
c) mating a known carrier to his own daughters (or the daughters of a known carrier).

Table 6.5 shows the three types of mating in terms of what will ensue assuming that in case (c) the daughters are out of normal (TT) mothers. Frequencies are shown as percentages. In the case of parents they are the percentage of sperm or ova bearing T or t^+ and, in the case of progeny, the percentages of actual progeny carrying the various genotypes. It would, of course be impossible, with present knowledge, to distinguish between the animals that were TT and those that were Tt^+ since both would appear normal.

Thus, in the random mating situation, 99.75 per cent of animals born would exhibit phenotype T and would therefore appear normal, and only 0.25 per cent would actually be affected by the disease. When using a carrier sire, half the offspring are known carriers but, in a random mating situation, only 2.5 per cent are affected whereas in the own daughter situation 12.5 per cent are affected. The extent to which inbred matings were undertaken would influence the existence of the t^+ allele in the population, and what are given in 2 and 3 in Table 6.5 are the incidences among progeny of that mating.

Table 6.5 illustrates how inbreeding increases the chances of deleterious recessives coming to the surface, but it also shows how inbreeding would show up that a suspect was or was not a carrier more easily than just

randomly mating him. Nevertheless, inbreeding to test for a deleterious gene would be potentially wasteful and costly in animal terms.

Obviously an increase in 'abnormal' progeny is undesirable, but more serious is what is termed inbreeding depression. This occurs as inbreeding increases and traits of low heritability, mainly reproductive traits, are harmed such that there can be an increase in infertility (of both sexes) and a reduction in litter size, as well as an increase in embryo and foetal mortality. Inbreeding depression largely affects fitness traits rather than conformational ones because the latter tend to be on the high side in heritability terms. Inbreeding can lead to serious damage in fertility terms but does not always, and a dog breeder will be less concerned with litter size than with conformational and character advances. Some people regard inbreeding with horror but it depends on what you are trying to achieve.

A pig breeder, for example, is concerned to breed large litters as uniform as possible, and any action which reduced fertility or litter size would be economically unwise. However, a dog breeder is not particularly interested in a large litter per se but more in the quality of the puppies. If, for example, a litter was small but it contained one or more outstanding animals, the dog breeder would probably be well pleased. The production of a top-class animal, especially a male, would bring more fame to a dog breeder than a large litter of uniform but less outstanding animals.

An American study in Foxhounds (Wildt et al., 1982) showed that inbred litters produced litter sizes averaging 6.7 compared with 7.9 for outbred litters, and that conception rates were 72.7 versus 87.3 per cent respectively. The major cause of this large and statistically significant discrepancy was that inbred sires were less fertile. For example, their sperm motility was a third of that of outbreds and they produced 17 million sperm per millilitre compared to 118 million for outbreds. In a Dutch study of Bouviers, Ubbink et al. (1992) examined several genetic defects and showed that affected individuals tended to have significantly higher inbreeding coefficients than unaffected controls. The median level of inbreeding was from 6.25 to 12.5 per cent.

Breeders should avoid deliberately inbreeding as routine, but this does not mean that some inbreeding cannot be successful and breeders should be very clear as to why they are inbreeding. It is usually said within breeding circles that inbred dogs are more prepotent, i.e. more likely to stamp their type on their offspring. It is certainly true that an inbred animal would be more homozygous and therefore produce fewer alternatives in sperm or ova, but prepotency would only apply if dominant genes were involved. One is thus likely to see prepotency only in respect of simple Mendelian traits or highly inherited conformational features.

Linebreeding is often praised in the same circles that would condemn inbreeding. In reality, linebreeding is simply inbreeding to a less intense degree. All the failings and virtues of inbreeding will simply be less obvious with linebreeding. Having a famous and, hopefully, very good animal several times on both sides of the pedigree within 3 to 5 generations is called linebreeding, but it is also what would be called inbreeding.

Figure 6.6 shows a linebred pedigree of the American Ch. Ashley v Bernerliebe CD, triple BOB winner at the BMDCA speciality and the sire of 28 Champions, who was born in the 1970s.

In Figure 6.6, Ashley was 'linebred' on the littermates Galen and Ginger v Senseboden 1:2 or 25 per cent. In actual fact, we cannot work the linebreeding like this since the same animal must appear on both sides. Thus the doubling-up is not to littermates but rather to their parents. It is more correct to state that Ashley was inbred on Sultan v Dursrutti 2:3 and Diana v Moosseedorf 2:3, in other words on the parents not the littermates themselves. This is an inbreeding coefficient of 12.5 per cent, half that of the previous calculation to Galen/Ginger. There is also more distant linebreeding to Arno v Baurnheim which brings the value to 13.3 per cent

Outbreeding is the opposite of inbreeding

Bari vd Tabenfluh

Sultan v Dursrutti

Am Ch. Galan v Senseboden

Kandi v Dursrutti

Galen v Mattenhof

Diana v Moosseedorf

Kaya v Moosseedorf

Am Ch. Hektor v Nesselacker

Am Ch. Grand Yodler of Teton Valley CDX

Bella's Clara

Am Ch. Dault Daphne v Yodlerhof CD   **Sultan v Dursrutti**

Am Ch. Ginger v Senseboden

Diana v Moosseedorf

Figure 6.6 Pedigree of Am Ch. Ashley v Bernerliebe

and is the mating of unrelated animals. Within a breed like the Bernese, it is impossible to find two animals that have no ancestors in common. All will trace back to the same nucleus of ancestors. However, within three-to-five generations, pedigrees with nothing in common can be found.

Importation of an American dog to Britain could show little or no commonality within that sort of generation study. The nature of outbreeding would be to create heterozygosity rather than homozygosity, but it is doubtful whether Bernese are so distinct that this would be very meaningful.

7 *MATING AND WHELPING*

ost Bernese are sold as companion animals and they live out their lives without being used for breeding purposes. As an estimate, in Britain about 30 per cent of KC registered females and some 11 per cent of males are used to breed at least one litter and the remainder are not used for breeding at all. As a purchaser of a companion animal, the idea of breeding may be the furthest thing from your mind. Certainly, there is no medical reason why a dog should have a litter and, in every breed, there is a need to ensure that only wanted puppies are produced. Ideally, a breeder would breed a litter only when he or she wants to produce something for him or herself, with surplus puppies being offered for sale to others. There are litters, bred with the intention of retaining something, in which the resultant puppies are of the wrong sex (for what the breeder wants), or in which none of them come up to the expected standard and as a result the whole litter may be sold. Nevertheless, the basic intent was for the breeder's purpose. There are, of course those who breed purely for commercial intent: "We need a new kitchen, what about a litter?" Breeding merely to

Am. Ch. Vombreiterwegs Swiss Lace and pup.

increase the numbers of the breed or purely for financial gain are the wrong reasons. No serious breeder should be in that situation.

In Britain, a reputable and thoughtful breeder will have sold puppies via a written contract in which it is specifically stated that the puppy is sold as a companion animal and where breeding is specifically excluded. Our puppies have their pedigrees endorsed by the Kennel Club to the effect that (a) they cannot be exported and (b) progeny cannot be registered. Clearly this does not preclude the would-be owner exporting the animal or breeding from it, but it does ensure that it will not be registered in the country of export and that in Britain puppies will not be registered by the KC. Since failure to register with the ruling body reduces the value of the animal it is hoped that buyers would not breed. However, if there are no terms stipulated under which these restrictions can be lifted, a breeder might find the new owner seeking the removal of these clauses

by the KC or by legal action. It is, therefore, imperative to have a legally binding contract which the KC cannot break. Similar situations may be feasible in other countries.

Our own contract stipulates that the export clause will be lifted if the owners want to live abroad and take the dog with them. The breeding clause would be lifted if the dog was hip and elbow scored at 12 months or more, and obtained scores that would be suitable for breeding and if, in our opinion, it was suitable to be bred from. The contract is signed by both parties and each side gets a copy. In effect it means that, if owners want to breed and register the offspring, the animal must have acceptable hips and elbows and must be of a suitable conformational and temperamental quality. In some countries, binding restrictions are placed by the breed club or the appropriate kennel club which prevent breeding from animals that are below par, or which have poor hips or elbows. This would mean that the need for controlling contracts may be less. We do, however, live in increasingly litigious times and it is important for both parties that the terms of a sale are written down and that both parties have signed copies. One of the things we insist on is a clause that if the buyers want to 'be rid of' their dog, for whatever reason, then it comes back home. In other words, we expect to do our own rescue. Even as a small kennel, we have a number of dogs returned, often through marital problems between their owners, sometimes for alleged failings, real or imagined, of the dog.

Of course, breeders and owners will, in the majority of cases, contract or not, have a good relationship with each other. We expect to keep in touch with owners at intervals, we enrol them in the NBMDC (if they are not already members), and we are at the end of a phone/fax line if ever they need help. Caring attention by breeders is essential. I have been successfully involved as an expert witness in about 40 court cases (mostly not Bernese cases and not our own animals) where relationships between breeder and buyer have broken down and litigation has ensued. Something has gone wrong, usually of a genetic kind, and, all too often, the breeder has sought to wash his hands of the issue. Every breeder, however skilful, will occasionally produce some problem of a genetic nature. While this cannot be rectified, the owner can be helped as to what to do, and maybe financial recompense can be made or another puppy supplied. What is disastrous is the all too frequent comment from the breeder: "You bought it, you sort it out!"

The Bernese Mountain Dog is not a numerically large breed in any country, and most breeders wish to see that situation preserved because they do not want it to become a breed which the 'get-rich-quick merchants' enter to exploit for purely commercial ends. Such people do exist and do not deserve the title of breeder; rather, they are 'reproducers of stock'. A companion owner may, at the time of purchase of their eight-week old cuddly puppy, have no intention of breeding, but time can change this. As the dog gets older and bigger, it may turn out to be a very nice-looking animal and the owner may be told as much, not only by lay persons but by those who do understand the breed. Even if the dog does not turn out to be a quality animal, the owner will, hopefully, love him or her and may be tempted to breed a litter simply to have one of the animal's descendants to carry on the line. I can sympathise with this viewpoint, but it is really no reason for breeding.

If you have a male, breeding from him is more difficult because, unless you have a bitch of your own to use him on (and they may not be of compatible bloodlines), you are reliant on someone with a bitch asking to use him. A dog that is unshown and virtually unseen is unlikely to attract that sort of attention. With a bitch, however, you can quite easily find some Bernese male, undertake a mating and end up with a litter. If the bitch is not really of breedable quality, the stud dog owner will, hopefully, advise the bitch owner of that fact and discourage or even not permit a mating. However, not all stud dog owners are so altruistic, and many will mate any bitch that passes their gate seeking a mating. The phrase "Have you got the stud fee?" may be all that the stud dog owner needs answering in the affirmative for a mating to be agreed. In which case, is that where you should be going?

If you are thinking of breeding from your Bernese bitch, there are certain questions you need to ask:

1. Is the bitch a good enough specimen to breed from?
2. Has she got acceptable hips and elbows?
3. Is she of acceptable character?
4. Do you have any idea which stud dog to use and why?
5. Do you have a potential market for the puppies you do not wish to keep?
6. Do you know how to whelp a bitch?
7. Can you afford it?
8. Can you be at home to whelp and rear a litter?
9. Have you got the space and facilities to rear a litter?

If you cannot answer all these questions positively, then maybe you ought not to be thinking about breeding. If you still do insist on going ahead, then you should have made a study of the Breed Standard and how well your bitch conforms to it (see Chapter Two). You must also understand something about breeding and genetics (Chapters Six and Ten) and try to learn something about the pedigree of your animal (Chapters Eight and Nine may help in this area). You also need to understand a little about the principles of mating and whelping.

Since Bernese puppies normally fetch a good price and, with a mean litter size of seven or eight, there is the prospect of a good income. However, you will first have to lay out a stud fee which could be as high as the price of one puppy. You will be involved in the extra costs of feeding, perhaps ultrasonic screening, the costs of whelping (which might be negligible – unless your bitch needs a Caesarian section, which can be the price of one or more puppies!). Then there are rearing costs, vaccinations, worming and the various expected and unexpected things that crop up. You might, after all, not get as big a litter as you expected but only one or two puppies or, more tragically, you could lose puppies at the birth or later. What about the ultimate tragedy that the bitch is lost during whelping or during a Caesarian? Can you rear a litter without their mother? You could even get a large litter of 12, and rearing that many puppies is a formidable task. Would you be up to it?

Of course, some of this is a worst-case scenario and everything may go swimmingly, but I am merely drawing your attention to the fact that a one-off litter is not necessarily an easy or rewarding option – certainly not a financially rewarding one. You may ask "What about breeders? How do they do it all?" The situation for a breeder is quite different. The worst-case scenario can happen to the breeder just as easily as to the novice, but a breeder is looking at a planned programme not just a one-off litter. We have had litters ranging from one to 13. We have lost, on one occasion, four out of six and, on three occasions, reared all 12 puppies successfully. The point is that a breeder is in a swings and roundabouts situation, not simply looking at one mating but at a whole series of matings over a long period of time. Some will be financial or biological disasters, others not so. Although every litter is wanted and worked on, it is not the individual litter that is crucial but the planned programme over a long period of time.

REPRODUCTIVE CYCLES

Wild canids, such as the wolf, tend to breed once per year and, in most wolf packs, only the dominant females and male may breed. The domestic canid male will mate at any time, whereas the bitch is a monoestrus animal. That is to say, the bitch will have only one oestrus during each breeding season and will probably have two seasons per year. This is in contrast to polyoestrus animals such as cattle and women whose cycle is at three-to-four week intervals throughout the year. Unlike in women, there is no menopause when oestrous cycles cease, which means that bitches may cycle throughout their lives, though their fertility might weaken with age. There are four stages of the oestrous cycle.

1. Anoestrus: This is the longest part of the cycle and is, in essence, the period of sexual inactivity between the cycles. It can last around 70-80 days and the length of anoestrus determines the frequency with which the bitch will cycle.

2. Pro-oestrus: This is the stage at the beginning of the season (heat) when the vulva becomes swollen and there is some discharge of blood. It will last just over a week, but could range from two days to a month. During this period, males will show interest in the bitch but she will not allow them to mount her.

3. Oestrus: This is the heat proper. It can last from three days to three weeks but, on average, will be about 8-10 days. The vulva becomes enlarged and the discharge is more a pale yellow than bloodstained. The bitch will accept mating during this period but ovulation will occur about two days into the oestrus proper, and it will occur spontaneously, i.e. whether she is mated or not.

4. Met-oestrus: During this period, hormone levels similar to those in pregnancy are seen and the bitch may exhibit a false pregnancy. Alternatively, she may be pregnant. This stage of the cycle will last about three months and eventually reverts to stage one, anoestrus. Otherwise the bitch is pregnant and in around 63 days she will produce her litter. The period from oestrus to oestrus may range from 5-10 months but, in the Basenji and racing Greyhound, may be sufficiently long that many animals will cycle only once per year. Animals with very frequent heats (every 3-4 months) are usually demonstrating some abnormal trait and are very often infertile.

Detecting signs of oestrus is not easy, since the difference between pro-oestrus and oestrus proper may be minimal. Some bitches may show discomfort before stage two, and may indulge in rather abnormal numbers of urinations when out for a walk or in her run. The need to detect oestrus from its start is obvious when one considers that ovulation – the release of eggs – lasts only for about 24 hours. One needs to mate just prior to, during, or just after the time of ovulation in order to be able to get a fertile mating.

There are certain hormones linked with the reproductive cycle which need to be understood. Hormones are substances, produced by glands, which are spread through the bloodstream and instruct specific organs to work or to stop working. In effect, these hormones control the body's activity. There are two sites or glands involved in reproduction. These are the ovaries, which are in the body cavity near to the kidneys, and the pituitary gland, which is situated at the base of the brain.

The pituitary gland produces a variety of hormones of which two are important in reproduction and two in lactation. The first three of these are called gonadotrophic hormones and are produced from the anterior pituitary. They are called Follicle stimulating hormone (FSH), which promotes ripening of the eggs in the ovaries, Luteinizing hormone (LH), which causes ovulation, and Prolactin, which stimulates the mammary gland so that it is ready to produce milk. The final pituitary hormone, produced from the posterior part, is Oxytocin which makes the pregnant uterus contract at whelping and also stimulates the release of milk from the mammary glands.

From the ovaries come Oestrogen and Progesterone. Oestrogen is responsible for the female characteristics and it also stimulates bleeding when the bitch is in season. It is also involved in mammary gland development. Progesterone prepares the uterus for the support of the foetuses. Progesterone is essential for the maintenance of pregnancy. It also causes mammary gland development which eventually helps milk to be produced.

In the brain there is the hypothalamus, which is concerned with reproduction in the bitch. The hypothalamus is sensitive to day length, in some species like the sheep, and to heat and light. It can also be influenced by pheromones (chemical substances secreted by animals), so that it may be stimulated by other bitches and by males. This accounts for why bitches in a kennels tend to cycle at around the same time. It is the hypothalamus which causes the pituitary gland to release gonadotrophins and there is interplay between these and the hormones produced by the ovaries.

At the end of anoestrus, the hypothalamus stimulates the pituitary to release FSH, which causes ovarian follicles to form, which, in turn, release oestrogen. This hormone is at low levels and stimulates the production of more FSH until the follicles mature. When the follicles are ready to rupture, oestrogen has reached higher levels and has a negative feedback, inhibiting FSH, but, at the same time, stimulating the production of LH. It is the presence of LH which stimulates ovulation or the release of eggs. The ruptured follicle then becomes what is called a corpus luteum. This structure secretes progesterone which, at high concentrations, stops the secretion of FSH and LH. Thus the cycle is one in which oestrogen and progesterone are implicated.

The bitch is unusual, in reproductive terms, in that she has low levels of progesterone before ovulation. Rising progesterone levels superimposed on falling oestrogen levels induce the bitch to stand for the male. Thereafter, there is a high level of progesterone for a long time. There are similar hormonal patterns in the pregnant and non-pregnant bitch, in that progesterone levels are maintained in both. In the pregnant animal they fall rapidly at the end of pregnancy, whereas in the met-oestrus situation the fall is more gradual.

Breeders normally try to calculate the right time for mating by physical signs and/or by timing from the start of the pro-oestrus period. If we consider the pro-oestrus start as day 1, then oestrogen levels gradually rise up to about day 9. They then fall rapidly, with ovulation occurring at about day 12. Progesterone is rising gradually from about day 5, while LH reaches a peak about two days before ovulation. The problem is that getting the start of pro-oestrus exactly right is not easy, the more so if you are not very observant about your bitches. If we do not get the start right, then the right time to mate may be missed and the bitch does not get pregnant. That means we have to wait another six months to try again.

Obviously, if you have a stud dog, you can daily test whether a bitch is ready to mate, but that is not an accurate test of ovulation and animals do vary in the length of their stages. It is highly probable that much so-called infertility in bitches is not infertility per se, but, rather, a failure to mate at the right time. Too soon, and the sperm is dead before ovulation occurs. Too late, and ovulation is long gone before the sperm is placed in the vagina.

Detecting the LH peak would be a clear indicator that ovulation will take place in a couple of days and thus time mating exactly. However, to determine the LH peak would necessitate sampling blood for about five days. It is known that the LH peak is closely associated with an increase in progesterone concentration. In Holland, Okkens et al. (1985) suggested that mating one or two days after progesterone concentration increased to 5ng/ml resulted in 93 per cent pregnancy (39 of 41 dogs). In a later study, also in Holland, Van Haaften et al. (1989) looked at 104 bitches with a reduced fertility and 112 bitches with normal fertility. Blood samples were taken at 8am and assessed by 3pm the same day. Owners were advised to mate within nine hours if the progesterone concentration was above 12ng/ml, to mate within 9-33 hours if the concentration was between 6 and 12 ng/ml, and within 33-57 hours if the concentration was between 5 and 6 ng/ml. Under this regime, the workers found that 86 per cent of the bitches became pregnant. Among the so-called reduced fertility bitches, the pregnancy rate was 78 per cent and among the normal fertility bitches it was 94 per cent. The start of vulval bleeding was reported exactly in 88 bitches and, in these, the optimal time for mating was 11.8 + 3.1 days. Mating more than once was not advantageous, provided the mating time had been determined by blood assay.

Most experienced dog breeders argue that mating should take place 11 or 12 days after the start of vulval bleeding, which is in good agreement with these Dutch figures. However, the standard deviation of 3.1 days implied that some 68 per cent of bitches would be mated between 8.7 and 14.9 days post the start of bleeding, and that 95 per cent were within 5.6 and 18 days post-bleeding. Clearly, blood testing of this kind is going to be effective, provided that the results can be fed back quickly to the bitch owner and that stud dogs can be available at relatively short notice. In a breed like the Bernese Mountain Dog, where stud dogs are not heavily used, this would be easier than in, say, the German Shepherd Dog, where some stud dogs are heavily used (three times per week).

MATING

Choice of stud dog is not something that you decide on the day the bitch first comes into season. Choice needs to be made in good time, not only for the sake of the stud and whether or not he will be available when you want him, but also because choice involves planning as to suitability. I have had people seeking help on stud dogs for newly purchased puppies and also for bitches that were well into their season, and these owners represent undesirable extremes. The choice of who to mate, in due course, to your newly acquired eight-week-old puppy, is a decision you can well leave for a year and more since, at eight weeks, you have no idea whether the bitch will even be worth mating. Hips, elbows, type and temperament are all unknown at this stage, and the stud dogs available when you buy may not be there when the time comes to mate. Other stud dogs, not available or known about today, may be possible later. In contrast, leaving the decision until the bitch is already in heat is likely to result in using a convenient or available sire rather than the one that is most suitable.

In broad terms, a bitch is more likely to conceive if she is on a rising plane of nutrition. Certainly, very fat or very thin animals are at a disadvantage and it is preferable to breed from a bitch in a very fit state and in good condition than with an overweight or a skinny animal.

Ideally, you should be seeking to mate a Bernese bitch when she is over 18 months of age. Preferably, aim to mate her so that she whelps for the first time at around two years and three months of age, or thereabouts. If your bitch is a successful show dog, do not sacrifice mating for her show career. I have known people who have kept on showing, perhaps seeking the last CC or points for a title, and, by the time they have contemplated mating, their bitch has been too old or, sadly, for some reason, she has not conceived. Pull your bitch out of the ring to mate her at a convenient time, and earlier rather than later. If she is a hard, fit animal, she is capable of coming back after a litter to carry on her show career, and, if she is not, then the litter should be more meaningful than a title.

Although some stud dog owners will come to the bitch, it is usual for the bitch to go to the dog, so plans have to be made in advance. As breeders, my wife Helen and I have always preferred to have the bitch arrive early, well before 11 days into her season, because the owner may be wrong about the start and, if the bitch is later on than was thought, she needs to be there early and not late. If the bitch is well past ovulation, no stud dog will get her pregnant and, if she is early, we would normally house the bitch and try her each day until a mating is possible. We would then mate in successive days for about three matings.

Our studs are used to mating outside on concrete. Some people mate indoors and the Guide Dogs for the Blind Association has a large mating room and claim that this assists the males, who begin to understand why they are in that room. If the mating is on grass, then a rubber mat or rug may be needed to give the dog secure footing.

When it comes to attempting the mating, having someone to assist is desirable, though it is possible to undertake a mating alone.

Some bitches are very eager and easy to mate, while others can be difficult and can appear nasty. As long as the bitch is even-tempered and not nasty, let dog and bitch play for a while and, if the dog will mate, let him do so naturally. If the bitch is nasty, either refuse to mate her (as we would do) or muzzle her, rather than risk getting the dog or yourself bitten. If your dog is a beginner, then you ought to try and get him an easy-going and experienced mate for his first litter, since some dogs can be put off if their first experience is not good. If the bitch is clearly not ready, she will resist all attempts to mate. Even some bitches who are ready resist. One of us does the matings and, on the owner's arrival, will check to see if the bitch really is ready otherwise it is pointless going ahead.

In normal circumstances, the bitch will turn her tail to one side thus allowing vision of and access to the vulva. The dog will mount the bitch, penetrate and hold her around her middle. He will then thrust to and fro a few times, rock sideways from foot to foot, shifting his weight, which may assist in pushing the bulbous base of the penis further in and thus locking the organ into a 'tie'. The dog will then thrust again and ejaculate. The tie is formed by the swelling of the base of the penis and the constriction occasioned by the sphincter muscles of the bitch's vagina. The dog will seek to lift one leg over the bitch's back, so that they are positioned behind to behind. Some dogs just dismount and stand alongside her while still connected. Either method will suffice, since it is the tie, not the posture, which is important. However, do not attempt to turn the two of them too quickly or the tie may become disconnected. Most people would seek to hold the bitch near the head and reassure her while mating is in operation, and we hold both animals during the tie to prevent the bitch trying to sit down or pull away. The tie may last a relatively short time or anything up to almost an hour. Then the penis will deflate, the vagina relax and the two animals will separate. Most ties are around 20 minutes duration. We find the most comfortable way of maintaining the tie is to get the two animals close to a fence, and then to encircle both sets of back legs with a pair of arms while holding on to the fence. That way, the two cannot sit down or split apart and the helper is crouching. Not good on the human back, but the dogs are fine! Never leave two tied animals unattended for whatever reason. Note that a tie is not essential for, or a guarantee of, pregnancy. A slip mating is one where no tie results (we have had 12 puppies from such a mating). Given the right time, one mating can be successful.

An experienced stud owner with a sensible dog can help enormously to effect a mating, even with troublesome bitches. A dog that trusts you and knows his job is worth his weight in gold. Some Bernese males lack interest in bitches or they are fairly clueless about what to do. Some bitches are so attached to their owners that they become almost impossible if the owner stays around. It may be wiser to send the owner of the bitch away to allow the mating to take place with minimal hassle. A good stud dog will be skilled at mating and, if he has been trained, will not object to being assisted. There is often a time when even the best stud still needs assistance with a particularly large or small bitch and, if he will accept a guiding hand, it can make a mating both easier and quicker. Some stud dogs get very excited when bitches are in season and stop eating, but the best ones are capable of carrying on as normal. They will not get upset if the bitch is not ready but simply go back and eat their tea then try again later!

FEEDING DURING PREGNANCY

There is no need to feed a bitch more, just because she has been mated. Although a demand does exist for foetal growth, it is not very important until the final third of pregnancy (the last 20 days), during which time the bitch should be fed more. We would be feeding a high-energy complete diet and increase it by some 10 per cent per week from about six weeks into pregnancy so that, by the time the bitch whelps, she is eating about half as much again as she was before the pregnancy. However, each bitch is an individual and you must exercise care in not letting her get too fat. We would not feed additional vitamins and minerals, and certainly not alter calcium feeding. There is a requirement for calcium during late pregnancy and lactation, but this will be met by eating more food rather than by altering the composition of the diet. Many bitches will eat less in the time immediately preceding whelping and this may be used as a clue to its onset. We do not weigh food, but assess matters by study of what the bitch looks like.

PSEUDO OR FALSE PREGNANCY

False pregnancy is a behavioural problem that can vary considerably in intensity. Because met-oestrus is similar in bitches that are pregnant and those that are not, the hormonal status of pregnant and non-pregnant bitches is very similar. Prolactin may, however, be implicated and, as progesterone levels decline, prolactin levels increase. The problem is probably greater than most veterinarians imagine, since experienced breeders may not seek veterinary help. To some degree it is a self-limiting problem, but the bitch may appear pregnant in that she becomes more sluggish and less interested in exercise and may actually increase in weight as if she were pregnant. Some bitches may show this after each oestrous cycle; others on a one-off basis. There is a suggestion that bitches prone to this may also be prone to pyometra.

PYOMETRA

Pyometra is the commonest reproductive disease in bitches. It can occur in any breed, at any age and in maiden or multiparous animals, though it is commoner in middle-aged and older animals (Sevelius et al., 1990). It is an inflammation of the uterus with an accumulation of pus. Affected animals may show depression, excessive water intake, excessive urination and vaginal discharge or even sickness. Sevelius et al. (1990), in their Swedish study, give detailed descriptions of the kinds of findings. Most treatment involves spaying and, if not treated, pyometra can be fatal. We had one German Shepherd Dog with pyometra and were able, with expensive antibiotic treatment, to avoid spaying but we had to mate her at the next season. She gave us a litter of 12 – all reared successfully, though produced by Caesarian section. That route is, however, costly, very time-consuming and not something we would have done with other than a very outstanding animal. In most cases, we would have taken veterinary advice and possibly spayed.

DYSTOCIA

Dystocia is the word used to describe difficulties at parturition or whelping. It is relatively common in cattle, but not particularly so in the dog. It can result from a variety of causes associated with the foetus, the mother, or the birth canal. Foetal problems are usually caused by faulty presentation or by oversize, which latter might be a breed effect or due to a small litter or to a singleton puppy. Maternal factors can result from a variety of features including uterine inertia. Problems of the birth canal can be due to pelvic immaturity or to problems with the uterus, cervix or vagina. Bennett (1974) produced an excellent review of the subject. Some breeds are prone to problems, especially those with large heads, but the Bernese Mountain Dog is not particularly implicated, though it can occur. Usually dystocia necessitates veterinary assistance and it will often result in a Caesarian section, as many veterinarians work on the 'better safe than sorry' principle. A skilled breeder can sometimes help to release a puppy that is stuck, but most people would be advised to call out the vet once a bitch appears to be having difficulties. This occurs when a bitch is obviously straining but nothing appears to be happening. The bitch may not be dilating and, in this event, nothing is going to get out and the bitch could rupture her uterus. At such a point, speed can be of the essence and a vet needs to be called. Parturition can, of course, be a speedy or a slow process and still be normal. The puppies in a large litter can be born at regular or irregular intervals and still be alive and well, but, once a puppy does appear to be stuck, it can die and can hold up those behind it.

WHELPING

Let us assume that you have got a pregnant bitch and that she is due to whelp. What do you need to do? First of all, you have to appreciate that, although the mean gestation length is about 63 days, a bitch can whelp as early as 55 and as late as 72 days, so you have to be prepared over a longer period than merely the standard 63 days. Moreover, if a bitch has been mated over a period of several days, she could be pregnant to the first or the last mating. You have to be ready well in advance. Most bitches tend to be regular in gestation lengths since it is about 40 per cent heritable so, if she 'goes off' the first time at 60 days, she is likely to do that on most occasions.

Your bitch should be introduced to the whelping box and whelping room early on so that she is not faced with new surroundings at the last minute. Midway through pregnancy, as her bladder comes under pressure from the uterus, she is going to need to be let out frequently to urinate and, from time to time, accidents may happen which just have to be lived with. As whelping approaches, she may be less friendly towards other dogs, so, if you have others, keep them out of the way, as a scuffle is the last thing you want. If you are whelping in the house, as we do, then you will have ready access to water (hot and cold), a kettle, a phone and to methods of heating the room if it is required. We use a plastic whelping box about 4 x 4 feet with an eight-inch-high edge around the rim. One of us sleeps near to the bitch for some days before whelping is due. Taking her temperature regularly is a useful aid to when things might happen.

Before whelping you need to have available certain things.
1. A plastic box about 24 x 12 ins with hot-water bottles and towels (into this you put puppies while the next one is being born).

MATING AND WHELPING
Photos: Courtesy M. Bärtschi.

1 A few days before parturition.

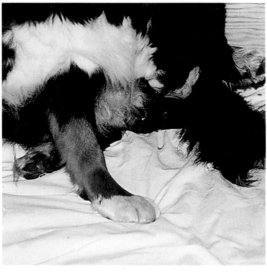

3 The bitch turns to investigate.

2 Bitch starting parturition (final stages), with blood appearing.

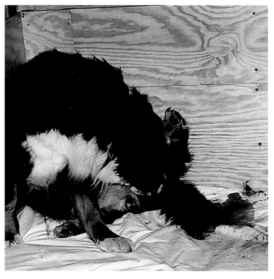

4 The water-bag, which eases the passage of the first whelp emerges.

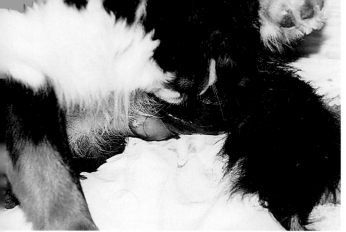

5 *The first whelp appears head-first.*

8 *The newborn puppy is licked dry.*

6 *The bag is broken.*

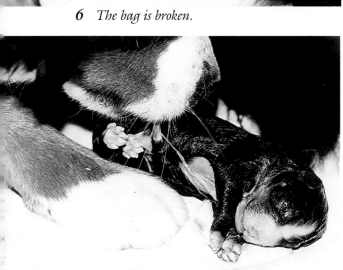

7 *The bitch bites through the cord.*

9 *The mother is calm and relaxed. Her puppies are in a box as she awaits further births.*

2. Plastic gloves (to avoid infection of the bitch).

3. KY jelly or some other lubricant (to help in easing delivery).

4. Scissors (for cutting umbilical cords) and a reel of cotton to tie them. You can use dental floss or, with forceps, you can clamp the cord.

5. Cotton wool swabs or baby buds.

6. Thermometer (to check body temperature of the bitch).

7. Notebook, pencil (to keep notes of what happens, birth intervals, etc.).

8. Scales (to weigh puppies as they are born).

9. Old towels and paper towel rolls (to help mopping up).

10. Refuse bin or black plastic bag (for discarded refuse and for afterbirths, etc).

11. A respiratory stimulant, in case the pups need it.

12. A flashlight if it is night-time. (If the bitch needs to go out you do not want her 'dropping' a puppy in the garden).

13. A clock by which you can time intervals, etc. (Your watch will do but if you are messing about in afterbirths you will have wisely removed it.)

14. A good book to take your mind off what you are waiting for.

There are lots of other things you can use, even down to incubators, but we are looking at basic essentials which any breeder has access to. It will be wise to advise your veterinary surgery that a litter is due so that, if the call-out comes, they are aware and ready.

In the final week of pregnancy the bitch is likely to show a decline in rectal temperature. Although normality can vary with the individual dog, the normal temperature is 38.6 degrees C (101.5 degrees F) and this will drop to 37.2 or even 36 degrees C (99 or 97 degrees F), which suggests whelping may take place within 24 hours. Experienced breeders start taking rectal temperatures several times per day as whelping approaches to ensure that they are ready. However, do not get hidebound by the figures cited. The important feature is the drop towards 37 degrees C or below.

There are three stages of the whelping process and it is the foetuses which initiate the procedure. As they grow in size, they become crowded in the uterus and the stress induced by this will serve to actuate the cardiac and respiratory systems which the pup will need once it leaves the safe confines of the mother's womb. During this first stage the bitch will be restless; she may stop eating and, if she is in a box with newspapers, she is likely to be busy ripping up paper. She may exhibit periods of restlessness, deep panting, paper-ripping and even just sleeping. The behaviour pattern can be short-lived or last for a couple of days. It is popularly believed that this is a nest-making exercise, but it may be a response to pain. During pregnancy, mucous discharges from the vagina may be seen and these may increase in volume as whelping approaches.

Dilation of the cervix will normally have occurred during stage one because, without it happening, puppies cannot pass from the uterus. In the uterus, puppies are usually lying on their backs with their heads towards the vagina. Each foetus will be in a double-layered water bag (amniotic sac) which is moved along towards the exit by the pulsating action of the uterus. Puppies are thought to be born alternately from each of the two uterine horns and, normally, they come out head first. As whelping approaches, the bitch will become quieter but there will be obvious signs of abdominal contractions. The first sign of a whelp will be the presence of the water bag, black in colour, which will appear and retract and then may burst expelling its liquid contents. This water bag is helping to ease the passage of the first whelp and you should not try to hold on to it or pull it out. A puppy should appear soon after the water bag has burst. The bitch may whelp lying down, crouching or standing and, once the puppy's head appears, the rest of it may slide out quickly. Ideally, let this happen naturally but, if help is needed, use plastic gloves or well-lubricated clean hands to give assistance. Hold the puppy with two fingers and slowly ease it out. This may be necessary only for the first, which is pioneering the way out to the world. Although puppies ought to appear head first as if diving out, many will emerge hind legs first, and this is still a normal presentation. An abnormal or breech birth occurs if the animal comes out behind-first with the back legs tucked under it, or head-first with the head to one side. Assistance must be minimal and non-violent, and it is imperative that, once the puppy is out, the amniotic sac should be removed immediately. Some breeders let the bitch do this, but we prefer to do the whole thing ourselves and get the puppy breathing as quickly as possible.

Getting the membrane off the head so that the puppy can breathe is more important that cutting the cord. Hold the puppy head downwards so that any fluid drains from the lungs, but make sure that you are always supporting the puppy. Clean the mouth and nostrils with swabs or baby buds and use a vigorous towelling to warm the puppy and get it breathing. Only when it is making a noise and actually breathing should you

attend to the cord. About two inches from the puppy, seek to effect a cut/clamp. Use cotton thread or dental floss (less slippery) to tie the cord and then cut it between the bitch and the ligature. Better still, clamp with forceps if you have them. If need be, take hold of the puppy between two fingers and, with a hand on the body, swing the puppy gently to and fro until it is resuscitated. Dry the puppy with a towel and then put it with the mother to see if it will suckle. However, you will have the plastic box mentioned above (item 1), in which there will be a hot-water bottle wrapped in a towel. If the bitch starts producing a second puppy, put the first one in this box to keep warm while the second one is dealt with. Thereafter, keep putting the puppies with the mother to lick and attend to, thus aiding maternal bonding, while replacing them in the box as another puppy appears. This not only keeps them dry and warm but also safe, as the bitch may be moving around quite energetically.

The final stage of whelping is the expulsion of the afterbirth (placenta) which should be expelled soon afterwards. It is important that all the placentas are expelled and, if any are retained, an injection from the vet after the completion of all the births will ensure that all puppies and afterbirths are out. Retention of an afterbirth can lead to infection. Most breeders would visit the vet within 24 hours of the last birth for an oxytocin injection to expel any retained afterbirths. Some breeders let the bitch eat the afterbirths but, since they can lead to bowel movements, other breeders discard them. In a wild state, consumption of the afterbirth would be useful to sustain the bitch, but domestic dogs do not lack for food, so the placentas can be readily discarded.

The intervals between births can vary

considerably without being abnormal. Some bitches will produce puppies as easily as shelling peas; others take a longish time. The interval may be ten minutes or thirty but, if the interval is getting beyond the two-hour mark, it may be as well to get the vet ready should an emergency arise. If the bitch keeps straining to no effect, there may be a puppy stuck. If she is resting contentedly and suckling her puppies, then she may well have finished. The whelping of a fairly large litter could last anything from 12 to 36 hours, depending upon litter size and the breed. We have had litters of 12, and one of 13, completed within 24 hours. A skilled breeder will know when to call out the vet because of an understanding of his or her bitches. Delay when a puppy is stuck (dystocia) can result in the loss, not only of that puppy, but of others lined up behind it. In broad terms, the bitch least likely to have problems is one that is in fit, hard condition, as opposed to one that is in soft condition and grossly overweight. However, a bitch whelping for the first time in middle-age (4-5 years) may not be as easy as a similar bitch whelping her third litter, even if both appear equally fit.

Oxytocin injections can usually expel a puppy within ten minutes of the injection, but this will not work if there is an obstruction and oxytocin must be used carefully under veterinary supervision. If a Caesarian section is called for, leave the existing puppies in a warm box on a towel-wrapped hot-water bottle and take the bitch to the surgery along with another box in which any later puppies can be brought back, also on a hot-water bottle. A flank entry for the incision may be preferable since it will not mean a wound between the teats.

Bernese puppies can be inclined to be very lethargic. Walkowicz and Wilcox (1994) describe them as having a low birth-survival drive and I would broadly concur with this. My experience with German Shepherd Dogs suggests that they tend be born 'raring to go' and that lethargy is not common among the puppies, though uterine inertia is known in German Shepherd bitches. Many Bernese are born flaccid and with no apparent will to live. In this respect, they are not unlike Charolais calves with which I have considerable experience. For this reason, vigorous rubbing and careful swinging may be called upon to get the puppies breathing and moving and interested in suckling. I have found differences between stud dogs in the enthusiasm with which their offspring greet being born. This statement is, however, an observation rather than a scientific finding.

Although most Bernese bitches will take well enough to people being present during the whelping, it is generally advisable not to have too many people around. Our bitches are all whelped by either my wife or myself, and the other is there only if the need arises. Once whelped, the bitch needs to be carefully observed to ensure that she is feeding the puppies. This is particularly true in the case of a large litter, when the bitch may not have enough teats for all to feed simultaneously.

Litter size is partly a breed feature, but is also a feature of the bitch upon which the sire has almost no influence. It is, however, some 30 per cent repeatable so that, in general terms, if a bitch has a large litter, she will probably continue to have large litters while those with small litters will tend to continue to have small litters. Inbreeding may reduce litter size, but only at relatively high levels of inbreeding.

LACTATING

Mortality of newborn pups can exceed 20 or 30 per cent (see Wilsman and Sickle, 1973) and weight gain is crucial to survival. In their study of Pointer puppies, Wilsman and Sickle (1973) showed that a favourable prognosis for survival was associated with two growth patterns. Puppies which gained weight from the start had a high chance of survival, as did those which lost less than 10 per cent of the birth weight within the first two days and then began to gain weight. There was a poor prognosis for pups which lost more than 10 per cent of body weight early on.

It is obvious that care over the first 48 hours is crucial for puppies. They have a body temperature of about 34.4-37.2 degrees C (94-99 degrees F), compared with adult temperature of 38.6 degrees C (101.5 degrees F), and thus they need to lie on something warm or be kept warm by the mother's body. I do not favour infra-red lamps, which tend to be dehydrating, but prefer to create warmth beneath the puppy. Newborn puppies tend not to be still and those who lie very still or who are constantly crying are the ones likely to be in trouble. Breeders should ensure that puppies are receiving milk from a teat and should also make sure that weaker puppies get an opportunity on the rear teats, which are usually the most productive. All puppies need to suckle the bitch as soon as possible because the first milk is colostrum-rich and this helps to provide immunity for the puppies. Ideally, they should suckle within 24 hours to derive the benefit. It is, however, possible to rear puppies who did not get the opportunity of colostrum, though it is something best avoided.

Most bitches have enough milk for their puppies and, if well fed, they will be stimulated to produce more if the litter is large. It is therefore unnecessary to supplement with artificial milk sources. It is, however, wise to have artificial milk powders available in the event of an orphaned litter or of the mother developing an infection which prevents her feeding the puppies. A proportion will be born dead, or die for a variety of reasons, and that is not abnormal. The larger the litter, the greater the chance of losses either at birth or subsequently. There is, however, no reason to lose those that can be saved, and a sensible breeder will handle puppies on a daily basis and check that all is well. Healthy puppies are smooth, warm, firm and plump and make murmuring sounds and occasional sharp yells if they are pushed off a teat or are squeezed. Abnormal ones tend to be cold, damp, wrinkled and plaintive in their mewling. A bitch will often push away a sickly puppy, so make sure you are not trying to rear a specimen with some deformity like a cleft palate which is better culled humanely.

Bitches' milk is highly nutritious compared with that of the cow or goat. The moisture content is about 77 per cent compared with 87 per cent for cows or goats. Protein at 8 per cent is much higher (3.4 per cent in cattle and goats), as is fat at 9.8 per cent, compared with 3.8 per cent in cattle and 4.5 per cent in goats. Similarly, energy level is of the order of 570 kJ/100g which is over twice that of cows. Calcium is 0.28 per cent of bitch milk, more than twice that of cattle and goats.

Given this diet, the first two weeks of a pup's life require no additional feed in normal circumstances. Additional feed can be introduced from about three weeks post-partum, sometimes later. We would use a complete puppy porridge initially, then gradually move on to a premium-quality dry puppy food. We grind this through a coffee grinder until it is a fine powder, then make it into a paste with the addition of boiled water. Once it has cooled to an acceptable temperature, this paste can be fed to puppies using one's finger or a small teaspoon. There are many feeds on the market but you should use highly palatable feeds dense in energy and nutrients. You can use milk-based diets, including goat's milk which puppies may love, but it is not essential to use milk and in some circles these days it is considered rather old-fashioned.

The weaning process involves additional feeds of this kind introduced gradually. Initially, it may be just once per day, then twice. Feeding has to be controlled and can be a rather messy process as the puppies can wander around in their food despite your best attempts to prevent this. Eventually, you will be feeding about six times per day and they will still be having a suckle from mum. The puppies become capable of eating from a tray rather than having to be fed by hand. They will increasingly make use of dry food as opposed to bitch's milk and this is particularly true as the bitch loses patience with her puppies. As they age, their nails need to be clipped so as not to harm the mother, but sharp puppy teeth can still hurt, and most bitches begin to lie to be suckled for short periods only. By about six weeks of age, the puppies can be fully weaned and by eight weeks they are ready to leave for new homes. It is important to let Bernese puppies grow gradually and not at their maximum potential, since growth disorders can result. Any dog that has been slightly retarded in growth during early life will, in time, compensate and reach the required body weight. All quality puppy foods list on the package the nutrients that are present and give feeding instructions. You can assess how much to give each animal in the light of this. High-quality puppy feeds will have higher calcium levels than adult feeds, but these should be matched to phosphorus levels. There is no need to give additional minerals or vitamins, and doing so to diets that are already balanced can be harmful.

Puppies should be wormed with a good-quality but mild wormer from about two weeks of age and again every two weeks until 12 weeks of age; thereafter at three-monthly intervals. Some breeders would worm less. Remember that worming is dangerous and the right quantity should be given, relative to body weight. If worming is not undertaken and a high worm burden results, growth can be markedly impaired.

THE NEW HOME
Check out puppy buyers before you sell or even let them visit. For example, if they are out at work for long periods each day, is it wise to sell them a puppy? Have they had a puppy before of this or any other breed? Do they already have a dog and what sort? Do they want a companion animal or are they seeking a breeding animal? Will they follow your instructions? If you are selling to a couple, does the woman really want a dog? In many cases, it will be the woman who is at home and will have the major task of looking after the puppy, so she needs to be as keen as the man is.

We find that the puppy will often not eat on the first day – not surprising in that he has changed homes, left his littermates and may have had a lengthy car journey. It is imperative that the new owners do not change the diet – you have probably given them some to take home or they have already bought what you told them to buy. No dog will starve himself for long, so, within a day or two, the puppy will be eating. Changing his diet could be more damaging than letting him ignore his food for a short time.

Make a contract with your buyers stipulating the price paid, the identity of the puppy, the purpose the dog is sold for, what restrictions there are and under what circumstances they would be lifted. Each puppy should be accompanied by a pedigree and the registration papers, and any tattoo papers if the litter is tattooed. There should also be a diet sheet telling the new owner what and how to feed the puppy. Do not buy or sell unregistered puppies. Sometimes, if the breeder has sent papers to the registration body late, they may not be back at the time of sale. In that event, the contract should specify that they will be sent within a specific time. If a dog is unregistered at eight weeks, it may cost more to register later and the animal cannot be shown or sensibly bred from if it is not registered. Kennels that do not sell registered stock should be avoided like the plague! Do otherwise and you could be building up problems for yourself.

The new puppy should visit the vet (do not put him down on the ground at the surgery) for a check-up within 48 hours of arrival at his new home, to ensure that he is healthy and has no obvious deformities or heart trouble. Sort out vaccinations (parvovirus, leptospirosis, distemper etc.) and do not take the dog off the home premises until it is vaccinated at least once. The second vaccination may be at 12 or 16 weeks and thus into socialisation time. It may be necessary to take a slight risk and socialise the puppy with various experiences of the outside world before the 12-, or certainly the 16-week, vaccination.

We recommend buyers use a crate for their puppy. These are like a metal cage and come in various sizes. The buyers should purchase one that is large enough for an adult Bernese and use this for the puppy. A crate is not to be treated as a punishment block or a prison cell, but everyone has to go out sometimes, which means leaving their puppy behind for a few hours. If the puppy is crated, then nothing can happen to him and any accidents caused by him relieving himself are easy enough to deal with. Failure to crate can result in chewed furniture (through boredom) or, more serious, the young dog chewing through phone and electric wires. The use of a crate can also avoid serious accidents such as stiletto heels on a foot or pans of hot water being tipped up over an animal. We found that our dogs become used to crates and will lie in them if they are open and there is no compulsion to be inside.

As soon as the puppy is vaccinated, he can be taken to training classes and the like (see Chapter Four). Remember that, in some hot countries such as areas of the USA for example, heartworm is a serious problem and your dog may need to be on tablets. There may be other local issues on which your vet can advise in order to keep your Bernese safe and healthy.

In a book such as this, no single feature can be dealt with as fully as would be the case in a book dealing solely with a single aspect such as mating and whelping. Some useful books in this field, here listed briefly, appear in the references at the end of this book: Evans and White (1988); Jackson (1994); Jones and Joshua (1982); and Walkowicz and Wilcox (1994). Note that these are the editions which I have, and later ones may now exist. Buy, or borrow from a library, the most up-to-date version.

8 IMPORTANT DOGS

This chapter deals with individual Bernese Mountain Dogs who have made some contribution to the breed. They are largely those from more modern eras. British-based dogs are included who were successful winners in the show ring, widely used in terms of the number of progeny produced, or successful sires and dams in terms of winning progeny. Within these broad areas they are my choice. Inclusion does not mean approval and exclusion does not mean disapproval.

The animals are mostly British-based but the list does include some from other countries where data is known. In this chapter, animals are listed in alphabetical order of affix and males are listed in upper case and females in lower. Each animal is given, together with its sire and dam. Then follows the inbreeding, if any. Thus, Duntiblae Nalle 3:4 means that Nalle appears in the third generation on the father's side and the fourth generation on the dam's, where generation 1 would be the parents of the dog being assessed. The inbreeding coefficient, based on 4 to 5 generations, appears in brackets and in bold (e.g **1.6 per cent**). If there is no inbreeding

ancestry, the value is given as **<1.0 per cent.** There follows the year of birth and of death where known, the hip status where known and then, in some cases, details of the dog's career and opinions as to his conformation etc. (which may be based upon show reports). Full names are given if the dog features in its own right, but abbreviations are used in parentage and inbreeding notes. When the year of death is unknown but the animal is known to be deceased the letter d is used thus: (1982-d). Comments and corrections on these dogs, especially factual data, would be most welcome.

BRITISH-BASED DOGS

Ch. and Irish Ch. ANNEALDON EMPEROR (Hayfell Dugald with Drumbroneth x Irish Ch. Annealdon Diadora) (**<1 per cent**) (1995) Hips 2/8. 57 progeny from 10 bitches with more to come. Unusual in that his sire was not hip scored but Dugald appears to produce well on the small number assessed thus far. Emperor is from a successful litter which also included Ch. and Irish Ch. A. Excalibur and the Irish Champions A. Ebony and Ivory, A. Enforcer and A. Early Eclipse. Emperor is over medium-sized, a well pigmented dog, slightly long cast, and stands slightly narrow through the chest. Excellent in pigmentation, coat and furnishings and in character. He has a good head and a dark eye. A good mover with excellent bone. He made up at two years of age and won the CC at Crufts in 1997 and 1998. Currently one of the heaviest used studs in Britain.

Ch. Annealdon Emperor: A top winning dog of the late 1990s, currently heavily used in Britain.
Photo: Carol Ann Johnson.

Irish Ch. Annealdon Diadora (Ch. Fero v Buetigen x Irish Ch. A. Beldora) (**<1 per cent**) (1992) Hips 23/10. Produced the Annealdon E litter of five Irish Champions, two of which made English titles. Her brother Ch. and Irish Ch. A. Dark Dazzler (Hips 5/3) was successful in the British ring with seven CCs. A very beautiful top-quality bitch of excellent type and body with a beautiful head and expression. Had she lived in England rather than Ireland she would doubtless have made her title easily.

Ch. Bernfold Dawn Chorus (Windlenell War Lord x Kernow Summerlove at Bernfold) (**<1 per cent**) (1991) Hips 4/4. An over medium-sized substantial bitch of excellent type and proportions. In her younger days she was as harmonious in stance as she was on the move. Strong-headed, well pigmented and excellent in character. I liked her so much that I gave her a CC – and so did my wife. After her only litter (seven offspring to Ch. Kernow Masterpiece) she was spayed and became rather too heavy and soft in condition, though she was still shown and did go BOB at Crufts in 1997. A top winner of her day with 10 CCs and 15 Res. CCs to her credit. To date, she has a double CC winning daughter (Kernow Patience Rewarded).

Ch. FERO V BUETIGEN OF GLANZBERG AT BERNFOLD (Int. Ch. Gaston v Nesselacker x Uta v Schofschurli) Astor v Chaindon 4:4.4 (**<1 per cent**) (1990) Hips 6/7. Elbows 2/2. Six CCs and nine Res. CCs. Imported as a puppy from Switzerland. A heavily used important sire, he produced 240 progeny from 34 bitches and, thus far, his UK Champion offspring are Annealdon Dark Dazzler, Fordash Fearless of Glanzberg, Kernow Masterpiece, Bernfold Star Jupiter and Kernow Waltz at Oldberne. Dazzler also made Irish Ch. as did a sister, A. Diadora. Very sire-typical, Fero was an over medium-sized, well boned, beautifully headed dog with excellent markings and character. He was inclined to be rather forward placed in scapula, which he transmitted to some progeny, and he could have used better rear pasterns. As he aged, his hind movement improved. He proved to be a sire of good hips and generally good characters.

Ch. Fero v Buetigen. One of the UK's mostly widely used sires.

Photo: Ann Wells

Carlacot Ebony: A top producing bitch of strong character. Photo: Russell Fine Art.

Carlacot Ebony (Ch. Jumbo v Waldacker x Ch. Carlacot Bracken) (**<1 per cent**) (1984-92) Hips 2/2. A very strong-charactered bitch of medium size and substance. Her strength lay in her producing ability. She produced 22 progeny from three different sires, including Champions C. Genesis, Heather and Jupiter.

Ch. CARLACOT FIDO (Carlacot Candyman x Glanzbergs Kirsch of Carlacot) Fox v Grunenmatt 5:5 (**<1 per cent**) (1985-94) Hips 4/4. Won 34 CCs and 11 Res. CCs, with his CCs all being from different judges. Won the Group at Blackpool, 1990. The current British breed record holder (in CCs won), he was an outcross and did not leave a great legacy among his progeny. He only sired 46 progeny from nine bitches and was then implicated in trembler and withdrawn from stud. He sired two Champions (Carlacot Carefree Kate and Clenojas Fido's Prince), and Duntiblae Dark Dexter died while on two CCs. An over medium-sized dog, Fido had a sound laid-back character, was well proportioned with good markings, bone and coat. Tragically, a bloat sufferer. One of a successful litter which included Ch. C. Flame and C. Fjord who won a Res. CC.

Ch. CARLACOT GENESIS AT NELLSBERN (Ch. Clashaidy Nordic Fire x Carlacot Ebony) Duntiblae Nalle 4.4:4 Kisumu Belle Fleur 4:4 (**2.3 per cent**) (1986-94) Hips 5/11 Elbows 2/1 Character Grade A (the only Bernese Mountain Dog thus far). Three CCs and two Res. CCs. A medium-sized dog (67 cms [26½ins]), weighing 41kg (90lbs) throughout his adult life. Well pigmented and masculine, though he could have used more depth of muzzle. Good front assembly but rather straight behind, he had a strong firm back, excellent bone and (like his father) was an outstanding side mover, though he threw out one forefoot. Won his title at Crufts 1992 with BOB. Noted for producing soundness, though not used a great deal (59 progeny from nine different bitches). He sired Ch. Allado Dark n' Delicious and the CC-winner Nellsbern Casablanca. His sister C. Gorse produced Ch. Carlacot Carefree Kate. Inbred to in his home kennel, he did not give rise to trembler so did not inherit it from his father.

Ch. and Aust. Ch. CHORISTMA MONCH OF VINDISSA (Ch. Tarncred Bullfinch x Ch. Tarncred Mutzi of Choristma) Tarncred Black Watch 3:3, Fox v Grunenmatt 4.4:4 (**4 per cent**) (1983-91). Won three CCs and 4 Res. CCs Hips 4/14. His sister C. Jungmutzi

Ch. Carlacot Fido: The top CC winning Bernese in Britain. Photo: Hartley.

Ch. Carlacot Genesis At Nellsbern, with owner Helen Davenport Willis, in the Group ring at Crufts 1992. Like his father, Nordic Fire, he made up with BOB at Crufts. Photo: Dave Freeman.

Ch. Aust. Ch. Choristma Monch Of Vindissa: A successful winner in Britain before going to Australia. Slightly over-marked on the face, he was a fine character. Photo: Twigg.

Oro de coin-Barre Of Kisumu, born 1969 (Astor v Gitzirain – Linda v Blaumatthof), a foundation sire in Britain.

was the youngest Champion in the breed and he won a Res. CC from minor Puppy at WELKS (West of England Ladies' Kennel Society) in 1984. A medium-sized, rather overmarked dog of good proportions with excellent angulations, excellent character and good bone with a level topline. Despite the markings, he had a nice head and a gentle expression though a darker eye might have helped. He was a good-moving animal. Taken to Australia by his owners in 1985.

Ch. CLASHAIDY NORDIC FIRE (Ch. Tarncred Bullfinch x Tarncred Tattoo of Clashaidy) Black Velvet of Nappa 4:3.3, Oro de coin-Barre 5.5:4.4 (**3.9 per cent**) (1983-92) Hips 2/3. Won seven CCs and one Res. CC. BOB at Crufts in 1989. A top-sized (69 cms), substantial (55 kg) and powerful dog of excellent bone and good backline. Well pigmented. Good strong character and general shape but rather lacking in hindquarters and in coat. Excellent mover. Sired 104 progeny from 16 bitches including three Champions: Carlacot Genesis, Cotshill Savannah and Parracombe Lunar Fire. He also had several CC winners including Manadoris Good To Be Alive, Musical Madam and Tophat 'n' Tails and Cotshill Rainbow Warrior. Sadly, Nordic Fire was implicated in trembler as was Lunar Fire, but Genesis missed this problem.

ORO DE COIN-BARRE OF KISUMU (Astor v Gitzirain x Linda v Blaumatthof) (**< 1 per cent**) (1969-76). Imported from

Switzerland at three months of age. Oro was not a large dog but he was very typical with good markings, good construction, especially in shoulder and arch of chest with a nice head and expression. Excellent in character, he appeared on the British TV programme *Blue Peter in* 1973 and helped to stimulate wide interest in the breed. He was an important foundation sire especially through the Kisumu and Nappa kennels. Produced 33 progeny to three different bitches before being given away to a pet home. His daughters mixed well with the Fox v Grunenmatt/Duntiblae Nalle combination.

Coliburn Shona at Materas (Tirass v Waldacker x Coliburn Cher) (**< 1 per cent**) (1987-) Hips 5/2. A small, rather plain, bitch of excellent character, who moved wide in front but with the ability to produce better than herself. Produced 12 puppies from three litters including two Champions to Eiger v Staalenhof, namely Materas Dizzy Lizzy and M. Sweaty Betty. Betty produced Ch. Materas Ready Teddy Go to Nellsbern Casblanca.

Ch. DUNTIBLAE DARK PROTECTOR (Ch. D. Forgeman Fusilier x D. Bernax Bardot)

Ch. Duntiblae Dark Protector: BOB at Crufts 1986 and 1987.

Ch. Duntiblae Dark Pleasure: Sister to Protector and a successful brood.

Photo: Dalton.

Duntiblae Nalle, who could claim to be the foundation dog of the British breed.

Photo: Pearce.

Duntiblae Nalle 2:4.3, Fox v Grunenmatt 3:4, Oro de coin-Barre 4:4 (**12.1 per cent**) (1982-88). Seven CCs and three Res. CCs, BOB at Crufts in 1986 and 1988. A very beautiful dog of excellent proportions and angulations with an equally beautiful Champion sister D. D. Pleasure (who produced Ch. Cotshill Savannah). Nicely marked, well coated and well angulated, he was widely used. He sired 148 progeny from 23 different bitches and was a source of excellent hips though, allegedly, implicated in elbow problems. His character was rather sensitive. Sired Ch. Husheen Balletrina of Meadowpark and the CC winner Clynymona Falken.

Ch. DUNTIBLAE FORGEMAN FUSILER (D. Nalle x Ch. Kisumu Belle Fleur) Carlo vd Grandfeybrucke 4:4 (**<1 per cent**) (1975-82) Hips 1/2. Sired 78 progeny from 13 different mates. Won five CCs and four Res. CCs. A large, well-marked, well-angulated, typy-headed and proportioned male of the Nalle/Fox/Oro combination and typical of his breeding. Good bone and gentle character. Moved well. Sired Champions D. D. Protector and Pleasure, two of the best animals of their day, as well as the strong-charactered and powerful Ch. Carlacot Bracken who was the dam of C. Ebony. He also sired Ch. Meadowpark The Brigadier who, in turn, sired Ch. M. Sensation.

DUNTIBLAE NALLE (Soderkullas Vivo x Soderkullas Orli) Eros v Gehrimoos 2:3 (**6.3 per cent**) (1972-75) Hips 5/9. Imported to Britain from Sweden as a puppy, he arrived before the breed had CCs. He was a rather light-framed, undermarked dog, much criticised later for not having substance, but he was very shapely, with very good shoulders and hindquarters, an excellent driving gait and an outstanding character. Sired only 67 progeny from nine different bitches before dying in a road accident, but he produced six Champions, including some of the best seen in Britain, being very successful with Fox v Grunenmatt daughters. His strength as a producer may have come from his sire who was a very big, strong dog. He developed OCD in the shoulder and may be implicated in hypomyelinogenesis, but the breed in Britain owes a debt to him. He was a very good hip producer and had the ability to produce better than himself. He features behind most leading British-born dogs. Top sire three years after his demise and an undoubted pillar of the breed in Britain, without whom the breed might not have developed so well.

Ch. DUNTIBLAE DARK VIKING (Ch. Choristma Monch x Ch. D. Dark Pleasure) Kisumu Belle Fleur 4:3, D. Nalle 4.4:3.5.4

Ch. Duntiblae Forgeman Fusilier Cochrane: A top-quality animal of his day.

Ch. Duntiblae Dark Viking.

(**6.9 per cent**) (1985-91) Hips 4/2. Widely used, leaving 145 progeny from 22 bitches. Beautifully headed, over medium-sized dog of good proportions and angulations. Brother to the very beautiful D. D. Vesper (rather weak in temperament), who produced D. D. Dexter (two CCs) who, in turn, gave Champions Jaybiem Polyanthus and Arrowmeet Chieftain, a Crufts BOB. Viking sired Ch. Vikings Dark Billymajigs out of Crensa lines. In turn, Billymajigs sired Ch. Jaybiem Billy the Kid.

Ch. Folkdance at Forgeman (Ch. Tarncred Puffin x Ch. Forgeman Folksong of Tarncred) Duntiblae Nalle 2:2, Fox v Gruncnmatt 3:3 Oro de coin Barre 4:4 (**17.2 per cent**) (1977-85) Hips 2/2. A member of a successful litter containing three Champions (the others were T. Tearose and T. Bullfinch). A large, well-boned, top-quality bitch of excellent conformation, head structure and substance with strong bone. She was slightly overmarked. A very sound mover, she won the BOB at Crufts in 1980 and went on to take the Working Group, the

Ch. Forgeman Footpad, born 1980 (Mustang v Nesselacker – Folkdance At Forgeman). Pictured at nine years of age, he was the one-time breed recordholder for CCs. Photo: Brenda Griffiths.

first Bernese Mountain Dog to win a Group. The dam of Ch. and Irish Ch. Forgeman Footsteps, Ch. Forgeman Footpad, who was the winner of 30 CCs and one-time breed record holder, and Ch. Forgeman Freelance. Sadly, both these males produced trembler. Produced 20 progeny from three mates. Won 10 CCs and six Res. CCs.

Ch. Forgeman Folksong of Tarncred (Duntiblae Nalle x Ch Kisumu Belle Fleur) Carlo vd Grandfeybrucke 4:4 (**<1 per cent**) (1975-85) Hips 5/5. A bitch of the Fox/Nalle/Oro combination, she was the first Champion in Britain, a bitch of substance, shape and outstanding type. She had a beautiful head with a dark eye and excelled in forehand. Good mover. She had 23 offspring from three different mates including five Champions. To her half-brother, Ch. T. Puffin, she produced Ch. Folkdance at Forgeman (see above), Ch. T. Tearose and Ch. T. Bullfinch. To Mustang v Nesselacker, she gave Ch. T. Kleine at Timberlog and to T. Drummer she gave rise to Ch. T. Tom Tom. Implicated in trembler. Won five CCs, including Crufts 1977, and two Res. CCs.

Ch. FORGEMAN FOOTPAD (Mustang v Nesselacker x Ch. Folkdance at Forgeman) Carlo vd Grandfeybrucke 4.4:6.6 (**<1 per**

cent) (1980-92) Hips 6/6. The top winning dog of his day, amassing 30 CCs, 19 Res. CCs and one Group win. However, three of his CCs came from one judge and two each from three other judges. A below medium-sized dog who perhaps took after his sire rather than his dam except in colour. He had a good deal of white on chest, muzzle and blaze but he had an attractive head and expression and a good neck and lay of shoulder. He could have used more bone and a touch more hind angulation. He had an excellent character and in his show career was an excellent ambassador for the breed. His photograph appears on numerous items. Little used (16 progeny from three bitches), he nevertheless had a long life. He was implicated in trembler.

Ch. FORGEMAN FREELANCE OF MEADOWPARK (Dingo de Froideville x Ch. Folkdance at Forgeman) (<1 per cent) (1982-89) Hips 5/12. Won five CCs and four Res. CCs. Sired 92 progeny from 16 bitches and sired seven Champions, a breed record. His strength came from his bitch line. An over medium-sized, shapely and typy dog with good shoulders and bone and an excellent head, a touch light in eye colour. Good-charactered, he was mainly used in his home kennel (Meadowpark) and was several times top stud dog. Sadly, he was implicated in trembler and was castrated. His

Champions were Lotsolove from Meadowpark, Ways and Means at M., M. Kissin' Cousin, Beevor Ballerina of Stirleyhill, Sir Stanley from M., M. Likely Lady of Margand and littermate M. Lancelot. He also had the two CC winner Lady Laura.

GILLRO FLAPJACK OF FORGEMAN (Gillro Gambler x Onka v Grunenmatt) Astor v Chaindon 3:3 (3.3 per cent) (1980-87) Hips 0/0. Produced 60 progeny from eight different bitches. A very typy, richly pigmented, well boned male with a good coat. Good construction especially in the shoulder with a good topline. Excellent in character. His mother was heavily marked on the head but Flapjack was very correctly marked. Sired the Champions Choristma Bliss and Einselmutz and Collansues Brigitta and Marta. Also produced the widely-used Gillro Ginger Tom (Res. CC) and NZ Ch. Clashaidy Winged Dagger, who was an important sire in Australasia.

Ch. GILLRO GENTLE GENIUS (Ch. Tarncred Tom Tom x Gillro Gadabout) Kisumu Belle Fleur 3:4, Fox v Grunenmatt 4.3:5 (2.3 per cent) (1982-91) Hips 6/9. Won six CCs and one Res. CC. Sired 29 progeny from eight bitches but his stud career was affected by trembler and he was withdrawn from stud. A very large, beautifully headed dog with excellent eye shape and colour. Nicely marked. Good proportions with a good shoulder, excellent

Ch. Forgeman Freelance Of Meadowpark b 1982 (Dingo de Froideville – Folkdance At Forgeman), a dog widely used by the Meadowpark kennels and sire of seven Champions. Photo: Dalton.

Ch. Gillro Gentle Genius: A big, strong dog of outstanding type. Photo: Hartley.

ribbing, strong bone, substance and plenty of coat. Tremendous character. Sired Ch. Gillro Gypsy Magic.

FOX v GRUNENMATT (Astor v Chaindon x Nadja v Burgistein) (<1 per cent) (1971-77) Imported from Switzerland, Fox sired 50 progeny from seven different bitches. He pre dated the hip scoring scheme and only had seven progeny scored, but they did not appear good overall. However, his mixture with Nalle was largely beneficial on hip grounds, type and general construction. The Fox/Nalle/Oro combination was highly successful in the early days of British breeding. Fox was a very beautifully-headed dog, although slightly dish-faced. Very good

Fox v Grunenmatt b 1971 (Astor v Chaindon – Nadja v Burgistein, a foundation sire in Britain. Winner of two CCs before his early death.

construction, albeit not very large in stature. He had excellent bone and substance and an excellent character. He won two CCs before his early death and would surely have made up had he not died young. One of the pillars of the breed in Britain.

Ch. Hildrek Jonquil (Pascha v Nesselacker of Glanzberg x Lady v Nesselacker at Hildrek) Wita v Nesselacker 2:2, Kai v Tonisbach 4:4. (13.3 per cent) (1993) Hips 12/12. An inbred medium-sized bitch of substance and proportions with good markings and

Ch. Hildrek Jonquil: Twice CC winner at Crufts, and the only Bernese to go BIS at a general Championship show in Britain. Photo: Hartley.

excellent type. Slightly forward placed in front assembly, she had a lovely head and moved very soundly. A very successful show winner, she won six CCs and three Res. CCs and was twice the BOB winner at Crufts, as well as winning BIS at the East of England general championship show in 1996, the only Bernese to do so, thus far, in Britain. Sadly, she was spayed on health grounds and did not reproduce.

Ch. Kisumu Belle Fleur of Forgeman (Fox v Grunenmatt x Kisumu Aphrodite) (<1 per cent) (1973-81) Hips 38/34. Made her title at six years but eventually won six CCs and one Res. CC. A bitch of Fox/Oro combination and sister to Ch. Kisumu Bonne Esperance of Millwire, she had poor hips. This was only discovered after her death when the scoring scheme began and her plates were submitted, but her descendants were generally good in terms of hip status as was usual with the Nalle combination. Dam of 18 progeny from three different mates. Foundation of the Forgeman kennels. She was of good size and proportions with a good shoulder, beautiful hindquarters and correct markings. She had good tail carriage, something not often seen in this breed. To Nalle she gave Champions F. Folksong and Fusilier and Swedish Ch. F. Fellini.

GROLL vd LECKENBECKE (Arno v Kiesenthal x Billie v Koblhang) (**<1 per cent**) (1970-77) An early import from Germany to Scotland in 1971. Sired 23 progeny from three bitches. He is found behind Majanco dogs and sired Ch. Meiklestane Black Benjamin to Tarncred Tara who had produced M. Dark Ace to D. Nalle. More importantly, Groll sired Tarncred Drummer out of an Oro daughter. Drummer sired Champions T. Tom Tom and T. Troika and appears close up behind several Champions. Groll was an above medium-sized dog with an nice head, a profuse coat and a good character.

used in his home kennel, Hans Christian produced Ch. M. Early Election, M. Early Embargo and the CC winning M. Early Exodus.

Ch. Ways and Means of Meadowpark (Ch. Forgeman Freelance x Meadowpark Friendly Persuasion) Duntiblae Nalle 4.4:4.4.4.4 (**6.7 per cent**) (1985-) Hip scored. Five CCs and three Res. CCs. Had only one litter of eight, the Meadowpark Early E litter to Hans Christian, two of which, Election and Embargo, made titles. A large bitch, very sire-typical, but sensitive in temperament.

LEFT: Groll vd Leckenbecke (Arni v Kiesenthal – Billie v Koblhang: A German dog imported to Britain in 1971.

Ch. Ways And Means Of Meadowpark: A successful winner and brood.
Photo: Russell Fine Art.

HANS CHRISTIAN OF MEADOWPARK (Danettas Hercules x Ina of Chantelle) (**<1 per cent**) (1986-1991) Hips 4/5. Widely used for a dog with a limited show record, he sired 152 progeny from 25 bitches. A Danish-bred animal, Hans had a good character and pigment but was rather lacking in angulation behind. Ina was a daughter of the very good dog Waddenzee Bas. Widely

MUSTANG v NESSELACKER OF GLANZBERG (Duc v Findlingsbrunnen x Zusi v Nesselacker) (**<1 per cent**) (1975-84) Hips 23/26. A widely used sire producing 151 progeny from 15 bitches. His dam was sister to Zyta v N. who was BOB at the first BMDCA Show. A Swiss-born dog of good head, type, substance, character, construction and bone but rather lacking in

Mustang v Nesselacker as a puppy in quarantine. An important sire in Britain.

Ch. Elnside Mayo Spirit b 1984 (Snowstorm Of Peninghane – Inchberry Annaliese): The first Scottish-bred Champion. A big dog, despite the fact that his dam was small. Sire of Ch. Elnside Fatal Attraction.

stature. Some show reports suggest that he was rather loose in movement but others disagree. Mustang was the best Assessed dog at the first BMDCGB Open show in 1979. His hip status was worse than he produced which, on the whole, was tolerable. His stud career was successful since he sired seven Champions (the breed record with Freelance), which were Champions Forgeman Footpad, F. Footsteps, Tarncred Kleine, T. Mutzi, Walchwil Classy Lassie, Glanzberg Helvetia and G. Edelweiss. He also had other CC winners.

Snowstorm Of Penninghame: An important sire in Britain.

SNOWSTORM OF PENNINGHAME (St Fillans Marksman x Temeraire Tombola) Tarncred Tarquin 3:2 (**6.3 per cent**) (1982-d) Hips 6/16. Sired 20 progeny from two bitches (three litters) including Champions Elnside Mayo Spirit, E. Huggy Bear and Dark and Handsome at Ursine. A rarely shown dog, he was a successful sire, bearing in mind his limited use, taking after his sire line. His Champion sons tended to be large dogs of good character.

EIGER v STAALENHOF AT COLIBURN (Pius v Nesselacker x Dora v Wolfgalgen) Grey Waldacker 3:2 (**6.3 per cent**) (1987-1997) Imported from Switzerland. Hip scored. A medium-sized, well constructed typy dog of good bone and substance with a somewhat curly coat. Rather light in eye he still had a good head and expression. Little shown, he was nevertheless widely used with 134 progeny from 20 bitches. He sired the sisters Materas Dizzy Lizzy and M. Sweaty Betty and the dog Coliburn Owen of Blumental, all of whom made titles.

Ch. TARNCRED BULLFINCH (Ch. Tarncred Puffin x Ch. Forgeman Folksong of Tarncred) Duntiblae Nalle 2:2, Fox v Grunenmatt 3:3, Oro de coin Barre 4:4 (**17.2 per cent**) (1980-85) Hip scored. Sired 22 progeny from four bitches. A very large, substantial, superbly boned, upstanding masculine dog who was well constructed front and rear with a good backline. He had a balanced head and dark eye and was a very good mover which can come through his line. Sired the youngest champion, Ch. Choristma Jungmutzi who made up at 14 months, and also Ch. and Aust. Ch. Choristma Monch of Vindissa as well as Ch. Clashaidy Nordic Fire who resembled him in many respects. Won four CCs and three Res. CCs. Died young of myelopathy.

TARNCRED DRUMMER (Groll vd Leckenbecke x Black Velvet of Nappa) York v Fluhwald 3:4 (**1.6 per cent**) (1972-1981) Hips 4/4. Sire of 32 progeny from five different bitches. A shapely, undermarked, well-coated dog of above medium-size with an excellent character and adequate bone for his size. He had a level bite until he was about five when it corrected. Produced Ch. T. Troika, reserve in the Group at Bath 1979 and the excellent Ch. T. Tom Tom. Found close up in several Champion pedigrees. Drummer's dam had a blue eye but did not produce it in her offspring.

Ch. TARNCRED PUFFIN (Duntiblae Nalle x Tarncred Black Watch) Carlo vd Grandfeybrucke 4:4 (**<1 per cent**) (1976-85) Hips 2/4. A very large dog, typical of the Nalle/Fox/Oro combination. Strong-boned and substantial, with a beautiful head and excellent type. Excellent shoulder and hindquarters. A fine mover, he was the first male Champion in Britain. Sired 55 progeny from nine different bitches, including the Champions Folkdance at Forgeman, T. Tearose and T. Bullfinch. Won eight CCs and four Res. CCs.

Ch. TARNCRED TARQUIN OF TEMERAIRE (Duntiblae Nalle x Tarncred Black Watch) Carlo vd Grandfeybrucke 4:4 (**<1 per cent**) (1976-85) Hips 3/7. Hips Clear (Sweden). Six CCs and seven Res. CCs. Brother to T. Puffin. An over medium-sized well pigmented animal with a good coat. Produced 112 progeny from 19 bitches. Sired the sisters Ch. Temeraire Tender Thymes and Temeraire Penny Black of Crensa (inbred on Nalle).

Ch. TARNCRED TOM TOM (T. Drummer x Forgeman Folksong at Tarncred) Oro de coin-Barre 3:4 (**1.6 per cent**) (1979-1986) Hips 3/3. Five CCs and two Res. CCs. 171 progeny from 25 bitches. Trembler carrier. A large, well marked and beautifully constructed dog, Tom Tom was one of the best-looking dogs of his day and proved a very good hip producer. Good head with excellent expression and excellent character. He took a long time to make up, largely because he did not handle well in the ring and was strong enough to do his own thing. Sired the very beautiful Ch. Millwire Forever Esperance and Ch. Gillro Gentle Genius.

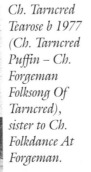

Ch. Tarncred Puffin: The first male Champion in Britain.

Ch. Tarncred Tearose b 1977 (Ch. Tarncred Puffin – Ch. Forgeman Folksong Of Tarncred), sister to Ch. Folkdance At Forgeman.

Ch. Tarncred Tom Tom: One of the UK's finest dogs.

Ch. Millwire Forever Esperance b 1980 (Ch. Tarncred Tom Tom – Millwire Diamond Cluster). Winner of seven CCs and four Reserve CCs, she was one of Britain's best bitches. She tended to lack coat, but not quality nor type.

Ch. TRANSCONTINENTAL BOY OF CLENRAW (Inchberry Great Bear of Clenraw x Boneidle Quickstep) Duntiblae Nalle 3:3, Black Velvet of Nappa 4.4:4 (**4.1 per cent**) (1982-95) Hips 2/2. Five CCs and five Res. CCs. An over medium-sized substantial dog who was graded B+ for character. Well proportioned, with a good front assembly, and a sound mover. Widely used, he sired 113 progeny out of 21 different dams and was a very good hip producer. He produced Ch. Bernalpen Welsche, who in turn produced Ch. B. Ketje. Also sired B. Sylvanner who won a CC.

Ch. JUMBO v WALDACKER AT COLIBURN (Arthos v Waldacker x Nora v Bernetta) Cresta v Bernetta 3:2 (**6.3 per cent**) (1979-87) Swiss hips 0/0 Hips 6/7. The first import to take a title in Britain, he won five CCs and five Res. CCs. He had a beautiful head but was known to fly his tail high and was not well angulated behind. He was a stocky dog of excellent character with excellent bone and pigmentation. A widely used sire producing 162 progeny from 22 different bitches of which four made up to Champion: Brick Kiln Matilda, Lacelaw Statesman, Meadowpark Captivation and Troublesome Lass. He also sired several CC winners including Coliburn Bea, Ember (BOB at Crufts) and Echo. Statesman was a particularly good Champion but he was sadly never used at stud. His mother had a blue eye but that should not have stopped his usage and he might well have been of value to the breed. Jumbo does appear close up in many Champion pedigrees and a trace of his 'blood' is useful. He seems to have 'clicked' well with Forgeman lines. Of the imports post the Nalle/Fox/Oro era, Jumbo was probably the most useful in that he gave character and head structure, though he was not particularly good in hip production. He tended to produce a couple of small incisors in the centre of the lower jaw which comes through in some of his descendants.

Below: Ch. Lacelaw Statesman (Ch. Jumbo v Waldacker – Taking A Chance Of Lacelaw, a blue-eyed sister to Footpad): Statesman won seven CCs and one Reserve CC, and was a very typey male with a gorgeous head. A combination of Jumbo with Forgeman. Tragically not used for breeding.

TIRASS V WALDACKER AT COLIBURN
(Hansi v Seewadel x Ira v Waldacker) (**<1 per cent**) (1984-97) Hips 5/4. A large, well pigmented dog of excellent character and strong bone and substance who was rarely shown. Inclined to be cow-hocked. He was the most prolific sire of Bernese Mountain Dogs in Britain, producing 294 progeny from 34 different bitches, many in the Coliburn kennels. Carlacot Heather is his only Champion to date. He had several CC winners, including the siblings C. Napoleon (two CCs) and Nadja (one CC) out of C. Bea and also C. Truce (one CC). Napoleon appears to have been a source of very good elbows though he was less successful in hip terms.

Ch. CHIVAS vd WIEDEWA OF COTSHILL (Pilatus x Ned. Ch. Grasja Uit't Groes) (**<1 per cent**) (1990-97) Hips 10/11. Five CCs and 10 Res. CCs. A nice-headed, well pigmented dog of excellent character brought in from Belgium as a puppy. His father, a very beautiful dog, was slightly short in the leg, a trait which Chivas also demonstrated, though he did not usually transmit this. Died of meningitis, but not before he had produced 205 progeny from 26 different bitches. His first Champion, Millermead Eternal Dream, made up in 1998.

Ch. Chivas vd Wiedewa Of Cotshill, at ten months of age.

AMERICAN-BASED DOGS

American Champions produced are correct to the end of 1997. Some animals may yet add more, but others are unlikely to do so. No comment is made for sires with fewer than six or dams with fewer than four Champion offspring.

Am. Ch. ALPHORNS COPYRIGHT OF ECHO (Tryarr Alphorn Knight Echo x Tryarr Alphorn Brio) Bellas Clara 3:3, Sanctuary Woods Black Knight 3:4 (**4.7 per cent**). Top winning conformation male 1976-78. BOB BMDCA 1977-8. Sired 11 American Champions.

Am. Ch. ARTHOS OCTOBER v BERNDASH (Aldo v Kleinholtz x Am. Ch. Grunberg Iridescent Fire) (1984-94). Top conformation male 1989. Sire of 27 Champions.

Am. Ch. ASHLEY v BERNERLIEBE CD (Am. Ch. Galan v Senseboden x Am. Ch. Dult Daphne v Yodlerhof) Sultan v Dursrutti 2:3, Diana v Moosseedorf 2:3, Alex v Bauernheim 4.4:5.5 (**13.3 per cent**). Top conformation male 1979. BOB BMDCA 1980, 1982, 1983. Sire of 28 Champions.

Am. Can. Ch. Bev's Jabbering Jody v BB CD (Am. Bermuda Ch. Darius v Rutherford x Am. Can. Ber. Ch. Alphorns Happy Talk) (**<1.0 per cent**) (1979-91). Dam of 14 Champions including a top sire, Jaycys Wyatt v Hund See who produced 23 Champions.

Am. Ch. BROKEN OAKS DIETER v ARJANA CD (Am. Ch. Wyemede Luron Bruce x Am. Ch. Broken Hills Arjana CD) Ultra v Oberfeld 5:5, Gretel v Langmoos 5:5 (**<1.0 per cent**) (1980-90) Hips OFA. Best of Winners at the BMDCA 1981/82 and BOB in 1984. Sire of 19 Champions. Large, free-moving, well-marked male.

Am. Can. Mex. Int. Ch. DALLYBECKS ECHO JACKSON CD (Am. Ch. Alex v Weissenberg x Am. Ch. Dallybecks Cresta v Bergita CD) (**<1.0 per cent**) (1986-98) Hips: OFA Good. Elbows: 0/0. A mixture of Swiss (sire) and American (dam) lines. A well-marked, small but shapely animal who was a successful show dog and who has sired more Champions (64) and working title holders (23) than any other dog in America up to the end of 1997. Implicated in PRA. He was from a good litter containing three other Am. Champions: D. Elsinor v Raven Mtn, D. Elga v Cresta, and D. Ein Kelsey v Mystik. The first two were OFA Good and the final one OFA Fair. Jackson sired Swiss Stars Taken for Granite at Duntiblae, exported to the UK where he sired the CC winner Duntiblae Designer Label (out of Ch. Majanco Loretta at Duntiblae).

Am. Can. Mex. UCI FCI Ch. Dallybecks Echo Jackson CD NDD (1986-1998): Sire of more American Champions than any other dog (68 to early 1998), also sired 23 offspring with working titles. He was a registered Therapy dog.

Am. Ch. DEERPARK HEARTLIGHT (Am. Ch. Ashley v Bernerliebe CD x Deerpark Daisy) (**<1.0 per cent**) Top conformation male 1987-8, BOB BMDCA 1988. Sire of 44 Champions.

Am. Can. Ch. Deerpark Heartlight: BOB at the 1988 BMDCA Specialty.

Am. Ch. HALIDOM DAVOS v YODLERHOF CD (Am. Ch. Grand Yodler of Teton Valley CDX x Am. Ch. Ginger v Senseboden) (**<1.0 per cent**). BOB BMDCA 1979. Sire of 44 Champions.

Am. Ch. Halidom Keri CD (Bari les Sommetres x Am. Ch. Halidom Kara CD) (**<1.0 per cent**) (1980-91). Dam of 11 Champions.

Am. Ch. DONAR v MUTSCHEN (Hansi v Seewadel x Assi v Mutschen) OFA G, EL 0/0. A Swiss import and the sire of 58 Champions.

Am. Ch. Halidom Keri (1980-1991): Dam of 11 American Champions.

Am. Ch. Nashems Taylor Made (b1993): The highest winning BMD bitch in American history. Twice Best Bitch at the BMDCA Specialty, once with BOB.

Am. Ch. Shersan Chang O'Pace (1978-1988): Sire of 26 American Champions, BOB BMDCA Specialty 1986, and the top winning BMD of all time.

Am. Ch. Nashems Taylor Made (Am. Ch. De-Li's Standing Ovation x Am. Ch. Nashems Becken v Woodmoor) (**<1 per cent**) (1993). A well-marked, substantial bitch with an outstanding show record, being BOS (1996) and BOB (1997) at the BMDCA Specialty and the highest winning Bernese bitch in history.

Am. Can. Ch. PIKES HARPO J ANDREW (Am. Ch. Pike's Siegfried v Edo x Am. Ch. Bellas Albertine Faymie) (**<1.0 per cent**). Top Conformation male 1980-83. Not as prominent in the production stakes as his show career might have implied.

Am. Can. Ch. SHERSANS BLACK TIE REQUIRED (Am. Can. Ch. Shersan Chang O'Pace v Halidom x Am. Ch. Halidom Keri) H. Kali v Muensterplatz 2:3 (**6.3 per cent**) Sire of 33 Am. Champions

Am. Can. Ch. SHERSAN CHANG O'PACE v HALIDOM CD (Am. Ch. Halidom Davos v Yodlerhof CD x Am. Ch. Halidom Kali v Muensterplatz CD) Galen v Mattenhof 4:4 (**<1 per cent**) (1979-88). BOB at the 1986 BMDCA Specialty, Top conformation male 1984-86. Chang was the top winning Bernese of all time in all-breed competition, winning 20 BIS and 56 Group Firsts, including the group at Westminster 1985. Widely used, he has sired 26 Champions so far. He was well angulated behind, especially for his day, and was well boned but looked very rangy in his youth.

Am. Can. Mex. Int. Ch. SWISS STARS BLUE BARON (Am. Ch. Dallybecks Echo Jackson x Am. Ch. Vombreiterweg's Swiss Lace) (1989). Medium-sized (Ht 65cms [25½ins]), substantial (Wt 50 kg [110lbs]) male with good pigment. BOB at BMDCA in 1992 and 1996. Sister was Am. Ch. SS Brandy Sniffer.

Am. Can. Mex. Int. Ch. Swiss Stars Blue Baron TT (b1989): Twice winner of BOB at the BMDCA Specialty (1992/1996) and a top winner.

SWISS-BASED DOGS

The following dogs are Swiss-based or were exported from Switzerland. Hips relate to grades so that a grade of 0/0 is not the same as a score of 0/0 under the British system. Brief details of show record, progeny/litters produced if known and hip and elbow status of progeny are given.

Int. Swiss Ch. PYROS v BARNERHOF (Castor vd Lehnflue x Essy v Barnerhof) (1987) Hips 0/0 Elbows 0/0. Klubsieger 1991. World Sieger 1992. Sired 23 litters. Progeny: Hips 28 dogs 0 = 46.4 per cent. Elbows 27 dogs 0 = 77.8 per cent, 2/3 = 3.7 per cent

Int. Ch. HONDO v BERNETTA (Astor v Chaindon x Int. Ch. Cresta v Bernetta) York v Fluhwald 3:4.3 (**4.7 per cent**) (1974-82). Produced 79 litters.

ASTOR v CHAINDON (Carlo vd Grandfeybrucke x Diana v Ruegsbach) Alex v Angstorf 3.3:3 (**6.3 per cent**). Highly important foundation dog seen in many pedigrees worldwide. Winner of a CACIB.

CYRUS vd DILLETEN (Arno v Dahlen x Calla vd Dilleten) (1980-86) Hips 0/0. Produced 43 litters. Sire of Int. Ch. Gallo v Leubschimoos who was grandfather of Ch. Bernalpen Ketje. Progeny: Hips 24 dogs 0 = 62.5 per cent.

DOMINO v DORFLI SchH1, SanH1 (Pat de Perreux x Hella vd Schwarzwasserfluh) (1988-96) Hips 0/0 Elbows 1/1. Sired 21 litters. Progeny: Hips 28 dogs 0 + 44.8 per cent. Elbows 29 dogs 0 = 48.3 per cent, 2/3 = 10.3 per cent.

COSAQUE de la GOTTAZ (Jerry v Rosiendlithal x Olma v Reuenberg) (1989-94) Hips 0/0 Elbows 0/0 Sired 19 litters. Progeny: Hips 17 dogs 0 = 5.9 per cent. Elbows 17 dogs 0 = 70.6 per cent 2/3 = 17.7 per cent.

CLEO de MONT-DEDOS (Udo vd Gotthelfsegg x Nadine v Saanenstrand) (1986) Hips 0/0. Sired 22 litters. Sire of Am. Ch. Arthos v Dorneckberg. One daughter, Berna v Aemmesteg, brought to the UK. Progeny: Hips 14 dogs 0 = 35.7 per cent. Elbows 11 dogs 0 = 18.2 per cent, 2/3 = 18.2 per cent.

BENY v NESSELACKER (Pius v Forst x Odette v Nesselacker) (1982-89) Hips 0/0. Sired 69 litters. Progeny: Hips 71 dogs 0 = 80.3 per cent. Elbows 22 dogs 0 = 50 per cent 2/3 = 13.6 per cent.

Int. Swiss Ch. GASTON v NESSELACKER (Kai v Tonisbach x Zuza v Nesselacker) Hasso v Hogebuur 3:4.3 (**4.7 per cent**) (1984-91) Hips 0/0. Klubsieger 1988. World Sieger 1990. Large powerful male with good type. Strong, well-marked head and good front assembly, rather straight behind. Sired 72 litters. Father of Ch. Fero v Buetigen. Progeny: Hips 85 dogs 0 = 51.8 per cent. Elbows 21 dogs 0 = 57.1 per cent 2/3 = 38.1 per cent.

Int. Swiss Ch. JERRY v ROSIENDLITHAL (Beny v Nesselacker x Berna v Rosiendlithal) (1986) Hips 0/0. Elbows 0/0 Klubsieger 1988-89. World Sieger 1989. Large, well-proportioned with well-marked head. Good front assembly and good topline. Sired Ch. Pia v Nesselacker, a strong bitch who made up in 1996. Progeny: Hips 44 dogs 0 = 72.7 per cent. Elbows 21 dogs 0 = 76.2 per cent, 2/3 = 9.5 per cent.

World Ch. Gaston v Nesselacker. An important Swiss dog found in pedigrees around the world.

GINO vd SCHEIDEGG (Beny v Nesselacker x Colette vd Scheidegg) (1989-) Hips 0/0 Elbows 0/0 Ht 68 cms. Progeny: Hips 22 dogs 0 = 22.7 per cent. Elbows 21 dogs 0 = 57.1 per cent, 2/3 = 14.3 per cent.

HANSI v SEEWADEL (Argo v Freibach x Cora v Seewadel) Cuno vd Dilleten 3:2 (**6.3 per cent**) (1982-92) Hips 0/0. Tough, slightly leggy dog who could be slightly dog-aggressive when I saw him at the 1987 Swiss Sieger. Produced 86 litters. Sire of Tirass v Waldacker and of the top Am. Ch. Donar v Mutschen. Progeny: Hips 67 dogs 0 = 65.7 per cent. Elbows 15 dogs 0 = 53.3 per cent, 2/3 = 33.4 per cent.

Swiss Ch. KAI v TONISBACH (Donar v Buschsischlossli x Ella v Tonisbach) Wacho v Dursrutti 3:3 (**3.1 per cent**) (1979-87) Hips 0/0. Sire of Am. Ch. Alex v Weissenberg, Can. Ch. Rambo vd Schwarzwasserfluh and grandsire of Eiger v Staalenhof. Progeny: Hips 104 dogs 0 = 76.9 per cent.

Int. Swiss Ch. WACHO v TONISBACH (Int. Ch. Igor v Vindonissa x Gora v Steinholzli) (1988) Hips 0/0 Elbows 0/0 Klubsieger 1990. Produced 96 litters. Progeny: Hips 66 dogs 0 = 42.4 per cent. Elbows 57 dogs 0 = 54.4 per cent, 2/3 = 33.3 per cent.

Int. Ch. SASSO LA VAUX (Carol v Wolflisried x Pira la Vaux) (1981-d) Hips 0/0. Large, powerful dog. Swiss Sieger 1986. Sire of Am. Ch. Tibor du Champs Paris. Progeny: Hips 67 dogs 0 = 52 per cent.

Int. Dutch. Lux. Ch. IGOR v VINDONISSA (Janis v Barnerhof x Vilja vd Hausmatt) (1985) Hips 0/0. Produced 14 litters and 81 progeny. Progeny: Hips 24 dogs 0 = 50 per cent. Elbows 20 dogs 0 = 70 per cent, 2/3 = 15 per cent.

ARTHOS v WALDACKER (Int. Ch. Hondo v Bernetta x Mirabella ad Steini) (**<1.0 per cent**) (1975-82). Sired 49 litters. Father of Ch. Jumbo v Waldacker and grandsire of Tirass v Waldacker.

GREY v WALDACKER (Arthos v Waldacker x Nora v Bernetta) (1978-89) Hips 0/0. Hip graded progeny 61 with 68.9 per cent grade 0. Sire of Am. Ch. Olly v Tonisbach and grandsire of the top stud Am. Ch. Donar v Mutschen.

MUTZ v WALDACKER (Arthos v Waldacker x Nora v Bernetta) (1982-93) Hips 0/0. Sired 47 litters. Sire of Can. Ch. Weron vd Schwarzwasserfluh. Progeny: Hips 34 dogs 0 = 52.9 per cent.

9 ROUTES FOR BREED IMPROVEMENT

Most dog breeders operate with relatively small populations of dogs. Outside of what are called puppy mills or puppy farmers – an insult to farmers – who are reproducers of dogs rather than true breeders, very few have more than half a dozen females of a breed and many operate with just one or two. Even a relatively small pig breeder would probably have 150 sows, while some hill sheep breeders would count their ewes in thousands. Genetics is very much a numbers game so that a breeder operating with, say, half a dozen bitches, might produce only six litters per year or about 44 puppies. Most breeders would consider that quite extensive breeding but, in genetic terms, it is relatively minor.

Not only do dog breeders operate on a small scale, they do so in relative isolation and with minimal information. A breeder of Holstein-Friesian dairy cows would not only have a large herd (70-150 cows in Britain on average), but he would have a great deal of genetic advice available through organisations like Genus. He would also have access to regularly produced information on the inheritance of traits and the quality of stud bulls. Information exists worldwide, so that a British breeder could know, or readily find out about, the performing potential of American, Dutch, New Zealand and other sires, as well as those in Britain. For a relatively small sum he could use frozen semen from a suitable bull located virtually anywhere in the world. Each country has a different way of evaluating bulls, but conversion formulae exist which allow American test figures to be converted to British ones and so on.

Dairy bull breeders have available various kinds of Estimated Breeding Values which are mathematically reliable and enormously useful. In contrast, the dog breeder, who is selecting for a variety of conformational traits, does not even know the heritability of the traits he is seeking. He is thus working to improve particular features without knowing to what degree, if any, that trait will be transmitted from father to progeny. Some data on conformational heritabilities were given earlier, but relate to South African German Shepherd Dogs and thus may not equally apply to Bernese. It is, however, reasonable to suppose that figures across breeds may be similar, so that a heritability of wither height of $65 + 17$ per cent may be

A group of Meadowparks with their breeder Bernice Mair. They are members of the Double E litter, several of which became title-holders.

similar in Bernese. Most of the heritabilities on conformational traits tend to be high, which is encouraging.

RELIABILITY OF INFORMATION

There is, clearly, a need to determine how specific traits are inherited and also to develop ways in which they can be used by breeders. Breeders have to realise that, even if they are relatively large in scale of operation, they cannot expect to progress effectively in isolation and that breeders have to cooperate through breed clubs or collections of breed clubs (breed councils). Given data on heritabilities, breeders can expect to know what emphasis to place on various items of information. No breeder can operate as an island and, if they do so, they are likely to produce inferior stock.

Most pedigree dog breeders place great emphasis on the pedigree of a dog and will wax lyrical about animals well back in the pedigree. Table 9.1 shows the reliability of the animal's own information and that of his pedigree and siblings as well as progeny data.

In broad terms, all information becomes more reliable as the heritability increases and as the amount of information increases. Thus, at 40 per cent heritability, a dog's own performance is 63 per cent reliable. This is more useful than the data on his parents, grandparents or the full pedigree, which never exceed 50 per cent at this heritability. Clearly, a breeder has data on a pedigree before he has the dog, because he can mix and match pedigrees of sires and dams before breeding them. However, once an animal has a record available, then that record is more useful than the whole pedigree. If the animal is a poor performer in the particular trait

Table 9.1 Reliability of various records for selectional purposes at different heritability values (Values as percentages)

Pedigree Data* P+				Dogs Own Data	Records of siblings						Progeny records					
					Full Sibs			Half Sibs								
h^2	P	GP	CP		2	4	6	5	10	20	5	10	20	40	80	120
10	22	27	29	32	22	29	35	17	23	29	34	45	58	71	82	87
20	32	37	39	45	30	39	44	23	29	36	46	59	72	82	90	93
30	39	43	45	55	36	45	51	27	33	69	56	70	79	87	93	95
40	45	49	50	63	41	50	55	30	36	41	60	73	83	90	95	96
50	50	53	54	71	45	53	58	32	38	43	65	77	86	92	96	97
60	55	57	57	77	48	56	60	34	40˙	44	68	80	88	94	97	98
70	59	61	61	84	51	58	62	36	41	45	72	82	82	95	97	98

*P=parents only. P+GP= Parents plus grandparents. CP=complete pedigree. Data in the table relate to a single record per animal. It is assumed that there are zero environmental correlations within and between progeny groups. Reliability is the relationship (in percentage terms) between the additive genetic merit of the dog being evaluated and the phenotypic measure being selected for and being measured.

being assessed, then it is no use arguing that his pedigree was "wonderful" because he clearly has not lived up to expectation. Data on littermates can be more useful than pedigree data but still do not achieve the level of the animal's own performance, unless siblings were very numerous, which is improbable. Half-siblings (usually by the same father out of different mothers) can be useful but are less valuable than full brothers and sisters, though largish numbers can, of course, be obtained more readily.

Progeny data is much more useful than anything else, largely because it is telling us what the parent (usually the father) *is* doing rather than pedigree data and own performance telling us what he *might* do. At 40 per cent heritability, ten progeny tell us more than does information on the dog or its pedigree. Thus, if a sire is giving very poor hips, for example, on ten progeny, this is likely to be more valuable data than everything that has gone before. If he is producing badly, it is not really important to tell us that he had a 0/0 or Excellent hip grading, because what matters more is the poor value for his progeny which countermands the dog's own excellent result. It is, however, likely that, in broad terms, the best producers will have good performance themselves and that poor performers are unlikely to give good results. The higher the heritability the more true the previous sentence is likely to be. Breeders must, however, appreciate that, if used often enough, any dog can give rise to a single good (or bad) performance in any specific trait and it is not the individual animal that must be considered but rather the full data on unselected progeny.

Progeny data on hips scored under the British (BVA/KC) scoring system are given in Table 9.2 for all dogs with 20 or more progeny scored up until April 3rd 1998. Dogs are listed in merit order based upon mean progeny score. In using this list, we must look at the number of progeny (the more the better), the number of dams (the more the better) and the mean progeny score (the lower the better). One must also look at the percentage of progeny in the low groups (0-10 or 0-20, preferably the former) which should be as high as possible, and the percentage of progeny in the high groups (30+) which should be as low as possible. Some of the dogs listed will have progeny added in future years but others will be complete. In breed club publications more data are produced than the abbreviated form given here for convenience. Note that all the sires listed were scored through the scheme. The percentage of progeny scoring high (over 30) ranges from 2 to 27 per cent, according to sire, while those scoring well (20 or better) range from 96 down to 45 per cent. Obviously, there is more to a sire than hip production and breeders must bear that in mind, but hip status is very important in animals that are sold and, increasingly, would-be buyers are wanting to be given data on hip status of pedigrees. Sadly, most of the sires listed in table 9.2 are now deceased and many will have no further additions to these lists. Reliability will depend upon numbers scored and also, in part, upon the numbers of different dams to which sires were mated. Some sires listed have over 30 per cent of registered stock scored. In others, the figure may decline to 15 per cent or so. Progeny numbers produced by some of these dogs are shown in Chapter Eight.

Table 9.2 Progeny test data for BVA/KP hip scores. BMDs

Sire	Progeny scored	Diff. dams	Range scores[1]	Average score[2]	percentage[3]		
					<11	<20	>30
Duntiblae D. Protector*	45	19	0-48	8.8	78	96	2
Transcontinental Boy*	40	16	0-41	11.1	63	88	3
Tarncred Tom Tom*	48	18	0-56	11.7	63	90	4
Duntiblae D. Dexter*	25	12	6-32	12.0	56	88	4
Bernerbakkens Froy*	59	24	0-59	12.5	62	82	5
Fero v Buetigen*	68	27	2-65	12.6	52	90	7
Hans Christian/M.*	49	20	0-66	13.2	57	88	10
Tarncred Tarquin/T.*	36	17	0-59	13.4	52	83	6
Mustang v Nesselacker*	24	10	3-36	13.8	38	84	8
Nellsbern Casablanca*	27	11	4-89	14.2	68	93	7
Chivas vd Wiedewa/C.*	60	19	5-76	14.9	44	87	9
Duntiblae D. Viking*	48	18	4-70	15.3	50	79	8
Ambros v Griesbach/G.*	28	12	6-45	15.4	50	79	11
Crensa Trafalgar/D*	23	8	1-37	16.2	35	74	9
Gillro Ginger Tom*	28	8	4-48	16.2	50	71	15
Clashaidy Nordic Fire*	52	15	2-96	16.3	55	79	16
Gillro Flapjack/F.*	23	7	4-49	16.6	43	78	13
Buganeezee Lochnivar*	21	9	6-64	17.3	19	71	5
Forgeman Freelance*	28	12	3-58	17.6	43	72	18
Carlacot Genesis/N.*	28	8	6-88	18.3	50	71	11
Alex v Buhlikofen*	26	13	8-60	18.9	28	78	12
Ambros v Griesbach*	32	11	4-62	19.2	37	68	12
Tirass v Waldacker/C.*	53	23	0-69	20.4	38	64	27
Jumbo v Waldacker/C.*	58	18	0-87	20.5	36	69	22
Meadowpark Lancelot*	22	7	5-71	20.7	32	59	19
Eiger v Staalenhof/C.(*)	21	10	4-81	22.7	34	53	20
Coliburn Napoleon*	27	10	5-65	25.3	12	45	12

[1]the best and worst scoring progeny [2]arithmetic progeny mean score [3]percentage of progeny scoring 10 or better, 20 or better or above 30. *indicates the sire is himself scored, (*) scored but not made public.

Table 9.3 shows the same type of data for Swiss Bernese Mountain Dogs. It relates to data taken from the Swiss Klub (1998) but relates only to dogs with at least 20 progeny graded, while the club publishes when there are 10 or more progeny. Dogs are listed in order of the percentage of grades 0 (A). Note that the Swiss system originally used grades 0-3, which was then altered to grades A-E so that data are pooled.

In looking at the data in Table 9.3, we have to realise that there has been an advance in hip quality over time, so that more recent sires would tend to meet up with better dams. In addition, the scheme changed from a 0-3 grading to an A-E grading, i.e. from four grades to five, which latter might be mathematically more accurate. Thus, in Table 9.3, sires born more recently have progeny in grade B which were not in earlier sires'

Table 9.3 Progeny tests for HD grade in Switzerland. BMDs

Sire[1]	Sire birth year	No. of progeny	percent of progeny in grade			
			0 or A	B	1 or C	2/3 or D/E
Beny v Nesselacker	1982	71	80.3		11.3	8.4
Kai v Tonisbach	1979	104	76.9		11.5	11.6
Jerry v Rosiendlithal	1986	44	72.7	4.5	15.9	6.8
Pat de Perreux	1982	25	72.0	4.0	16.0	8.0
Fertek v Chujerhof	1981	30	70.0		20.0	10.0
Grey v Waldacker	1978	61	68.9		18.0	13.2
Kuno v Schoneggschwand	1984	88	68.2	9.1	14.8	8.0
Hansi v Seewadel	1982	67	65.7	3.0	23.9	7.5
Cyrus vd Dilleten	1980	24	62.5		20.8	16.6
Udo v Gotthelfsegg	1981	69	62.3		23.2	14.5
Pius v Nesselacker	1985	43	55.8		16.3	27.9
Mutz v Waldacker	1982	34	52.9	2.9	26.5	17.6
Sasso la Vaux	1981	67	52.2	1.5	28.4	17.9
Gaston v Nesselacker	1984	85	51.8	2.4	18.8	27.0
Heiko z durstigen Bruder	1988	33	51.5	36.4	9.1	3.0
Igor v Vidonissa	1985	24	50.0	16.7	29.2	4.2
Pyros v Barnerhof	1987	28	46.4	32.1	17.9	3.6
Domino v Dorfli	1988	29	44.8	34.5	20.7	0.0
Kay v Blaumatthof	1987	58	44.8	15.5	25.9	13.8
Zar v Oberfeld	1982	25	44.0		36.0	20.0
Donald v Gammenthal	1987	47	42.6	27.7	17.0	12.8
Wacho v Tonisbach	1988	66	42.4	28.8	19.7	9.1
Gregor vd Scheidegg	1989	27	40.7	33.3	22.2	3.7
Fedor v Galgenveld	1989	39	35.9	33.3	17.9	12.8
Gino vd Schneidegg	1989	22	22.7	31.6	13.6	31.8

[1]All sires graded 0/0 except Zar v Oberfeld who was A/A.

(Schweizerischer Klub fur Berner Sennenhunde, 1998)

progeny. Some of these B grade animals might have been in grade 0, others in grade 1, in earlier times. Thus, comparing grade 0 or A is difficult for dogs born early and those born late. In that event, grade D/E would give some idea of poor hip production in respect of sires that might be comparable over time. Comparison over years is not easy but, in general terms, the sires closest to the top of the table are likely to be the best hip producers in Switzerland. Many, probably the majority of those listed, will now be deceased but availability of such lists on a regular basis would be highly valuable for Bernese breeders both in Switzerland and those abroad using Swiss lines. For example, many of the dogs listed in Table 9.3 appear in the pedigrees of British-born Bernese Mountain Dogs.

Table 9.4 shows hip data for Australian /

Aust. Ch. Meadowpark Beta Bravo b 1988(Hans Christian Of Meadowpark – Markmiss Of Meadowpark): Imported to Australia from the UK.

New Zealand dogs. In these two countries, the hip scheme used is identical to that in Britain, namely scoring, but the means tend to be slightly lower. On 378 dogs from the two countries' schemes (AVA and NZVA), the mean score is 11.25. Sires with at least 10 progeny are listed in Table 9.4.

Table 9.5 shows the progeny test data for elbows published by the Swiss Klub (1998) citing dogs with at least 20 progeny. Some of the earlier dogs were not themselves assessed, but a large range can be seen between the best and worst elbow sires. Note that there are two litter brothers Gino and Gregor v Scheidegg and they produce quite differently even though of identical elbow score themselves. This is in contrast to hips, where they scored identically to each other and

Table 9.4
Progeny tests for AVA/NZVA tests of Bernese

Sire Percentage	No. progeny	range of scores[1]	Mean score	Progeny <11	<30
Zeigen Accolade*	13	2-13	6.8	76.9	0
Zeigen Forest Glenn*	10	5-12	7.7	80.0	0
Tudorhill County Squire*	16	5-12	8.1	68.8	5.9
Jojans Woody*	17	2-30	10.3	70.5	5.9
Meadowpark Beta Bravo*	19	4-33	10.8	52.6	5.3
Zeigen Fine Favin*	10	5-17	11.1	40.0	0
Clashaidy Winged Dagger*	18	2-33	11.2	55.5	5.6
Vindissa Night Voyager*	22	6-32	13.0	50.0	4.5
Balahu Reddy Teddy*	10	2-63	13.0	60.0	10.0
Glanzberg Ingot	17	6-50	15.1	35.3	5.9
Marketing Time*	12	3-40	16.2	33.3	16.7
Vindissa Sir Ralph*	14	2-13	42.8	42.8	14.3

[1] Best and worst progeny score * sire is scored.

Routes for Breed Improvement

Table 9.5 Progeny tests for elbow scores in Switzerland. BMDs

Sire[1]	Sire elbow grade	Sire birth year	No. of progeny	percent of progeny in grade		
				0	1	2/3
Fedor v Galgenveld	0/0	1989	34	88.2	11.8	0.0
Pyros v Barnerhof	0/0	1987	27	77.8	18.5	3.7
Jerry v Rosiendlithal		1986	21	76.2	14.3	9.5
Heiko z durstinger Bruder	0/0	1988	28	75.0	14.3	10.7
Gregor vd Scheidegg	0/0	1989	23	73.9	21.7	4.3
Igor v Vindonissa		1985	20	70.0	15.0	15.0
Kay v Blaumatthof	0/0	1987	50	66.0	20.0	14.0
Kuno v Schoneggschwand		1984	41	63.4	19.5	17.1
Gino vd Scheidegg	0/0	1989	21	57.1	28.6	21.3
Gaston v Nesselacker		1984	21	57.1	4.8	38.1
Wacho v Tonisbach	0/0	1988	57	54.4	12.3	33.3
Donald v Gammenthal	1/0	1987	41	53.7	31.7	14.7
Beny v Nesselacker		1982	22	50.0	36.4	13.6
Domino v Dorfli	1/1	1988	29	48.3	41.4	10.3

produced more similarly for the better grades (see Table 9.3). This emphasises the importance of progeny test data.

Data of this kind are produced for British dogs, and Table 9.6 relates to dogs with at least 15 progeny elbow-scored. Sires are listed in order of the percentage of 0 scores and, as in other countries, an animal is assessed on its worst elbow so that a 0/3 and a 3/3 both count as scores of 3.

The number of dogs listed in Table 9.6 is small but, had a minimum of 10 progeny been used, it could be doubled and, of course, numbers are coming in all the time. However, Table 9.6 illustrates some of the problems of how to deal with data. On the basis of percentage of progeny grading 0, Casablanca is easily the best but, if we worked on the percentage of 0 + 1 (which are the grades recommended for breeding), he would drop to fourth place. Ambros

Aust. Ch. Bernerbakkens Amber Autumn (left) b 1993 (Little Norways Tango – Bernerbakkens Umbrella) and Aust. Ch. Jojans Woody b 1994 (Tertzos King Shahzaman – Four Wuimi): Two Scandinavian imports which were mated together in Australia.

Aust Ch. Millwire Clockwork Soldier b 1978 (Duntiblae Dark Fortune – Millwire Ace Of Diamonds): An early British import to Australia.

would go top, followed by Genesis and Ginger Tom. If we worked on the lowest percentage of grades 2 + 3, this order would of course remain. Thus, Genesis, who ranks eighth out of eight on one system, would rank second on most others. This emphasises the importance of looking at sire data in detail and examining individual scores. For example, Casablanca's poorest results largely relate to a specific litter rather than a wide spread. There may be a case for looking at mean score giving each progeny points

according to its score. The lowest mean by this basis would be Ambros at 0.78 as an average, followed by Ginger Tom at 0.89 and Genesis at 1.11. However, the breeder wanting the highest percentage of zero scores would find the odds favouring the dog with the most zeros.

Similar analysis could be made on tables 9.2 through 9.5 inclusive. We are seeking to identify the best elbow or hip producers and thus we have to examine data in detail and not simply in one set way. What is really needed is Estimated Breeding Value (EBV) calculations for each trait, which would encompass the dog's own performance and that of his/her parents and siblings in one figure for the trait with a reliability attached. In time, as progeny become available, these would be added in and would be more reliable than the previous data.

CHARACTER EVALUATION

Breeders are seeking to bring about advances, not only in things such as hips and elbows which can be assessed on a mathematical scale, but also in various aspects of conformation and character. In character terms, dogs can be trained and their abilities measured but, often, we are measuring the skill of the trainer as much as

Table 9.6 Progeny tests for elbow scores in Britain

Sire[1]	Sire elbow grade	No. of progeny	percent of progeny in grade			
			0	1	2	3
Nellsbern Casablanca	0/0	18	50.0	22.2	11.1	16.7
Ambros v Griesbach	0/0	23	39.1	43.5	17.4	0
Gillro Ginger Tom	-	18	38.9	38.9	16.7	5.6
Chivas vd Wiedewa	-	30	36.7	16.7	23.3	23.3
Fero v Buetigen	2/2	53	35.6	24.5	32.1	9.4
Buganeezee Lochnivar	3/0	15	33.0	6.7	26.7	33.0
Alex v Buhlikofen	0/0	20	25.0	20.0	50.0	5.0
Carlacot Genesis	2/1	19	15.8	63.2	15.8	5.3

140

Dingo de Froideville (Int. Ch. Dingo de la Ciderie – Andra v Grederhof): The sire of Ch. Forgeman Freelance.

the ability of the dog. In Switzerland, dogs are sometimes trained to Schutzhund as described earlier but this is not necessarily a useful test to assess working potential or trainability (Pfleiderer-Hogner, 1979).

Hallgren (1975) argued that six factors are important in assessing genetic influences on character and that tests should seek to examine these. They are:

a) willingness or ability to learn
b) temperament
c) stability of nerves
d) fear
e) aggressiveness to humans and/or other dogs of the same sex
f) dependence or independence in relation to owner.

I have been assessing trainability and working potential for the Northern BMD Club using a 16-point test that was originally developed in the USA. The tests vary from simply fastening the dog to a stake in a field and leaving him to see how he reacts to being 'abandoned', through to a final gun test reaction. In the interim, the dog, fastened to a stake on a long chain, is approached by a man bearing a sack of cans (an ordeal for some nervous dogs). There are friendly and unfriendly reactions from

assessor to owner, retrieving tests, hearing test reactions, play skills, finding the owner in a room and repeating the exercise and simply being made to lie down for examination, much as might be required during a visit to the vet. In broad terms, these tests evaluate nearly all of the features listed by Hallgren (1975) in the previous paragraph.

Dogs were graded A, B+, B, B-, C and D, with the more acceptable grades being first, though grade A is not necessarily better than B+ but does indicate a dog that is extremely self-confident. To date, 143 dogs have been assessed, of which 100 were Bernese Mountain Dogs. These tests include a very small number made by other assessors and a few made for the BMDC of Great Britain. Dogs have to be 10 months of age or older, and younger ages are preferable to older ones. The non-Bernese breeds were mainly Newfoundlands, but included some Leonbergers, Hovawarts, Briards and isolated examples of other breeds. The percentages of dogs in each category are shown in Table 9.7 for Bernese and other breeds separately. To date, only two dogs have been graded A; one Bernese Mountain Dog and one Leonberger. In broad terms, if we score the grades as 5,4,3,2,1 and 0 working from A through to D, the mean score for Bernese would be 2.05, and that for other breeds would be 2.63. Thus the Bernese sample is less successful than the other breeds' sample. Though the modal grading is B for both groups, the Bernese has a higher proportion in the C/D grades which are largely unsuitable for training. The grade A Bernese was our own Ch. Carlacot Genesis at Nellsbern, assessed by Mr G. Mabutt (the instigator of these tests in Bernese), who described him as "what the breed must have been designed to be". Bogie, as he was called, was in no way aggressive but he had a tremendous love of life, great courage and was afraid of nothing. Yet he was gentle with children, cats and puppies. He gained top marks in all the tests, hence his A grade. Some breeders, who should have known better, but clearly did not, dismissed an A grade as undesirable, but such views are erroneous because a true grade A is an expression of total confidence, not aggression. I have lived, not only with Bogie, but with two grade A German Shepherds and I believe that, in the right hands, the A dog is the best dog that one can share one's life with. However, I also believe that an A dog is not for the uninitiated or inexperienced owner.

Using these tests it would be true to say that, as a general rule, Bernese Mountain Dogs tend to be largely unsuccessful at retrieving and at play but most tolerated the gun test. Thus far, no Bernese have been shy biters but one of the others, the only German Shepherd Dog tested, was. Mostly, breeders would be wanting B grade dogs, especially those in the B+ and B divisions. Some of the failure to play may be attributed to owners' failure to play with puppies, but Bernese are prone to stress and, in strange surroundings, they may react adversely unless they are the

confident type which the higher grades would indicate.

This type of testing is a means of evaluating a dog's potential to work which may be more vital than actually demanding working tests. Many Bernese have owners that are incapable of training them for working trials and obedience, still less to Schutzhund, and thus tests have to be aimed at the potential of the dog, not at the level of training. The tests used by the NBMDC are useful in this respect, and allow evaluation of a dog's potential that is simply not possible in the confines of a show ring. A skilful handler may be able to hide character weaknesses under judges who lack ability, of which there are many. Thus the show ring is not really an ideal place to assess character. We have a real need to understand and evaluate the character of breeding stock, and tests such as those described would be of paramount importance. It is, however, crucial that potential breeding stock are assessed, not only pets. The NBMDC have assessed some nine Champions and a number of CC winners, and this can only be desirable. In time, it may be that genetic conclusions can be drawn from such tests; certainly there is evidence that some of the better progeny grades have stemmed from sires which themselves graded high. Ch. Carlacot Genesis at Nellsbern (A) and Ch. Transcontinental Boy at Clenraw (B+) are cases in point.

WITHER HEIGHT AND SIZE

Wither height is stipulated in the Standard but, in Britain, few breeders understand or can estimate size. We have proved conclusively at several breed seminars that most owners will overestimate the size of their dogs by several centimetres. This

Table 9.7
Working potential test results

Grade obtained	BMD %	Other Breeds %
A	1.0	2.3
B+	10.0	16.3
B	29.0	44.2
B−	25.0	18.6
C	23.0	16.3
D	12.0	2.3
No. Dogs	100	43

Table 9.8 Wither heights of German Bernese in the Korbuch

Wither height (cm)	Males		Females	
	percent	cumulative percent	percent	cumulative percent
57			0.37	0.37
58			7.32	7.69
59			6.59	14.29
60			14.29	28.57
61			10.26	38.83
62			18.68	57.51
63			21.24	78.75
64	7.22	7.22	11.72	90.48
65	17.53	24.74	6.96	97.44
66	21.65	46.39	2.56	100.00
67	16.49	62.88		
68	17.53	80.41		
69	11.34	91.75		
70	4.12	95.87		
71	4.12	100.00		
No. of animals	97		273	
Mean height	66.91		61.86	

probably stems from failure to measure, and failure to possess a measuring stick such as those produced for the Verein für deutsche Schaferhunde (SV). In effect, owners do not develop an 'eye' for height because they do not actually assess it at any time.

Breed surveys do require height to be measured, and Table 9.8 shows the heights of breed survey Bernese taken from German stud books (SSV 1987-90). The heights were measured to the nearest centimetre and the percentage of each sex in each height range is given. Using survey data does mean that animals too small or too large to be admitted to the survey are excluded, but it can be seen that, while smaller dogs are rare, some do exceed the maximum size of 70cms (27½ins), as do some bitches (max 65cms [27½ins]).

Looking at the data in Table 9.8, we find that 55.6 per cent of the dogs are in the ideal

(66-68 cms [26-26¾ins]) range and 64.4 per cent of the bitches are within their ideal (60-63cms [23½-24¾ins]) range. If we assume that the heritability of wither height is about 65 per cent, then selecting animals at the higher ranges would quickly elevate the overall height of the breed. Some 20 per cent of the dogs and 33 per cent of the bitches exceed the ideal height range, and these would be the ones to use if the objective was to raise height. However, if breeders use dogs within the ideal height range – which is the central area – they are selecting to retain height at, or slightly above, its current level. It is probable that, in Britain, mean heights are below those given above but, since heights are unknown, this illustrates the point about working without data. It is little use breeders in Britain complaining that the breed is not 'big' enough if those self-same breeders do not measure a single dog and have no idea of the current height status. I have known estimates that exceed the true height by as much as 5 cms (2 ins). The Swiss are right to seek an ideal height rather than go for increased size. Not only does size bring with it certain genetic problems, but it could lead to difficulties in conformation aspects. For example, hind angulation will tend to worsen if dogs exceed ideal heights. Nevertheless, many Bernese Mountain Dogs are simply undersized and that detracts from the impressive nature of the breed.

The Berner-Garde Foundation in the USA was set up to look at genetic disease and other things within the breed, and has engaged in measurement studies which breeders have supported to varying degrees. It is an open register which means that data are non-confidential and it operates with data of varying levels of reliability. The foundation is measuring Bernese at shows, which will help understanding in due course. In Table 9.9 I have listed the heights of 251 American Bernese, all of whom were Champions in the period 1994-97 and thus correspond to the type of animal listed in Table 9.8. Wither heights were measured in inches and have been converted to the nearest centimetre, but it is unclear who took the height measurements. If made by owners, they might be biased.

In looking at the ideal height ranges, only 48.8 per cent of males were in the 66-68 cms (26-26¾ins) range compared with 54.7 per cent of the bitches in their ideal range of 60-63 cms (23½-24¾). Thus, the situation is somewhat reversed compared with the German data in Table 9.8. Nevertheless, the mean values are similar to those in Germany.

BREED SURVEY
In Europe, it is common policy in certain breeds to submit dogs for Breed Survey. This

Table 9.9 Wither heights of American BMD champions

Wither height (cm)	Males		Females	
	percent	cumulative percent	percent	cumulative percent
58	1.63	1.63	3.91	3.91
59				
60			7.03	10.94
61	2.44	4.07	17.97	28.91
62	1.63	5.69	19.53	48.44
63			1.07	50.78
64	5.69	11.38	25.00	75.78
65	15.54	26.83	9.38	85.16
66	26.83	53.66	13.28	98.44
67	19.51	73.17	0.78	99.22
68	2.44	75.61		
69	15.45	91.06	0.78	100.00
70	8.13	99.19		
71	0.81	100.00		
No. of animals	123		128	
Mean height	66.49		62.95	

was pioneered by the German Shepherd Verein (SV) in Germany during the 1920s and has been extended in that breed to other countries throughout Europe, Australia and New Zealand, as well as being undertaken by the German Shepherd Dog Breed Council in Britain. I am one of the ten surveyors used by the GSD Breed Council to survey dogs of that breed.

A survey system is used by the German SSV in Bernese and Figure 9.1 shows a typical report on a dog. In the SSV system, each dog is evaluated and a mark is given on the scale of 0-9 for each feature examined. Dogs of a stipulated standard are then approved for breeding. The GSD system used in Britain is rather better, and an example is given in Figure 9.2. In this, dogs are measured and assessed in a subjective way but each feature is evaluated and the dog is then placed in either Class 1 (Recommended for Breeding), Class 2 (Suitable for Breeding) or is failed. Dogs have to be at least 24 months at survey but there is no upper limit. There are rules which bind the surveyor. For example, there is a maximum hip score for each sex (higher in females) if a dog is to receive Class 1 and a somewhat higher maximum for Class 2. Dogs above these maxima would be automatically failed. There are also rules about missing teeth and about height. The British GSD system allows a maximum height of 66 cms (26ins) for males and 61 cms (24ins) for females, which is 1 cm (¼in) over the standard maximum in each case. Animals which exceed this cannot get a Class 1. Similarly, there is a gunshot test and any animal which fails this is placed one Class lower than it would otherwise have been. Other character failings usually result in failure.

It is my considered opinion that, although individual breeders will be successful, Bernese breeding in Britain and many other countries will be fraught with dangers until a system of Breed Survey is introduced. It is essential to find surveyors who understand what the principles of breeding and animal evaluation are, and we need surveyors who are not afraid to do what they think fit within the rules laid down. There can be no place for surveyors who are not competent or those who do not have the courage of their convictions, still less for those who think surveying is an opportunity to aid their friends. We have enough of that in the show ring without extending it to other areas.

It is my view that the implementation of a Breed Survey system would be highly beneficial for countries which do not have one. Getting started is more important than making sure everything is absolutely perfect at the start. There may well be teething troubles, but getting under way is vital and using surveyors of the right type is important, even if some may need training. That can be done by surveying each dog with a team or by having a skilled surveyor operating with a trainee.

Once surveying is under way and breeders realise that they should only be using surveyed stock for breeding, there will be a definite advance in overall quality. Moreover, as data begin to accumulate, survey information can be valuable as a system of progeny testing. If a particular sire has had, for example, ten or more progeny surveyed and a high percentage of them have been described as having forward-placed front assemblies, then it may be logical to assume that this is a feature of that sire's production and thus a feature of his genetic make-up. He would not be a choice of mate for a bitch with a forward-placed scapula. A survey

Berner Sennenhund   Rude
Bar von der Reglersruh
Vater: Rick vom Nesselacker HD-F   SSZ/BS 19807/ 9516
Mutter: Jorker vom Nesselacker
Wurftag: 5.6.88   SSZ/BS 17407
Zuchter: Rieck, Manfred, 8480 Weiden
Besitzer: Weib, Alfred, 8570 Pegnitz

Widerristhohe	cm 67	Typ	7
Knochen	9	Pigmentierung	8
Kopf	9	Scheitel	8
Stirnansatz	8	Fang	9
Lefzen	7	Gebiss	9
Gebissausformung	8	Augenform	8
Augenfarbe	5	Augenfehler	0
Ohrenansatz	9	Ohrenhaltung	9
Ohrform	9	Brust	5
Schulter	6	Oberarm/Ellenbg	6
Rucken	8	Kruppe	8
Rutenhaltung	7	Rutenlange	9
Stand (vorn)	7	Vorderfuss-Wurzelgel.	8
Stand (hinten)	7	Winkelungen VH	7
Winkelungen HH	8	Pfoten	9
Gangwerk	6	Haare	9
Haarlange	8	Brand	8
Zeichnung	9	Wesen	9
Gesamteindruck	6	HD-Befund	9
Fehlzahne Keine			

Figure 9.1

A SVV Breed survey report on a German Bernese (SVVV/1990).

system would need some basic character test, either in the survey itself or by using a scheme such as the NBMDC system described above and only giving survey status to dogs that grade B- or better. There is certainly no point in breeding from grade D animals, however shapely they may be.

DATA COLLECTION
If breeders wish to advance the breed, then they need to establish a data collecting system. Hip/elbow schemes and Breed Surveys are the basis for this in Europe, but,

although hip/elbow data are published in Britain, the Orthopedic Foundation for Animals (OFA) data are still not publicised in the USA unless the dog actually passes. This is counter-productive and needs to be changed. Berner-Garde is an American attempt to evaluate and assess some aspects of the breed via data collection.

In many European countries where breed clubs control registrations, breeders submit data on all litters whether pups live or die and this helps to build up valuable data which is not possible through the KC or

Jemness Alas

D.O.B. 24.9.92   Male   H.S. 4-5

K.C. No. S4370005 S04   Owner: E. Stephenson   Tattoo No. HØB 0876

Sire:	Int. Ch Rosehurst Chris
Lindanvale Vegas	Becky of Lindanvale
Dam:	Cello Vom Aschera
Kemnad Danielle	Zoe She's The Boss

Line Breeding:
Uran 3-4

1. (a) Height at Wither... 66cm.
   (b) Chest Measurement - depth...................... 29cm. circumferences....83cm.
   (c) Bodylength... 73   testicles...............Correct
2. Colour.. Black/Gold; depth in markings: very good
3. Sex Characteristics....................................... Normal
4. Character/Temperament................................ of sound nerve: lively: alert:: attentive
5. Expression.. typical: alert
6. Outline in stance
   (a) Outline... correct
   (b) Body.. correct: very slightly narrow
   (c) Bone... med. strong
   (d) Muscles... suff. strong: dry
7. Front Assembly... v. good; u. arm/correct: long: shoulder correct
8. (a) Hind Assembly....................................... angul/v. good; upp.thigh/long;low.thigh/long
   (b) Tail... correct
9. Wither.. normal
10. Back... correct
11. Croup.. slightly short
12. Feet... correct
13. Pasterns.. correct
14. Nails.. correct
15. (a) Coat condition....................................... healthy
    (b) Type of coat... normal: undercoat/present
16. Pigmentation.. adequate
17. (a) Head.. strong; masculine, pronounced
    (b) Ears... correct; firm; smallish for size
    (c) Eye colour/Shape.................................. match with surrounding colour: almond
    (d) Upper Jaw... strong
    (e) Lower Jaw... strong
    (f) Bite.. scissor
    (g) Dentition... complete: healthy: strong: correct spacing
18. Movement...
    (a) Gait... very good: spacious: rhythmic: co-ordinated
    .... retains outline
    (b) Firmness of back................................... very firm
    (c) Forereach... very good
    (d) Hind Drive.. powerful
    (e) Firmness of Elbows................................ firm
    (f) Firmness of Pasterns.............................. firm
    (g) Firmness of Hocks................................. suff. firm
    (h) Soundness Behind.................................. close: toes in with left fore
    (i) Soundness in Front................................. toes in with left fore
    (j) Overall Verdict....................................... well co-ordinated: spacious: far reaching
19. Reaction to Gunshot...................................... steady
20. General Remarks:- Large brightly coloured well proportioned male of excellent type with good angulations and firm topline retained in movement. Takes after sire line but caution with further linebreeding on Uran v Wildstiegerland

Survey Classification..........Class 1   Signed.........M.B. Willis   Date..........29.7.95

Figure 9.2 A GSDBC Breed survey report on a GSD

AKC systems since they merely accept registrations at the breeder's discretion. Sadly, we now have at least two breeders in Britain who are either not registering their Bernese with the KC or are registering only the occasional animal, presumably because a buyer has insisted. In addition, some use of Newfoundlands is going on in the Bernese breed in Britain which, though currently unregistered, could lead to the introduction of 'foreign blood' into the breed. Although we all have Pluto v Erlengut in our pedigrees (see Chapter One), there is little to be gained by adding in further Newfoundland material. In the first place, it could seriously damage hip status (in most countries Newfoundland hips are worse than Bernese) and, secondly, it could introduce heart conditions, with which the Newfoundland has serious problems and which are relatively unknown in the Bernese.

There is a need for national Kennel Clubs to move with the times, and either let breed clubs control registrations or insist that all members of a litter are registered within a short time (e.g. three months) of birth and that the whole litter be noted, including those stillborn or dying subsequently. This would help in understanding reproductive performance and, in conjunction with Surveys, hip and elbow scores and PRA status could be collected by a breed club. The PRA status will be dependent upon genetic mapping finding the PRA gene, but that should hopefully come within a few years.

The final chapter of this book looks at various features connected either with genetic disease in the Bernese Mountain Dog or with other important features, and any data collection system needs to be aware of all of these. Data systems do exist and can be valuable. Deciding what to keep and divulge is not easy, and there has to be a very well-laid-down procedure for the admission of data and for its divulgence. Certainly, 'witch hunting' should not be part of the system and data should not be divulged for someone to score debating points with, but producing data to help breeders with their breeding programmes is crucial. The solution lies in the hands of clubs and of their members who – if they want things done – have to elect those people to office who will do what is wanted. Serving on a Bernese Club committee should not be a sinecure or a way to get judging appointments but should be a means of working to aid advancement of the breed we all profess to love!

PRODUCING CHAMPIONS

The Champions produced in a country should be the best available animals in conformation and character. In Britain, making a title is relatively hard because Champions continue to compete against non-Champions for the top awards, whereas, in most other locations, this is no longer true. In some countries, a title can be won with almost no competition or very minimal competition. In America, for example, in the period 1993 to 1997 inclusive, there were 805 animals made up to Champion or an average of 161 per year. Even allowing for total registrations in this period of 8,604 Bernese Mountain Dogs, the odds were about one in 10 that a dog would make up (gain his/her title). In Britain, over the whole period from 1977 to 1997 during which time CCs have been on offer, there have only been 129 Champions, which equates to about one in 80 of the total number of Bernese registered since 1971. In Britain, there have been 443 sets (pairs) of CCs available during this time, an average of 21 sets per year. If dogs had to win three CCs to

Table 9.10 Top sires in USA for champion production

Champions	Name of sire[1] year of birth	Sire Dam
64	Dallybecks Echo Jackson 1986-98	Alex v Weissenberg Dallybeck Cresta v Bergita
58	Donar v Mutschen	Hansi v Seewadel Assi v Mutschen
44	Deerpark Heartlight	Ashley v Bernerliebe Deerpark Daisy
44	Halidom Davos v Yodlerhof	Grand Yodler of Tenton Valley Ginger v Senseboden
40	De-Li's Foreign Touch 1985-89	Bev's Black Jack v BB Tonia v Barenreid
33	Shersans Black Tie Required 1984-91	Shersan Chang O'Pace v Halidom Halidom's Keri
31	De-Li's Standing Ovation	De-li's Foreign Touch De-Li's Heart of Gold
28	Ashley v Bernerliebe 1977-d	Galan v Senseboden Dault Daphne v Yodlerhof
27	Arthos October v Berndash 1984-1994	Aldo v Kleinholz Grunberg Iridescent Fire
27	Bev's Baron v Greybern 1987-1992	Pike's Barnard O'Languardo Greta v Rosiendlithal
26	Shersan Chang O'Pace v Halidom 1979-88	Halidom Davos v Yodlerhof Halidom Kali v Muensterplatz
24	Kusters Jocko of J Bar	Clara's Christopher Alpstein's Knight Bell
23	Jaycy's Wyatt v Hund See 1982-1991	Jaycy's Oliver v Hund See Bev's Jabbering Jodi v BB
22	Ami vd Swiss Top Farm	Ami v Hasli Xandi v Nesselacker
21	Alex v Weissenburg	Kai v Tonisbach Erika v Saedelbuur

[1] All the sires are American Champions, some also had Canadian titles.

make a title and Champions won no more than three before moving to a separate Best of Breed class, as in USA, then there would have been a maximum of 148 champions per sex or 296 in total, which would amount to one dog in every 35 registered. Of course, some dogs would win one or two CCs and not make up – just as dogs in the USA take points but do not make the required 15 points including majors; thus one in 35 is a maximum figure using an American-type system where Champions do not hold back other dogs. With these figures, an American sire or dam needs to produce many more Champions to equate with British sires.

However, even allowing for some easy Champions (and there are unworthy champions in Britain just as there are in most locations), the performance of some American sires and dams is outstanding. The top 15 sires of all time in the USA, based on numbers of Champions produced, appears in Table 9.9, and the top 10 dams are given in Table 9.10.

REASSESSING PROGENY DATA
In looking at progeny test data, such as has been given earlier in this chapter, it is sometimes possible to examine the data in alternative ways. Table 12 shows the results of hip test data presented in the magazine

Table 9.11 Top dams in USA for champion production

Champions	Name of sire[1] year of birth	Sire Dam
19	Shersan Bernhugel Hot Gossip	Bernhugel Augustus v Odin Shersan Baroness O'Bernhugel
18	Trilogy's Title Role	Broken Oaks Dieter v Arjana Texas Tiffany Vombreiterweg
16	Texas Tiffany Vombreiterweg 1977-d	Kusters Jocko of J Bar Fireball Vombreiterweg
15	Deerpark Ferkin v Buttonwillow	Klause v Buchsischlossi Deerpark Brta v Buttonwillow
14	Bev's Jabbering Jodi v BB 1979-90	Darius of Rutherford Alphorns Happy Talk
12	Sunnyhills Anna v Jimco 1973-d	Argon v Wil-Lancer Andra v Mannenbuch
12	Windy Knobs Legacy de Grasso 1986	Bernhugel's Augustus v Odin Shersan's Brite-N-Shining Star
11	Halidom Keri 1980-91	Bari Les Sommetres Halidom Kara v Davos
11	Mentmore's Hollysprig v Bev's	Bev's Baron v Greybern Arak's Helga v Bevs
11	Vombreiterwegs Swiss Lace 1987-94	Harlaquins Thor the Bear Nikki Vombreiterweg

[1] All the dams are American Champions

Hunde in 1990, looking at hip grades by sire. I have extracted the data so as to examine nine Swiss sires with at least 19 progeny assessed. All these sires were mated to some daughters of Grey v Waldacker, and results are presented for all sires and for progeny out of Grey daughters.

In five cases, the progeny out of Grey daughters were better in terms of grade OS than all sires. Numbers are not large, but they do indicate ways in which data can be re-examined.

Table 9.12 Hip grades by sire of dam

SIRE	SIRE OF DAM	Progeny	% 0	% 2-4
Beny v Nesselacker	All sires	47	74.5	10.6
	Grey v Waldacker	8	62.5	25.0
Fertek v Chujerhof	All sires	30	70.0	10.0
	Grey v Waldacker	9	77.8	11.1
Gaston v Nesselacker	All sires	40	72.5	12.5
	Grey v Waldacker	19	84.2	5.3
Hansi v Seewadel	All sires	41	70.7	2.4
	Grey v Waldacker	12	75.0	8.3
Kai v Tonisbach	All sires	104	76.9	10.0
	Grey v Waldacker	46	80.4	8.7
Pat de Perreux	All sires	19	68.4	15.8
	Grey v Waldacker	15	60.0	20.0
Sasso la Vaux	All sires	52	51.9	17.3
	Grey v Waldacker	24	62.5	16.7
Udo v Gotthelfsegg	All sires	62	59.7	17.7
	Grey v Waldacker	21	47.6	33.3
Zar v Oberfeld	All sires	20	45.0	20.0
	Grey v Waldacker	9	44.4	11.1

Source: Hunde (1990)

10 GENETIC TRAITS, DEFECTS AND DISEASE

All breeds of dog, as with any other species, have their share of inherited disease and the Bernese is no exception. It is well established that the breed has problems with elbows and with cancer, while hip dysplasia is somewhat variable, depending upon the country being studied. On the credit side, eye disease is a relative rarity and many diseases that do occur are at comparatively low levels. The following discussion considers specific diseases known to exist in the Bernese Mountain Dog and uses data from a variety of countries. Some of these problems are known to have a genetic basis; others may not have been proven, but doubt still exists. This chapter also examines features which are inherited but are not necessarily problems; thus coat colour and reproductive performance are examined. References have been used, because it is crucial that readers know that information is based on scientific analysis and not on opinion. There is an increasing need in canine circles to show where data have been derived from because, all too often, we are working with anecdotal information that may be of limited value.

ASEPTIC SUPPURATIVE MENINGITIS

Meningitis is comparatively rare in dogs. It is associated with fever, stiff gait, cervical pain, vomiting, anorexia and general weakness. Usually, meningitis is associated with an infection agent, most frequently the Staphylococcus and Pasturella species. Aseptic suppurative meningitis refers to inflammation of the meninges, but with no infectious agent being identified as being present.

In 1986, Meric et al. reported three cases of aseptic suppurative meningitis in the Bernese in America. The animals were littermates. In Norway, Presthus (1989) reported on 11 cases in Bernese. Three (one male and two females) were examined by the author, and a further six females and two males were not seen by Presthus but were reported by vets and showed a typical clinical pattern. The animals stemmed from several litters as detailed in Table 10.1.

All the animals traced back to one extensively used sire, but a random sample of 23 pedigrees showed that 17 of these animals also traced back to the same sire. It is not therefore possible to ascertain that this is an inherited trait. Of the 42 animals in Table

151

Table 10.1 Occurrence of meningitis in BMD litters

Litter Number	Total		Affected	
	Males	Females	Males	Females
1	6	2	0	2
2	3	5	0	1
3	3	2	0	1
4	2	2	2	2
5	4	6	0	1
6	3	4	1	0
Total	21	21	3	7

in addition the dam of litter 4 was herself affected

(after Presthus, 1989)

10.1, ten (23.8 per cent) showed the problem. This is similar to a recessive trait but, if litter 4 is excluded because the dam was herself affected, the data do not conform to a simple autosomal recessive. The relationship may be similar to that which we expect in this breed, though Presthus did suggest that the Bernese Mountain Dog was more susceptible than other breeds. Where known, all the animals were relatively young (3-28 months).

Although not a proven inherited trait, this condition is listed for information and because inheritance has not been ruled out.

BEHAVIOUR (ABNORMAL)

Most dogs spend their lives as companion animals and, to do so successfully, their behaviour must be such as to fit in with the criteria desired by their owners. Some behaviour patterns are established by faulty upbringing or lack of correct socialisation, which is more a failing of the owner than of the dog. However, some behaviour patterns may be intrinsic to the dog and have a genetic basis. For example, the so-called Cocker rage syndrome which is more frequent in solid colours than parti-colours

and in reds more than in blacks has been examined by Podberscek and Serpell (1996). They found that there was a genetic and neuroendocrine basis for the within-breed differences. In a later paper (Podberscek and Serpell, 1997) they found that owners of high-aggression dogs were significantly more likely to be tense, emotionally less stable, shy and undisciplined than the owners of low-aggression dogs. In an earlier study of canine aggression, Borchelt (1983) listed eight major types of aggression, related to fear, dominance, possessiveness, protectiveness, predation, punishment, pain and intra-specific. Much of the genetics of behaviour has been reviewed by Mackenzie et al. (1985) and by Serpell (1995), both of which are publications worth reading for those interested in the inheritance of behaviour.

The Bernese is required to be a self-confident, fearless but non-aggressive dog. As with any breed, dogs can be found that fail on several counts, many of which may have a basis in inheritance but some of which are socialisation-induced. In 1970, the Dutch Club began to get reports on unprovoked attacks by Bernese, often against children and totally out of character for this breed. A survey was undertaken among 800 owners and using the 400 or so replies, Van der Velden et al. (1976) published an interesting report. Dogs were classified into five grades from 1 (normal) through to 5 (intermittent unprovoked attacks on owners). The study comprised 214 males and 190 females, of which 76 per cent of the males and 24 per cent of females were placed in category 5. Table 10.2 is based upon the original work and shows the status of parents and progeny. There were some flaws in the original work, in that not all parents were graded for behaviour. Nevertheless there are indications

Table 10.2 Aggression in Bernese Mountain Dogs in Holland

Parents (at least one)	Number of progeny	Progeny grades (%)					Mean grade
		1	2	3	4	5	
Grade 1	131	58.8	5.3	28.2	2.3	5.3	1.90
Grade 2	63	41.3	9.5	36.5	6.3	6.3	2.27
Grade 3	136	36.8	4.4	36.8	4.4	17.6	2.62
Grade 4	41	19.5	4.9	51.2	9.8	14.6	2.95
Grade 5	114	25.4	0.9	31.6	6.1	36.0	3.62
Total	485	39.2	4.5	34.4	4.9	16.9	2.56

after Van der Velden *et al.* (1976)

that, as the parental status worsens (scores higher), so the mean score of progeny increases. The original data did not allocate scores but I have done so to emphasise the effects. The information is indicative of a genetic trait, but one that is polygenic rather than simple. No full explanation was achieved but the problem did serious damage to the Bernese in Holland and certain sires were said to be implicated.

It is clear that, as parental status worsens, so does progeny status with an almost linear relationship in respect of parental grade and mean progeny grade (end column).

BLUE EYES
Blue or 'wall' eyes are found in many breeds. Puppies are born with blue eyes and the colour changes in infancy, but some blue eyes remain. In certain breeds they are never seen but they are common in others. The Bernese has its share of blue eyes (either singly or both) and there is ample anecdotal evidence to suggest that the anomaly is connected with white markings. Certainly, blue eyes are most often seen in animals with considerable white on the head. Mode of inheritance is unclear and there is no evidence that blue-eyed Bernese are deaf or that they see less well. The defect is aesthetic rather than

biological and can occur in many lines. Some quite famous animals used in Britain were blue-eyed, so it is not surprising that the condition crops up at intervals. In effect, it is a disqualifying feature in the breed. I would not remove a blue-eyed bitch from breeding if she was otherwise a good specimen.

CANCER
Cancer is a disease characterised by abnormal cells which proliferate in an uncontrolled fashion, whereas normal cells do not. By the time a tumour is detectable by palpation it will probably have diversified in respect of the cell types and their behavioural characteristics (Dobson and Gorman, 1993). These cancers are often called neoplasms, but neoplasms can be benign (which expand but do not invade normal cells and do not diversify) or malignant (which are invasive and destructive and can spread to other sites). According to Dobson and Gorman (1993), a tumour is unlikely to be detected radiographically until it is about one centimetre in diameter or weighs about 0.5 to 1 gram. By this stage, the tumour will contain some 10,000 million cells. Tumours grow rapidly and then slow down and are usually detectable at about the latter stage. Table 10.3 shows a simplified version of the major types of tumours found in dogs.

153

The causes of cancer are uncertain but usually involve some changes in the cellular basis of DNA. It is certainly true that some types of cancer are known to have a genetic basis and this may eventually be proved true of all cancers, though this could not be said at this stage. It is well established that cancers exist in most breeds of dog, but that the incidence of specific cancers is greater in certain breeds. There has been no shortage of literature from the 1940s onwards. It is outside the scope of this book to deal with the risks in other breeds, but rather I will deal with the Bernese only. In a study of mammary cancer in the USA, Priester (1979) found that 752 out of 1,187 were adenocarcinomas but the Bernese did not appear in the listings. The same is true of a similar British study (Else and Hannant, 1979). However, at that time, the number of Bernese in the UK and the USA was very small. It does seem that mammary tumours are the commonest neoplasms seen in dogs but that, even in later studies when the Bernese has been numerically meaningful, it has not often appeared in the major breeds affected. On the other hand, the breed is known to suffer from bone cancers, but this is a relatively small part of canine cancer. Grondalen (1975) in a Norwegian study suggested that bone cancers accounted for only some 5 per cent of canine cancer, but that larger breeds were predisposed and the average age at autopsy was 7.3 years. Osteosarcoma was the commonest bone cancer and this is known to occur in the Bernese Mountain Dog.

In 1983 Olsson et al., working on Swedish data, found a significantly higher incidence of tumours in 14 breeds, of which the Bernese was one. In a later study, Olsson et al. (1986) did not list the Bernese among the worst breeds but the breed did rank high in cutaneous tumours.

Table 10.3 Types of tumours found in dogs

Name	Location
Skin	
Basal cell carcinoma	Nodular growths front of body
Histiocytosis	Single or multiple nodules legs, feet, scrotum
Mastocymas	Rear half body under skin
Melanomas	Oral cavity and scrotum
Papillomas	Projecting nodules on head, feet, mouth
Squamous cell carcinoma	Near body orifices
Mammary Gland	
Females rather than males and mainly rear glands	
Carcinomas	Epithel origin spread by lymph system
Sarcomas	Mesenchymal origin spread by blood
Other Organs	
Adenocarcinomas	Digestive/respiratory tract, kidney, testicle
Fibromas	Connective tissue, vagina
Lipomas	Back, chest, abdomen
Hepatomas	Liver
Sertoli-cell tumours	Testicle (esp if retained)
Seminomas	Testicle

This could be explained by the breed's predisposition to histiocytosis. The disease is characterized by anorexia, weight loss, abnormal respiration and conjunctivitis. Multiple nodules occur on the body but especially in the nasal, scrotal and eyelid regions. Some authors have differentiated between systemic and malignant histiocytosis, but it may be that these are simply different expressions of the same disease. The condition appears to be fairly lethal. In a Californian study, Moore (1984) reported six cases in related Bernese dogs, mainly males, which were diagnosed in the timescale of 2-8 years and all of which were euthanised within a relatively short time, though the oldest animal had a 48-month duration. Malignant histiocytosis was reported in ten Bernese (nine males) by Rosin et al. (1986) and in 13 cases (11 males) by Moore and Rosin (1986). All these stem from the same school and may involve cases being reported in more than one paper, but the lethal nature of the condition and the pedigree relationships are important. Systemic histiocytosis in six Bernese Mountain Dogs in Britain, all males, was reported by Paterson et al. (1995). A more extensive study by Padgett et al. (1995) from Michigan covered 127 cases of histiocytosis in the Bernese. They found that histiocytosis accounted for 25.4 per cent of the 500 tumours studied in the Bernese and concluded that it was an inherited condition. They suggested a polygenic mode of inheritance with a heritability of 30 per cent (SE 2 per cent). This study reported that 40 different tumour types had been identified in the Bernese, of which histiocytosis (malignant or systemic) was the most common. The condition is known in other breeds (but is rare), whereas it is certainly common in American Bernese and probably occurs more often in British stock than has been reported. It was notable that the sexes were equally represented in the Michigan study, suggesting that sex involvement in genetic terms is improbable.

In data on age and causes of death in over 500 Bernese, presented to me by British owners, the incidence of cancer as a cause of death in Bernese was around 40 per cent, with a variety of cancers being noted, and an average age at death of about seven years. It is true that in many cases diagnosis was by local vets and only on some occasions following autopsy or biopsy testing, but there seems little doubt but that the Bernese Mountain Dog is a high cancer-risk breed and that histiocytosis, lymphosarcoma and osteosarcoma are major cancers. This high cancer-risk is the same in other countries, such as Switzerland (M. Bartschi, 1998 personal communication) and Denmark (L. Ramsing, 1998 personal communication). In a recent study in Sweden (dealt with later under longevity), Bonnett et al. (1997) found that, among 70 breeds, the Bernese ranked the highest risk for tumours, with 32.7 per cent of breed deaths being due to this cause. Some breeders argue that they do not have a cancer problem, but you should regard such claims with caution. Cancer is widespread in the Bernese in all countries and it is doubtful that any kennel can claim 'immunity'.

CLEFT PALATE (HARE-LIP)
The condition of cleft palate occurs in various species including man. It is probably known in most breeds of dog but rarely reported upon. It is described in the Bernese (Heim, 1914; Weber, 1955, 1959) but the genetics of the condition is unclear. Cleft

palate may be just one symptom of a series of similar conditions. Weber postulated a dominant autosomal gene causing nasal cleft as well as cleft palate. The nasal clefts were seen in the Bernese he referred to and were well known in the early years of the breed's development. In a German study covering 10,609 animals from 1,327 litters, Turba and Willer (1987) found an incidence of hare-lip plus cleft palate of only 0.6 per cent over the period 1977-84. However, litters with affected pups increased with time from 0.95 in 1979 to 6.62 per cent in 1984. They postulated a single autosomal recessive gene as the causal factor. It is interesting that Dreyer and Preston (1973) showed a relationship between aggressive tendencies and cleft palates which might reflect abnormal metabolism. Most affected pups die or are culled, this seems the best solution.

COAT COLOUR

There are many genes implicated in the coat colour of the dog. All breeds have these genes, but they do not have all the versions of them. For example the Merle gene (M) is not present in most breeds and thus most breeds are mm, as is the Bernese. The Bernese Mountain Dog is, in fact, homozygous for most coat colour genes as shown below.

All Bernese are CC (coloured), DD (non dilution), EE (extension of pigment), gg (black not altering to blue), mm (non merle) and tt (non ticked). They may have alternative alleles at two gene loci.

At the Agouti series locus the breed is $a^t a^t$, which permits a black body colour with tan points. This colour pattern is common in the dog and is the one seen in the Dobermann and the Rottweiler, for example. There are several other alleles in the Agouti series but it is probable that none of them exist in the Bernese, which would make the breed homozygous for the $a^t a^t$ state. However, it is possible that some Bernese are black and white and devoid of the tan markings. Though we have not seen them, the possibility does exist and would suggest that the A allele may exist, albeit rarely, so that some Aa^t animals may be found.

The white markings come from the S series. This contains S (solid colour with no white), s^i Irish spotting which is the basic Bernese pattern of white, s^p piebald spotting, as seen in the Landseer Newfoundland or the particoloured Cocker Spaniel and, finally, s^w which is extended white, leading to a white dog with perhaps a black eye patch, as seen in the Bull Terrier. The Irish spotting allele is found in many breeds, such as Boxer, Border Collie or Rough Collie, but, in these, the white neck band is acceptable. Although white neck bands were common in the early days of the Bernese development (and called 'Ringgi'), they were eventually selected against. This was made possible because the S series has minus and plus modifying genes which can increase or decrease the white expanses. Over the first few decades of the breed, selection against the Ringgi pattern took place by using 'Blassi' dogs (white blaze but no collar) or 'Bari' dogs which had little white on the head and no collar. A breeder producing $s^i s^i$ animals, which virtually all Bernese are, but who selected against excessive white and against the Ringgi pattern, would gradually reduce white and would be selecting for minus modifying genes of this locus. From time to time, white neck markings, complete or incomplete, and even white heads will appear but will be rare and particularly so in lines which seek the minimum white markings.

Most Bernese also carry the allele B which allows the body colour to be black. There is only one alternative to this, which is the recessive version called b. This is undetectable in animals that carry B. Thus BB or Bb animals would both have the black body colour and be indistinguishable. However, a bb animal would have no black pigment. It would be red in all the places a normal BB or Bb animal would be black, and this would include not only coat, but also nose, flews and pads. Moreover, the bb combination would lead to a lighter eye colour. The bb combination is found in many breeds but seems to be given a different name in each. In Labradors it is called chocolate, in Springers liver, in Newfoundlands brown, and in Dobermanns red. In some breeds it is an acceptable Standard colour and in others, like the Bernese Mountain Dog, it is non-Standard.

In the Bernese, the red/brown animal is a rather light red colour and the $a^t a^t bbs^i s^i$ combination is very, very rare. I have never seen one, but a photograph of one is provided by Stevens (1984) and another

A red, tan and white animal, illustrating the undesirable coat pattern in the breed.

photograph appears in this present book. A black and white photograph is given by Chesnutt Smith (1995) and she mentions a mating of red tricolours to red tricolours, which produced all red, tan and white offspring, exactly as should be the case. Such dogs will be red, tan and white in the Bernese pattern, though the one shown by Stevens and photographed in 1981 had one white foreleg. A Bernese that was $a^t a^t Bbs^i s^i$ would be a normal-coloured Bernese and we would only know about the recessive b allele if such a dog were mated to a Bernese with the same genotype as itself. Since this is highly unlikely, the probable consequence is that owners of such dogs will remain ignorant of the fact that they carry b. A red/tan and white dog would, of course be disqualified because the ground colour is not black. Chesnutt Smith (1995) mentions four American litters, born in the late 1970s, which contained red tri-colours, and all pedigrees contained Arno vd Grasburg, Bella's Albertine and Bobi v Bauernheim and there seems good evidence that Arno, at least, was a carrier of the b allele.

A Bernese which turned white when adult has been reported in the USA and a photograph of the dog appeared in the catalogue of the 1998 BMDCA Specialty show. The cause is unknown.

CRYPTORCHIDISM

Failure of the testicles to descend can take many forms. Total absence of the testicles in the body is anorchia and very rare. Similarly, monorchidism, the presence of only one testicle, is also rare. Most normal dogs have both testicles descended into the scrotum by the time they reach eight weeks of age or soon afterwards. In some dogs, descent can take much longer but, by six months of age, most testicles that are going to descend have done so. Those adults with only one descended testicle are called unilateral cryptorchids, while those with neither descended are bilateral cryptorchids. An American study (Pendergrass and Hayes, 1975) on 1,266 dogs affected with the problem showed that testicular tumours were 10.9 times more likely in retained testicles than in descended ones. Some breeds were at higher risk than others but, at that time, the Bernese Mountain Dog was relatively rare. The mechanisms of descent have been studied by Baumans et al. (1981) and Romagnoli (1991), and an extensive study on the condition in animals was made by Brandsch (1962), who concluded that it was an autosomal recessive trait. Willis (1989, 1992) has reviewed the subject and concludes that a threshold trait is more likely to be the cause. The condition is, of course, sex-limited in that it is only expressed in males, but it may be carried by females.

A Japanese study of 2,356 mongrels (Kawakami et al., 1984) found an incidence of 1.2 per cent and there is no reason to suppose that this is much different from the incidence in most pedigree breeds. It is well established that the bilateral cases are sterile because sperm cannot form inside the testicle retained in the body cavity, but the Japanese workers found that unilateral cryptorchids also had impaired fertility, with lowered sperm motility and increased numbers of abnormal sperm, a finding reported earlier by French workers (Badinand et al., 1972).

Practical experience suggests that the condition is not common in Bernese, but that it does exist, and I feel that it should be treated as a serious defect because it affects fertility. I would not normally recommend using affected animals in a breeding programme and would reject females who produced a moderate or high incidence of the problem.

DENTAL FAILINGS
The type of dental failings that can occur were mentioned in Chapter Two. In a study of 175 Bernese born in Switzerland in 1981, Burgi (1991) found that 43.4 per cent had abnormal jaws, but that missing premolar teeth were relatively rare, affecting only 4 per cent of dogs. Inheritance is unclear, but Byrne and Byrne (1992) suggested a simple autosomal recessive inheritance for overshot jaws in German Shorthaired Pointers. In Dobermanns, Skrentny (1964) suggested that missing teeth were also inherited as a simple autosomal recessive. Whether these modes of inheritance are correct, and whether they apply to the Bernese, is unclear. At present, though most British judges examine bites, few check dentition and thus the status of the breed in this connection is unknown and most breeders and judges operate in blissful ignorance.

ELBOW ARTHROSIS
The elbow is a hinged joint that involves three bones. The distal end of the humerus actually sits on the proximal end of the radius and ulna, which makes for difficulties if the three bones do not grow in a synchronized manner. Several conditions affect the elbow, notably osteochondritis dissecans (OCD), ununited anconeal process (UAP), and fragmented coronoid process (FCP). In essence, OCD is the faulty conversion of cartilage to bone, such that the calcification does not occur uniformly and slivers of cartilage may break off. Both UAP and FCP involve bone structures (processes) which break away from the elbow joint or which

Table 10.4 Incidence of elbow arthrosis in various breeds in Sweden

Breed	Radiographs seen	Arthrosis %
Rottweiler	1500	48
Bernese Mountain Dog	1300	48
Great Swiss	54	48
Newfoundland	82	27
Golden Retriever	86	25
GSD	207	21
Labrador Retriever	377	15

Audell (1990)

fragment. For some time it was felt that these conditions were separate entities but, in more recent years, the prevailing view is that these may all be symptoms of a general malaise which might be termed elbow dysplasia or, more accurately, elbow arthrosis. These conditions lead to foreleg lameness, usually commencing at about five months of age. In the case of UAP, it may give rise to intermittent lameness, depending upon where the anconeal process moves once it is broken off. However, the general consequence of these various conditions is that they can, and frequently do, lead to osteoarthritis which is a painful and potentially debilitating condition in the dog.

In a Swedish study, Bergsten and Nordin (1986) argued that the incidence of OCD was significantly higher in Rottweilers, St Bernards, Great Danes and Golden and Labrador Retrievers than in other breeds. In a series of papers (Grondalen, 1979abc, Grondalen and Rorvik, 1980, Grondalen and Grondalen, 1981), Norwegian workers reviewed the literature, examined the incidence and the effects of surgery. They considered it an increasing problem, concluding that specific breeds were more at risk and that rapid growth was involved which accounted for a higher incidence in

males than females. Swedish workers (Ernborg, 1986, Klingeborn, 1986) implicated the Bernese in this problem. In his study, Klingeborn (1986) found that 53.3 per cent of the first 105 Bernese radiographed had elbow lesions. Audell (1990), also working in Sweden, examined several thousand animals and listed the incidence of arthrosis in various breeds. These data are given in Table 10.4.

There is no doubt that the Bernese ranks among the worst breeds for elbow arthrosis. Audell considered that the heritability of elbow arthrosis was in the 25-45 per cent range. Grondalen and Lingaas (1991) put the heritability of elbow arthrosis in a similar range, based on Rottweilers, while, in a British study of guide dogs (mostly Labradors), Guthrie and Pidduck (1990) found heritabilities of 77 per cent in 2,489 males and 45 per cent in 2,641 females. These British figures are probably excessive. Studdert et al. (1991), looking at Labrador guide dogs in Australia, put the heritability of elbow OCD at 27 per cent. In a Swedish study, Swenson et al. (1997b) found that the heritability of elbow arthrosis in Bernese, based on the regression of sons on fathers was 34 per cent and for daughters on dams it

159

was 28 per cent. Corresponding figures for Rottweilers were 34 and 40 per cent respectively. All this does suggest that we are dealing with a moderately heritable trait, that the Bernese Mountain Dog is one of the worst-affected breeds, and that the various features may be linked.

The linkage of OCD, UAP and FCP is emphasised by the work of the American, Wind (Wind, 1986, 1990; Wind and Packard, 1986). She held the view, increasingly being accepted, that the problem stems from the three-bone joint and that minor differences in growth between the radius and ulna could lead to the faulty siting of the humerus and hence arthritic problems arising. She examined the ratio of proximal ulna (the part nearest the elbow or that part of the ulna above the radius) to the length of the radius and found that, where this ratio was low (as in most sight hounds), the incidence of elbow arthrosis was minimal but, in breeds where this was high (as in the Bernese), the incidence of elbow problems was greater. The proximal ulna/radius ratio in Bernese was around 0.22-0.23, second only to the Entelbucher, which compared with about 0.17 in Afghans and Salukis, who have good elbows.

This does not exclude a genetic explanation but suggests that the mode of action may be radius/ulna growth. Slater et al. (1992) in Texas suggest that high levels of dietary calcium and playing with other dogs can contribute to an increased risk of OCD. The 'abuse' of calcium, in the mistaken idea that it will give rise to 'good bone', is frequently practised among breeders and, where they are using complete diets and hence balanced calcium levels, the policy is fraught with danger. However, it is questionable that elbow arthrosis can be laid entirely at the door of nutritional inadequacies.

Klingeborn (1986), in his Bernese Mountain Dog study in Sweden, showed that, in the progeny of five sires each mated to 8-12 bitches, the incidence of elbow lesions ranged from 4.1 to 43.8 per cent among the progeny. This is again indicative of genetic involvement and of the need to examine what sires are producing.

There is a Bernese elbow scheme in Britain and, to date, almost 700 dogs have been examined through it. Data by sex are shown in Table 10.5. Animals were scored on the scale 0 (best) to 3 (worst) on each elbow and the data in Table 10.5 refer to the worst elbow, so that an animal scoring 3/0, 1/3, 2/3 or 3/3 would be classified as a score of 3. Alongside British results are those from Australia and New Zealand using the same principles and covering 142 Bernese. The general patterns look fairly similar overall.

In Switzerland, Morgenstern et al. (1997) reported that, from August 1st 1992, all animals under five years of age at that time had to be elbow scored and that only grades 0 and 1 would be admitted for breeding. They present graphical data on the proportion of animals in each grade from 1980 to 1996, but numbers submitted tended to be small in the early years. In the period 1987-91, of the 374 dogs examined, 24.6 per cent were in grades 2 or 3. From 1992-95, this dropped to 12.5 per cent of the 376 animals examined. Grade 0 rose from 56 per cent in the period 1988-91 to 66 per cent in the period 1992-5. The authors presented data by sire which are referred to elsewhere.

A comprehensive analysis was undertaken in Sweden by Swenson et al. (1997b). They showed that, in the period 1976-82, less than 10 per cent of Bernese breeding stock

Table 10.5 Elbow scores of BMD in Britain and Australia/New Zealand

	Britain			Aust/NZ		
Score	Males %	Females %	Both sexes %	Males %	Females %	Both sexes %
0	39.4	40.2	40.0	44.2	48.1	46.5
1	25.2	29.8	28.2	14.8	25.9	21.1
2	19.7	21.7	21.1	16.4	19.8	18.4
3	15.5	8.3	10.7	24.6	6.2	14.1
Mean score	1.11	0.98	1.03	1.21	0.84	1.00
No. Animals	238	460	698	61	81	142

were elbow scored but, by 1985, some 70 per cent were scored and, a year later, the figure had risen to 90 per cent. Surprisingly, in view of weight effects, they found elbow arthrosis was slightly less in male Bernese (41 per cent) than in females (46 per cent) and that age had an effect. Mean elbow score increased by 0.04 in males and 0.02 in females for each additional month of age at X-ray. Overall, the incidence of elbow arthrosis in Swedish Bernese decreased from over 60 per cent in 1983 to 38 per cent by 1988, with grades 2+3 declining from 42 to 14 per cent over that period. Data for different kinds of mating are shown in Table 10.6.

Table 10.6 Prevalence of elbow arthrosis in Swedish BMD born 1976-89

Parental status	No. of Progeny	% with arthrosis	% with marked arthrosis (2+3)
N x N	614	31	11
N x 1	363	44	19
N x 2/3	216	56	27
A x A	91	59	29
N x ?	262	40	18
? x ?	228	60	32
A x ?	161	51	29

N=normal A= arthrosis (1-3) ?=unknown status
1.2.3 indicates grade of arthrosis

(Swenson et al. (1997b))

Swenson and his colleagues examined the benefit:cost ratio, looking at the expected savings associated with a decrease in arthrosis against the costs of a screening programme. They found an economic benefit did ensue, though it was higher in Rottweilers than in Bernese Mountain Dogs.

In the USA, the OFA has published a report on trends in elbow dysplasia for a variety of breeds (OFA, 1997). For the Bernese, they showed that 545 dogs born in or before 1990 were examined, of which 30.6 per cent were dysplastic. In the period of birth 1993-4, 538 Bernese were examined and the dysplasia rate was 29.7 per cent, though this improvement of 2.9 per cent is unlikely to be meaningful. Of the six breeds examined, the Rottweiler had higher values in both periods than the Bernese. In 1990, the Institute for Genetic Disease Control (GDC) was set up and, from 1990 to 1997 inclusive, it certified 589 Bernese as being unaffected. This rose from 8 in 1990 through to 166 in 1997. The GDC publishes results, both passes and failures, and is thus an open registry.

ENTROPION and ECTROPION
These two diseases often occur in the same animal and may be influenced by the same factors, so are discussed together. Entropion is the inversion of the eyelid, while ectropion

is the reverse situation. The former can lead to painful irritation because of the contact of the lashes on the eyeball; the latter is more likely to be unsightly rather than painful to the dog. It is possible that the exposed haw, usually seen with ectropion, can lead to infections and irritating eye disorders. Many breeds are affected by these conditions, though some breeds show minimal problems and others have the diseases as a commonplace feature.

Both conditions can be operated upon with sufficient success that the original failing may be totally hidden and the observer may be unaware that the dog ever had a problem. These surgeries are considered cosmetic, making subject dogs ineligible to be shown. It is probable that, in some breeds, a vast number of dogs have been operated upon and returned to the show ring undetected.

Both diseases may be inherited but that is by no means proven. It may be that they are selectional defects, in the sense that selection for a certain type of eye brings about entropion/ectropion. In other words, they may be selectional defects rather than the result of specific genes for the actual condition. Certainly, some Breed Standards calling for small eyes or for diamond-shaped eyes would be conducive to the occurrence of these problems. This has been highlighted by Barnett (1976) but he admits that the genetics are unclear. In sled dogs, Bellars (1969) produced data that suggested a recessive trait but the information presented was limited.

It is known that both conditions are seen in the Bernese, though some dogs appear to have the problem early in life and then 'grow into' their eye and spontaneously recover. However, Burgi (1991), in his study of the problem in 175 Swiss Bernese animals born in 1981, found that 34.2 per cent had abnormal closure of the eyelid, that 10.8 per cent had entropion and 20 per cent had ectropion. These are appreciable incidences and give no cause for complacency. The data related to dogs of two decades ago, but the incidence today is unknown.

EPILEPSY
Epilepsy simply means a seizure and is a rather vague definition. Cunningham (1971) categorised extracranial and intracranial conditions which could give rise to fitting and which covered trauma and tumours through to mineral imbalances, vitamin D utilisation and even severe teething problems. None of these are inherited problems and, in view of this, need not concern us in this chapter. However, it is well established that epileptiform seizures are known in many breeds for which there is no explanation other than inheritance.

Inherited epilepsy is usually termed idiopathic or primary epilepsy. It is known to be common in a variety of breeds, notably the Beagle, Belgian Shepherd, Bloodhound, German Shepherd, Golden Retriever, Keeshond, Labrador Retriever, and Welsh Springer, among others (see Willis, 1989, 1992). Most idiopathic epilepsy occurs from 15-36 months of age. The fits are of short duration (30 seconds to two minutes) and mostly occur when the dog is resting, even sleeping, but almost never when the dog is being active. As a result, fitters are never seen indulging in a fit at a show though many fitters are exhibited and have been over the years.

In some studies there is a preponderance of males and, in all studies, there are familial relationships. Some explanations of a simple mode of inheritance have been put forward (see Willis, 1989 for a review) but the general view is that a single gene is unlikely and that a polygenic threshold explanation is most probable. A genetic counselling scheme has been set up for Keeshonds, a breed in which a simple autosomal recessive explanation appears to have been accepted (Hall and Wallace, 1996).

Recent Swiss work put forward by Srenk et al. (1994) in Golden Retrievers, and by Faissler et al. (1998) in Labradors, suggests that the most probable explanation is that idiopathic epilepsy is inherited in a polygenic way. The condition is known in the Bernese (Oliver, 1987; Chrisman, 1991) and one must assume that the problem is inherited in like manner until other evidence comes forward. At present, in Britain, I have to admit that the condition is very rare in the breed, but it is known to be causing anxiety in Switzerland.

GASTRIC DILATION VOLVULUS (TORSION)

Gastric dilation (GD) and gastric dilation linked with gastric volvulus (GDV) are problems associated with the rapid accumulation of gas in the stomach, increased intragastric pressure, varying degrees of stomach movement, and torsion. Heart attack can follow and many dogs can die once torsion (the severe malposition of the stomach) takes place. In a pet dog study in Holland, Van Sluijs (1991) found that, over the period 1984 to 1990, there was a decrease in post-operative mortality (from 63 down to 29 per cent) and a decline in recurrence rate (from 82 to 15 per cent). In an American study looking at the cause of death of German Shepherds and Malinois working as military dogs, Jennings (1992) found that 3.4 per cent of 914 deaths were due to GDV.

It seems to be established that gastric dilation is a precursor of torsion and that it is torsion which is often fatal and which can recur in the same dog over time. Many features are thought to increase risk including: large body size; deep chests; rapid eating; overeating; high water consumption; exercise soon after eating and certain types of processed foods. Some Bernese seem prone to GD and GDV and some have been operated on several times, including having the stomach stitched to the abdominal wall to prevent torsion. The Bernese Mountain Dog would fit some of the criteria, in that it is a large breed with a deep chest, but there is minimal evidence to suggest any genetic involvement in this or any other breed. It would seem that GDV is genetic in the sense that it is linked to genetic features like body size and chest depth, but not in the sense that specific genes exist for GDV per se.

In a comprehensive American study involving 1,934 affected animals and 3,868 controls, Glickman et al. (1994) assessed some of the features influencing this disease. They concluded that the risk of GDV was associated with increasing age and increasing adult body weight and they also found five breeds with a high risk of GDV, none of which was the Bernese. There was some evidence that chest depth was implicated, but little evidence for a sex effect. The absence of the Bernese from this study may reflect the relatively low numbers of the breed rather than any lack of predisposition. There is certainly no evidence to suggest that the Bernese is one of the highest-risk breeds, but there is no doubt that some members of the breed are susceptible to the condition and that, once begun, repeat attacks can occur. It is notable that, in the study by Glickman et al. (1994), there was a high mortality rate.

Of 998 dogs with GD, there were 28.6 per cent deaths. Of 934 dogs with GDV, the death rate was 33.3 per cent. Both these are causes for concern.

A more recent study by this group (Glickman et al., 1997) found that predisposing factors for GDV were: being male, being underweight, eating one meal per day and a fearful temperament. Factors decreasing the risk were a happy temperament and the inclusion of table scraps into the normal diet. Stress could precipitate an acute episode of GDV and, as I have already emphasised, the Bernese Mountain Dog is particularly prone to stress.

HERNIAS

A hernia refers to the protrusion of an organ from the abdominal cavity through an opening in the cavity wall. All hernias have an opening through which the organs protrude and a swelling below the skin consisting of the herniated organ. In broad terms, there are umblical, inguinal, perineal and diaphragmatic hernias. The last-named is mainly a trauma-induced problem, though some breeds are thought to have a genetic version (see Willis, 1992). However, the Bernese is not among these, so we can ignore this type of hernia.

Umbilical hernias result in the natural opening of the abdominal wall failing to close, while inguinal hernias are akin to scrotal hernias, where the inguinal canal through which the testicle passes is not sealed. Perineal hernias occupy the area between the anus and the genital organs.

In a US/Canadian study, Hayes (1974) studied over 300,000 patients and found that the rate for umbilical hernias was 2.4 per 1,000 patients in the dog and for inguinal hernias it was 0.54 per 1,000 patients.

Perineal hernias are probably even more rare but epidemiological data are not readily available. Robinson (1977) postulated a threshold mode of inheritance for umbilical hernias in the cat, and this may also apply to the dog. Although data on the Bernese are not readily available, there is reason to suppose that umbilical hernias are not uncommon in the breed. Small ones are likely to either disappear or to be of minimal concern. Larger ones are more serious and may require surgery. Many vets advocate not breeding from any dog with an umbilical hernia; if carried out, such a policy would decimate the breed. We have to use discretion and, certainly, small hernias can be safely ignored until evidence to the contrary is made available.

HIP DYSPLASIA

Hip dysplasia is the faulty fitting of the hip joint. This is a ball and socket joint, in which the head of the femur (ball) fits into the acetabulum of the pelvis (socket). In broad terms, joint laxity is the principal cause of the disease. Sometimes called Congenital Hip Dysplasia, the term is a misnomer since the condition is not seen until at least two months of age and hence, unlike in man, is not congenital (present at birth). (See Figure 1.) Joint laxity, through a shallow acetabulum or incongruity of the acetabulum/femoral head, contributes to the disease but the degree of effect upon the dog may vary enormously. Some animals are so badly affected that they need major surgery, including hip replacement, or may even be euthanised, while others appear to cope well enough with hips that, on X-ray, look particularly poor. Individual dogs vary enormously in the effect which the disease has upon their movement. However, diagnosis on the basis of clinical signs is not accurate enough and all schemes set up to combat the disease are based upon diagnosis from radiographs taken at or above a minimal age.

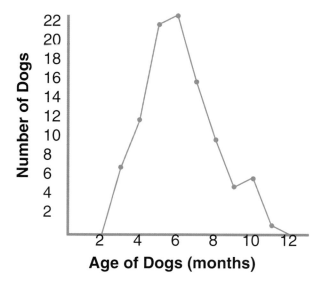

Figure 10.1
Age at onset of radiographic signs of HD based on 102 Labradors from 17 litters born to dysplastic parents
(from Lust, 1997)

Hip dysplasia has been known in man from Roman times, and has been found in the horse, cat, beef cattle and even in a timber wolf. It was first reported in the dog by Schnelle (1935), working in the USA, but began to attract attention during the mid-to-late 1950s, mainly in the German Shepherd Dog, though this was by no means the most affected breed. Scandinavian countries set up schemes involving diagnosis via X-ray in the late 1950s, and others in many areas of Europe followed, with the first British scheme for German Shepherds being started

in 1961. This was replaced by a BVA/KC scheme in 1965 and that, in turn, by the current scoring scheme in 1978 for German Shepherd Dogs and for all breeds in 1983. The OFA scheme began in the USA in the mid-1960s.

Diagnosis is based upon examination of a radiograph taken with the dog lying on its back with legs extended and turned in slightly. Most schemes involve reading by experienced veterinarians in some kind of panel using two or more readers. Dogs are then graded into a series of 4-7 grades or, in the case of the British scheme, are scored on the basis of nine radiographic features of the hip using a hedonic scale of 0 (best) to 6 (worst) with one feature running from 0 to 5. The original scheme used only three categories, namely Normal, Near Normal and Failure – inadequate as a grading scheme since, ideally, we need about seven grades for mathematical precision. All schemes throughout the world operate on a minimum age at X-ray of 12 months, except for the OFA scheme which used a minimum age of 12 months until the end of 1973 and a minimum age of 24 months thereafter. It is likely that a 24-month minimum is slightly more accurate, but the late starting age encourages breeders to examine animals provisionally and perhaps to discard many of those which look poor. Accordingly, from the point of view of assessing breed incidence, the 12-month starting age is likely to be much more reliable. Most Bernese schemes in Europe were on a five-point scale 0-4, with grades 0 and 1 being acceptable for breeding. For example, in Switzerland Bernese were graded as 0 (free), 1 (light), 2 (medium), 3 (moderate), and 4 (severe). This was in force from about 1971 until the end of 1991. At that point, the Swiss accepted the FCI five-point scale, identified as A, B, C, D and E, which can be made into a ten-point scale by dividing each letter grade into 1 and 2, such that the best grade would be A1 and the worst E2. When only the five letter groups are used, the letters A and B accord with grade 0, C with grade 1, D with grade 2, and E with grades 3 and 4. Graphical data were presented by Morgenstern and Reinmann (1997) showing a gradual increase in grade A and a marked decline in grades D and E. They also present data on sires which is used elsewhere.

The Danish scheme now uses the ten-point scale from A1 through to E2 and classifies A1 to B1 as being the same as HD Free, B2 to C2 as HD Grade 1, D1 to D2 as HD grade 2, E1 as HD grade 3, and E2 as HD grade 4.

It is known that age has some effect on HD but this is by no means certain in all breeds. An effect of age was reported by Swenson et al. (1997a) in Swedish Bernese Mountain Dogs such that they suggested assessing all dogs at a constant age. Sex effects occur in some breeds. Swenson et al (1997a) found that females had a greater prevalence than males in German Shepherds, Golden Retrievers and St Bernards, but that there was no effect of sex in Labradors, Rottweilers, Newfoundlands or Bernese. In man, females are at greater risk.

It is well established that HD is a polygenic trait, but the heritability of the trait varies from breed to breed and from location to location. This is to be expected (Mackenzie, 1985) because different schemes are in operation in different locations and there are differences between breeds, levels of inbreeding and the like. In their Swedish study involving seven breeds, Swenson et al. (1997a) found heritabilities ranged from 18 to 68 per cent, with the highest value applying to Bernese and based upon the regression of daughters upon dams. The error attached to the value was 18 per cent, suggesting that heritability in the breed ranged from 50 to 86 per cent, but it is likely that the higher of these values overestimates the heritability. Willis (1997) put the heritability for Bernese in Britain at 40 per cent based on paternal half-sib correlations, and most studies in other breeds suggest values in the 10-60 per cent range,

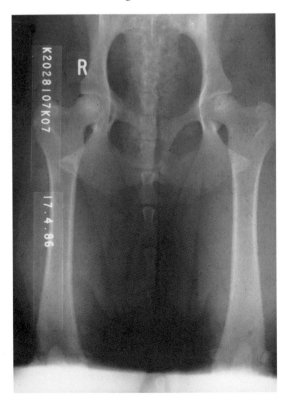

A hip radiograph of the Bernese, Redinka Rose at Nellbern, born 1985 and X-rayed at 13 months of age. Note that the X-ray should have the dog's registration number (or tattoo) filmed on to the plate along with the date of X-ray, and an indication of right (or left) side. Note that the hip score of 3:3 is indicative of Near Normal.

depending upon breed. In Norway, Lingaas and Heim (1987) put the heritability of HD in Bernese at 20+10 per cent using half-sib correlations, and 20+5 per cent for offspring parent regression.

At the time of writing, 2,603 Bernese Mountain Dogs have been scored through the BVA/KC scheme. The mean breed score based on a range of 0-102 (maximum range 0-106) was 16.29, which placed the breed 27th worst out of 71 breeds with 40 or more animals scored. The worst was the Clumber Spaniel, scoring 43.42 on 421 animals, and the best the Irish Wolfhound, scoring 6.00 on only 61 animals. In terms of numbers scored, the Bernese ranked seventh highest – which is very good, bearing in mind that only 700-800 Bernese are registered annually with the Kennel Club. There was a slight

tendency for females to score higher than males, in that 1,732 females averaged 17.00 and 871 males averaged 15.02. The split of about 33 per cent males and 67 per cent females is fairly typical of the split in submissions in Britain for all breeds and probably reflected breeders having more bitches than dogs.

The mean scores by year of birth are shown in Table 10.7 for British Bernese. Over the years, there has been little change in mean score or in the proportion of dogs scoring 10 or better and those scoring 30 or worse.

Many critics of HD schemes argue that selection against the disease is not only expensive, but that it leads to a loss in type. In countries where there are strict controls about what can or can not be bred from in respect of hips (Germany, Switzerland and the Nordic countries), there is no evidence to support the view that type has suffered. It is, of course, a fact that the more features one tries to select for the harder is becomes. It would certainly be easier to maintain type if no attention were paid to HD at all, but, in

Table 10.7 BMD scores by year of birth (BVA/KC scheme Britain)

Period born	No. Animals	Mean Score	0-10%	30+%
1964-82	217	15.12	47.0	11.5
1983*	107	12.60	61.7	4.7
1984	133	14.02	54.9	10.5
1985	173	15.36	54.3	12.1
1986	155	15.81	45.2	12.9
1987	191	14.95	53.4	12.0
1988	201	16.66	46.8	14.4
1989	205	18.24	48.3	16.1
1990	191	18.87	35.6	17.8
1991	158	15.94	45.6	9.5
1992	177	16.75	41.2	13.0
1993	166	17.70	42.2	13.3
1994	181	17.22	42.0	11.6
1995	195	16.83	39.0	12.3
1996-7	153	16.18	39.9	13.1
OVERALL	2603	16.29	45.9	12.6

*scheme began in this year for the breed

Table 10.8 Offspring HD relative to mating type in BMD

Parental status	Offspring X-rayed	% with HD 1-4	% with HD 2-4
1. N x N	3374	20	8
2. N x HD1	210	29	13
3. N x HD2-4	17	24	6
4. HD x HD	9	56	33
5. N x ?	321	28	14
6. ? x?	80	34	16
7. HD x ?	19	32	16

N=normal, HD=grade 1-4, ?=unknown, HD1=grade 1, HD2-4=grades 2-4

(Swenson et al. 1997a)

Table 10.9 Hip results for BMD in Germany (SSV)

Year examined	Number of dogs	Frei %	Verdacht %	Leicht %	Mittel %	Schwere %
1986	n/a	48.4	18.3	19.4	13.7	
1987	211	40.8	19.9	20.8	14.2	4.3
1988	257	46.3	17.5	18.7	13.6	3.9
1989	249	58.2	20.5	12.1	7.6	1.5
1990	277	49.5	22.8	17.7	7.2	2.9

(Schweizer Sennenhund-Verien fur Deutschland, 1987-90)

the intermediate and long term, hip status would degenerate because some animals of excellent type but poor hip status would be used extensively with disastrous consequences.

Swenson et al. (1997a) showed that a hip screening scheme was economically viable on a cost:benefit analysis for each of the seven breeds studied, which included the Bernese Mountain Dog. They examined the results from 3,197 Bernese of whom age at X-ray was known for 53 per cent, and showed that the mean age at X-ray was 16.6 months (SD 7.4 months) with a median point of 14 months. They found an age effect and suggested that all dogs be X-rayed at a similar age to avoid bias. The importance of X-raying is shown in Table 10.8 which looks at the results from different mating combinations.

Matings 3, 4 and 7 have insufficient numbers to be meaningful and all involve at least one dysplastic parent. The best results clearly stem from mating 1, which is Normal to Normal and which led to 20 per cent dysplastic of which only 8 per cent were in the worst grades (2-4), and therefore are not allowed to be used for breeding. Normal to unknown (?) matings gave similar results to Normal to Grade 1 matings, but remember that some of the unknowns would have good hips and others not. There is little doubt that, in this breed and even more so in some

of the other breeds examined, the benefits of using better-hipped parents was obvious.

Results for a few years of SSV (German Club) Bernese hips are shown in table 10.9. 'Frei' indicates Normal hips (grade 0), 'Verdacht' is Near Normal (grade 1), 'Leichte' is Light HD (grade 2), 'Mittel' is Medium HD (grade 3), and 'Schwere' indicates Severe HD (grade 4). Although there is not a marked trend over the five years, the Medium/Severe animals have been declining and the Normal and Near Normals have increased.

The American OFA scheme has been in operation since the late 1960s using a 12-month minimal age criterion. In January 1974 the minimum age was altered to 24 months. Dogs are graded into seven grades: Excellent, Good, Fair and Borderline, which are given OFA status, and Mild, Moderate and Severe, which are failures. Corley (1992) produced data on all breeds. They showed that, from January 1974 to July 1991, 2,491 Bernese were evaluated, of which there were 4.9 per cent Excellent, 47.5 per cent Good, 20.6 per cent Fair, 1.5 per cent Borderline, in other words a pass rate of 74.5 per cent. The failures comprised 12.2 per cent Mild, 11.2 per cent Moderate and 2.1 per cent Severe. On the basis of the percentage of dysplastics (failures) the Bernese ranked 8th worst out of the 82 breeds with 100 or more evaluations. This is a poorer position than is seen in the UK. The worst breed was the St Bernard with 47.4 per cent dysplastics of the 1,027 dogs assessed. More detailed results for American OFA data appear in Table 10.10.

The OFA (1997) suggested that there has been an improvement in hip status in many breeds, which they assessed by examination of Excellent OFA grades. They looked at three birth periods: 1980 and earlier, 1986-7 and 1993-4. The total Bernese examined in each period were 566, 622 and 842 respectively, and the percentage of Excellent was 2.8, 5.9 and 10.3 per cent respectively

Table 10.10
Hip evaluations from the OFA (1974-1992)
Bernese Mountain Dogs

Year	No. Dogs	Percentage in categories[1]						
		Excellent	Good	Fair	Borderline	Mild	Moderate	Severe
1974	12	0	16.7	8.3	0	25.0	50.0	0
1975	20	10.0	25.0	20.0	0	25.0	15.0	5.0
1976	35	11.4	42.9	22.9	0	5.7	8.6	8.6
1977	41	4.9	39.0	22.0	0	12.2	19.5	2.4
1978	50	5.0	55.0	20.0	0	11.7	6.7	1.7
1979	71	2.8	54.9	18.3	1.4	5.6	14.1	2.8
1980	81	0	40.7	22.2	2.5	16.0	16.0	2.5
1981	85	1.2	44.7	15.3	1.2	14.1	18.8	4.7
1982	90	0	50.0	15.6	1.1	4.4	25.6	3.3
1983	122	1.6	45.1	28.7	0.8	5.7	17.2	0.8
1984	163	2.5	47.2	19.6	1.8	11.7	15.3	1.8
1985	158	3.2	48.1	22.2	0	11.4	13.3	1.9
1986	187	5.3	49.2	19.8	1.6	12.8	8.6	3.2
1987	218	5.0	46.8	22.5	0.9	13.8	10.6	0.5
1988	293	5.8	49.5	19.8	2.0	10.6	10.2	2.0
1989	307	6.8	53.4	16.6	0.3	14.7	6.8	1.3
1990	357	5.6	48.2	24.6	0.3	12.3	6.2	2.8
1991	330	9.7	45.8	19.1	3.6	14.5	6.4	0.9
1992	407	6.1	50.6	24.1	2.5	9.3	6.1	1.2
1993[2]	350	8.9	69.4	21.7				
1994	438	11.6	70.1	18.3				
1995	411	18.7	62.3	19.0				
1996	413	10.4	70.0	19.6				
1997	449	10.7	68.6	20.7				
TOTAL	3037[3]	5.3	48.3	20.9	1.4	11.8	10.2	1.9

[1]Dogs graded Excellent through to Borderline inclusive receive an OFA pass and their names are published. Failures are not published. [2] From 1993-1997 inclusive the numbers relate only to dogs graded Excellent through Fair and those failing are unknown at time of writing. [3] The Total figures relate to 1974-92 inclusive.

for the three periods, with dysplastic percentages being 32.8, 23.4 and 12.6 per cent respectively. A similar cohort study in certain breeds by Kaneene et al. (1997) showed similar progress. This is, however, not confirmed by Packard (personal communication 1998) who showed that there was an abrupt change in a cohort study at cohort 25, corresponding to the period in mid-1991. One problem with American studies is trying to assess the extent to which pre-selection and the non-submission of poor plates influences figures. This is likely to be greater with a 24-month minimal age than one of 12 months.

The Institute for Genetic Disease Control in Animals (GDC), set up in 1990 in the USA, uses a 12-month minimal age. It also publishes failures, and owners of failing animals have their submission fee returned. The number of Bernese certified as being unaffected for HD has risen from 29 in 1990 to 242 in 1997, and totalled 967 over this period.

In Norway, Lingaas and Heim (1987) showed that, in the period 1972 to 1984, there were 2,174 Bernese registered, of which 923 (42.4 per cent) were radiographed. The incidence of HD was 23 per cent, very similar to the OFA figures and 7th worst of the breeds examined. In a Swiss study looking at 24 years of HD study, Fluckiger et al. (1995) showed that, of over 3,700 pedigree dogs examined, 42 per cent were dysplastic, i.e. in grades C, D or E of the FCI system. For the Bernese, the incidence of grades D and E combined was 25 per cent in the period 1971-4, 29 per cent in the period 1981-4 and 32 per cent in the period 1991-4. Similar lack of progress was seen in other breeds, and the authors concluded that it stemmed from inadequate breeding controls.

Failure to improve HD status is largely due to a tendency for breeders to use, to excess, some sires that are poor producers. Many breeders do not distinguish between phenotypic merit and genetic merit. There is a need to produce progeny data and Estimated Breeding Values if progress is to be greater than at present. Matters are not helped by some club officials in Britain arguing that radiography induces cancer and that X-rays should be avoided. There is more chance of getting cancer watching the TV, and the high cancer rate in Bernese is nothing to do with X-raying but a genetic predisposition in the breed. I have heard a similar argument that vaccinations cause cancer, and people perpetuating such fallacies do dogs a great disservice. It is astounding that they should hold office within breed clubs.

One should certainly not regard HD as the primary item of selection, but failure to take account of hip status is both foolish and dangerous. It is high time that kennel control groups such as the KC and AKC started to enforce rules that make assessment of hips mandatory in specific breeds. Mandatory rules will not affect those breeders who do screen their stock, but it will force those who do not either to comply or to get out. Those breeders who argue that they "do not believe in hips or elbows" – and I have heard such statements made – are walking a dangerous tightrope and doing no good to the breed.

HYPOMYELINOGENESIS

Hypomyelinogenesis occurs when there is inadequate myelin around the nerves of the spinal cord and brain. It leads to a kind of reduced insulation which results in trembling symptoms in the dog. Animals exhibiting this problem were observed around 1985 in the Bernese in Britain. In total, a dozen or so cases resulted. In an examination of the data, Willis (1986) suggested an autosomal recessive trait, which was the view published by Palmer et al. (1987). The condition had been reported in Springer Spaniels by Griffiths et al. (1981), and in Hereford cattle by Duffell et al. (1988). A similar disease was reported in the Tibetan Mastiff (Abbott, 1986) and the Rottweiler in Holland (Wouda and Van Nes, 1986). A genetic explanation was not given for the Rottweiler cases, but an autosomal recessive was considered for the Tibetan Mastiff.

Several important Bernese Champions were implicated in Britain and most ceased to be used for breeding. All cases traced back to Duntiblae Nalle on both sides of their pedigree, and the suggestion was that he might be the causal dog. However, most Bernese Mountain Dogs in Britain trace back to Nalle. Recessive traits can be lost since, in each generation, they are halved in risk; so this does mean that all Nalle descendants were at risk.

Many breeders became somewhat paranoid about 'trembler', as it was called, but it was an early-onset disease identifiable in most cases by eight or, at the latest, twelve weeks of age. Dogs had a constant trembling status except when asleep and most cases were euthanised, though I did hear of one who survived for some time. We owned Ch. Carlacot Genesis at Nellsbern, whose father was Ch. Clashaidy Nordic Fire, a proven carrier of the condition. This meant that Nordic Fire was Hh in genetic terms and Genesis had a 50 per cent chance of being HH (free) or Hh (carrier). Genesis never produced the problem in some 62 progeny, nor did inbreeding to him. His best son,

Nellsbern Casablanca, did not produce the condition, even in inbred matings, and he was mated to a bitch who subsequently produced the problem to another sire, but not in the Casablanca-sired litter. I therefore feel that Genesis was HH, and that would be true of his progeny. Thus, although a son of a proven carrier, he was a safe animal.

Although little is now heard of 'trembler' in Britain, there is no doubt that it still crops up, however rarely, and a living Champion has produced a case but is still at stud.

LITTER SIZE

Information on reproductive performance of dog breeds is not readily obtainable. It is known that there is a positive relationship between litter size and wither height (Kaiser, 1971) and between litter size and body weight (Robinson, 1973). This means that, as breeds get taller or heavier, they tend to have larger litters, certainly until one reaches giant size, when the relationship may tail off. Mean litter sizes of many breeds have been summarised by Willis (1989) and examined in detail for the German Shepherd Dog (Willis, 1992).

In his study of Swiss breeds, Kaiser (1971) looked at 995 Bernese litters in Switzerland covering 6,724 puppies, and established a mean litter size of 6.76 with a standard deviation of 2.8. The maximum size seen was 15 and the sex ratio was 106 males per 100 females, or 51.4 per cent males. On average, 12.07 per cent of puppies were born dead or died within the first 24 hours and these are usually considered as stillbirths. This appeared to be at the high end of the scale (see Willis, 1989) though Kaiser found a higher stillbirth figure for the Great Swiss (13.14 per cent) and the St Bernard (17.89 per cent).

When using registration data in some countries (e.g. in the UK or the USA), we are faced with results only for those pups surviving to be registered, and thus information on deaths and culling is unknown. In all studies, regardless of location, litters where all the pups died at birth or were lost before eight weeks are usually not known about because they may not be reported to the breed club since there are no puppies to register.

The German Club for Swiss Breeds (SSV) does produce litter details in its Zuchtbuchs which, by sex, give the number born, the number reared and the numbers stillborn, culled or being fostered. Data calculated for the years 1989 and 1990 are shown in Table 10.11. These data comprise 357 litters.

The mean litter size was 7.35, which is higher than Kaiser's figures, but the stillbirth rate is also higher than his. The sex ratio, unusually, was 99.3 or 49.8 per cent males. Normally one expects more males than females to be born (usually around 52 per cent males, 48 per cent females). The most common litter size was 9 and the maximum was 16, with the standard deviation at 3.75 pups. According to Robinson (1973), litter size should be given from the formula: $Y = 3.32 + 0.136X$, where Y is litter size and X is the breed body weight in kg. The actual litter size cited above (7.35) is equivalent to a body weight of about 30kg (66lbs) which is less than the mean size for a Bernese,

Table 10.11 Litter data for BMD in Germany 1989 & 1990

Item	Males	Females	Total
Total born	1307	1316	2623
Stillborn %	16.6	15.3	15.9
Culled %	3.8	3.9	3.9
Survived %	80.8	80.8	80.1

Table 10.12 Distribution of litters in German BMD

Number in litter	No. of litters	% of Total	Cumulative %
1	9	2.52	2.52
2	13	3.64	6.16
3	15	4.20	10.36
4	29	8.12	18.49
5	37	10.36	28.85
6	40	11.20	40.06
7	39	10.92	50.98
8	38	10.64	61.62
9	52	14.57	76.19
10	31	8.68	84.87
11	23	6.44	91.32
12	18	5.04	96.36
13	7	1.96	98.32
14	4	1.12	99.44
15	1	0.28	99.72
16	1	0.28	100.00

suggesting that the Bernese Mountain Dog is probably slightly less reproductively effective than it ought to be for its size.

The litter distribution is given in Table 10.12 for numbers born.

The median litter size is around the 7 to 8 mark, but the mean number weaned at eight weeks is likely to be reduced to around 6 as a consequence of stillbirths and subsequent losses. There seems minimal difference between the sexes, though a slightly higher tendency to stillbirths among males is to be expected.

LONGEVITY

I have been collecting mortality data from breeders for some time, and data on over 500 deaths suggest that the mean age at death is around seven years. About 40 per cent of the deaths with known cause are attributable to some form of cancer. Some breeders do not like to accept this; they believe

Ninth Birthday reunion of a Swiss Stars litter sired by Dallybecks Echo Jackson ex Vombreiterwgs Swiss Lace, born June 5th 1989. Seated (left to right): Truff, Maggy, Baron and Magic. Lying (left to right): Toya, Brandy and Bekka. It is quite a feat to get a litter to this age in the breed.

that we should not publicise this so as not to affect sales, and suggest that the data are in some way biased. It is therefore interesting that Bonnett et al. (1997) undertook a comprehensive study of causes of death in various breeds in Sweden. The study covered the years 1992 and 1993 and analysed over 222,000 dogs. The average death rate was 260 per 10,000 dog years at risk. The study covered 70 breeds and, because so many dogs in Sweden are insured, causes of death are more accurately known. The Bernese ranked as a high-risk breed. There were 441 dogs at risk in 1992 and 1,460 in 1993. The breed-specific mortality was 771 and 836 per 10,000 dog years for 1992 and 1993 respectively. Only the Irish Wolfhound exceeded this rate in both years. The Great Dane did so in 1992, and both are giant breeds in which longevity is well established to be limited.

Proportional mortality, which was effectively the percentage of deaths from a specific cause, showed that tumours (cancer)

accounted for 32.7 per cent of Bernese deaths, followed by locomotor systems problems at 28.8 per cent. The breed ranked first, above all other breeds, in these two causes of death. In fact, the Bernese Mountain Dog was more likely to die (or be euthanised) from tumours than the Boxer, which is popularly believed to be a high cancer risk breed. The cancer risk in Bernese is thus firmly established, while locomotor problems in this breed will be largely associated with elbow and hip difficulties.

We do a disservice to would-be owners if we seek to deceive them or do not make them aware of the lack of longevity of the breed. The short life is a tragedy that we have had to face but the pleasure that the breed gives us should not be lost sight of.

Pictured (right): correct toes; pictured (below): litter brother with an extra toe. Note this is not a dewclaw, but a genuine, if rudimentary, toe.

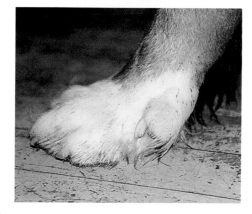

POLYDACTYLY

It is well accepted that some Bernese have an extra toe on the hind feet such that, instead of four toes, there are five. This is often claimed to be a dewclaw, but the genuine dewclaw is a vestigial item and is devoid of any pad, even if the dewclaw is double. Packard (1992), speaking about toes, claimed that the fifth toe in the front was used by the dog. It does seem that she was referring to the dewclaw which, though it can be removed under most KC rules, rarely is removed in Britain. In a rather ambiguous clause, she seeks to hear from those who leave the front dewclaws on but continue to amputate the rudimentary fifth or more toes on the hind feet. Chesnutt Smith (1995) refers to a 'monkey paw' and does state that these are additional toes, not just rudimentary dewclaws. She advocates removal. Simonds (1989) also refers to six toes and suggests having her puppies done at about 48 hours after birth. She admits that some vets will not remove hind toes but states that, ideally, only four toes should be left on the hind foot.

The presence of dewclaws on the hind foot is a simple autosomal dominant allele. Most German Shepherd Dogs are born without hind dewclaws and, when mated together, such dogs do not produce dewclaws in their progeny. This is indicative of the recessive nature of 'missing' hind dewclaws. I have not seen a hind dewclaw on a German Shepherd for decades. Most other breeds have hind dewclaws which are usually removed, but some breeds have a double dewclaw (e.g. Briards and Pyrenean Mountain Dogs). These are left on and, for some incomprehensible reason, are actually encouraged by the Breed Standard. I had never seen extra hind toes on any of our

Bernese puppies and some of our animals were even born without hind dewclaws. Then we mated our Ch. Carlacot Genesis at Nellsbern to bitches originating from Coliburn and Swiss lines. Some of these produced an additional toe and the bitch owners were surprised that we had not expected this, since almost all their stock were born with additional toes.

Examination of these additional toes, which are usually on the inside of the foot in much the same position as the thumb on a man's hand, will reveal that they clearly are toes, not dewclaws and that they have a pad beneath. Under KC rules in Britain, removal of these toes would be a cosmetic action and should be reported to the ruling body. In Denmark, removal of toes is prohibited by the DKC but there are many dogs born with these additional appendages (J. Ramsing, 1998, a personal communication). It is certainly true that these additional toes can be awkward, can look unsightly and can lead to slightly odd movement. Moreover the nail of the extra toe may need to be trimmed regularly because it does not take pressure on the ground. By the same token, its removal can lead to deformed action, with dogs that have their hind feet turned out in a sort of 'Charlie Chaplin' type of gait. Some breeders argue that dogs with these toes have stronger bone, but scientific evidence for this is not available. At a time when the veterinary profession has qualms about the docking of tails, it is astonishing that any vets would contemplate amputating (there is no other word for it) actual toes.

In the guinea pig, polydactyly is a threshold trait and it is probable that this is true of the extra toe in the hind feet in Bernese. The fact that dogs born without the extra toe can produce them is indicative that we might be dealing with a threshold feature, and it is feasible that the toe could be bred out by concentrating on animals born without it and those who did not produce the problem. However, desirable though this may be, it would give additional selection pressures that breeders might not be able to follow. It is interesting that Alberch (1985) put forward the theory that large breeds (St Bernards and Newfoundlands) frequently have extra toes, while small breeds may be missing digits. He argued that, by selecting for size, these breeds had larger embryos and larger limb buds (i.e. composed of more cells) and that this would lead to additional digits. Thus, by selecting for size, breeders cannot actually eliminate the atavistic appearance of an extra toe.

PROGRESSIVE RETINAL ATROPHY

Generalized Progressive Retinal Atrophy (PRA) has been known in the dog for the best part of a century, and is known to be common in gundog breeds in which it was first discovered. Although the condition brings about a gradual destruction of the retina leading initially to impaired night vision and eventually to total blindness, the exact form of the disease does vary from breed to breed (see the excellent review by Petersen-Jones, 1998).

In the Irish Setter, the gene causing the disease has been identified and thus any Irish Setter can – from a blood sample – be accurately assessed as to genetic status by DNA analysis. It is well established that generalised PRA is a simple autosomal recessive (see Chapter Six) and this is true in all breeds in which it has been studied (see review by Willis, 1989). However, the form seen in the Irish Setter has not been located in other breeds where, although symptoms are fairly similar, the trait is fractionally different and obviously caused by a different gene to that in the Irish Setter.

It should be only a matter of time before the PRA gene in other breeds is located, which would enable genotyping to be done for all dogs in affected breeds. It does appear that PRA has been located in the Bernese in America and, though this may not have been reported elsewhere and Bernese do not feature in Petersen-Jones' (1998) list of affected breeds, it would imply that the condition can be found in other locations. The incidence is low and should remain so if testing is undertaken but, like PRA in all breeds save the Irish Setter, the disease is late in onset and thus may not be identified until after some animals have been used for breeding. The DNA 'fingerprinting' of the disease would be a large step forward and, with global testing of Bernese Mountain Dogs, once this is established, the disease could be eradicated. Any Bernese with PRA will carry the recessive allele in duplicate (pp) and both its parents would have to be Pp at best, but could be pp. Affected dogs should not be bred from and there is minimal justification for using carrier (Pp) animals once they have been identified from progeny. As soon as a DNA test is discovered, all Bernese can be tested and only PP animals used for breeding, which should eliminate the disease from the breed. Some careful use of otherwise outstanding animals that are Pp could be undertaken, along with DNA testing, and this would allow virtues to be retained without the p allele being retained in the breeding population. However, this needs to be undertaken with strict controls. Table 10.13 shows the various matings with PRA.

Table 10.13 PRA possible matings

Mating	Parents (either round)	Progeny percent		
		Normal PP	Carrier Pp	Affected pp
1	Normal x Normal (PP) (PP)	100		
2	Normal x Carrier (PP) (Pp)	50	50	
3	Normal x Affected (PP) (pp)		100	
4	Carrier x Carrier (Pp) (Pp)	25	50	25
5	Carrier x Affected (Pp) (pp)		50	50
6	Affected x Affected (pp) (pp)			100

Only in matings 1 and 6 is the percentage accurate, regardless of numbers born. In all other cases, the percentages are those expected, given enough numbers to be meaningful. Note that PRA cases (Affecteds) are only possible when *both* parents carry the p allele. Although matings 2 and 3 involve the defective allele (p), no Affecteds can occur because only one parent carries the p allele. Matings 3, 5 and 6 involve at least one Affected parent and are thus unlikely to be undertaken, certainly once the Affected parent has been identified through blindness. The commonest way of producing Affected cases is mating 4 when Carrier to Carrier occurs, usually without the breeder knowing that the parents were Carriers. Once DNA testing is in operation, mating 2 could be undertaken using outstanding Carrier animals. All progeny could be assessed and DNA tested so that the PP can be distinguished from the Pp. The latter could be culled from the breeding programme by being spayed/castrated and the PP cases could be bred from with impunity.

SUBAORTIC STENOSIS (SAS)

Aortic stenosis is a thickening of the outflow tract of the left ventricle of the heart, which slows down the emptying process and leads to hypertrophy of the left ventricle. Usually, the problem is not with the valves but just below them, hence the term subaortic. Affected dogs have a typical heart murmur and the disease can cause fainting and sudden death. The disease is known to affect the Newfoundland, and, though the mode of inheritance is unclear, it does appear to be either dominant or polygenic, but not recessive. The disease is not strictly congenital, but appears to be present from about six months of age, though some murmurs may be noticed earlier.

Recent cases have been observed in the Bernese Mountain Dog in the USA (Robin Camken, 1998, personal communication), with many of the affected animals dying suddenly and with a variety of bloodlines implicated. If found in the USA, then it is likely that the condition exists elsewhere in the breed, so the collection of pedigree and litter data now seems of paramount importance.

Appendix I
References

(Citations to books on the breed are given at the end of this section).

Abbott, D.P. (1986) Canine inherited neuropathy of Tibetan Mastiffs (C.I.N.) Mimeograph.

Alberch, P. (1985) Developmental constraints: why St Bernards often have an extra digit and Poodles never so. Am. Naturalist. 126: 430-3.

American Kennel Club (1935) Pure Bred Dogs: the recognized breeds and standards, New York.

Anon (1995) Wheelchair Assistance Dogs. Hampshire College, Amherst, Massachusetts.

Archibald, A., Haley, C. (1993) Mapping the complex genomes of animals and man. Outlook on Agric. 22(2): 79-84.

Audell, L. (1990) Heredity of elbow dysplasia: can elbow dysplasia be controlled by judicious breeding? 57th Annual meeting. Am. Anim. Hosp. Assoc.: 730-3.

Badinand, F., Szumowski, P., Breton, A. (1972) Etude morphobiologique et biochemique du sperme du Chien cryptorchide. Rec. Med. Vet. 146: 655-89.

Barnett K.C. (1976) Comparative aspects of canine hereditary eye disease. Adv. Vet. Sci. Comp. Med. 20:39-67.

Baumans, V., Dijkstra, G., Wensing, C.J.G. (1981) Testicular descent in the dog. Zbl. Vet. Med. C. Anat. Histol. Embryol. 10: 97-110.

Bennett, D. (1974) Canine dystocia – a review of the literature. J. Small Anim. Pract. 15:101-17.

Bergsten, G., Nordin, M. (1986) Osteochondros som ersatningsorsak I ett material forsakrade hundar. Svensk Vet. 38:97-100.

Bartschi, M. (1986) History of Bernese Mountain Dogs. NZ Kennel Gazette. Sept 77-78.

Bellars, A.R.M. (1969) Hereditary disease in British Antarctic Sled dogs. Vet. Rec. 85:600-7.

Binns, M.M., Holmes, N.G., Marti, E., Bowen, N. (1995) Dog parentage testing using canine microsatellites. J. Small Anim. Pract. 36: 493-7.

Bonnett, B.N., Egenvall, A., Olson, P., Hedhammar, A. (1997) Mortality in insured Swedish dogs: rates and causes of death in various breeds. Vet. Rec. 141: 40-4.

Borchelt, P.L. (1983) Aggressive behavior of dogs kept as companion animals: classification and influence of sex, reproductive status and breed. App. Anim. Behav. Sci. 10: 45-61.

Brandsch, H. (1962) Vergleichende Untersuchungen zur Vererbung des Kryptorchismus und der Intersexualitat bei Haustieren. Kuhn-Archiv. 77: 323-425.

Burger, I. ed. (1993) The Waltham book of companion animal nutrition. Pergamon, Oxford.

Byrne, M.J., Byrne, G.M. (1992) Inheritance of 'overshot' malocclusion in German shorthaired pointers. Vet. Rec. 130: 375-6.

Burgi, I. (1991) Untersuchungen bezuglich der Vererbung von Zahnfehlern , mangelhaftem Lidschluss und unerwunschter Rutenhaltung beim Berner Sennenhund. Dissertation Vet. Med. Fac. Univ. Zurich. 109pp.

Chrisman, C.L. (1991) Seizures in: Problems in Small Animal Neurology. 2nd ed. Lea & Febiger. Philadelphia. 177-205.

Clutton-Brock, J. (1995) Origins of the dog: domestication and early history. In The Domestic Dog (ed. J.Serpell) Cambridge Univ. Press. Cambridge p 7-20.

Corley, E.A., (1992) Role of the Orthopedic Foundation for Animals in the control of canine hip dysplasia. Vet. Clinics. N. Amer. 22: 579-93.

Cunningham, J.G. (1971) Canine seizure disorders. J. Am. Vet. Med. Assoc. 158: 589-97.

Dobson, J.M., Gorman, N.T. (1993) Cancer chemotherapy in small animal practice. Blackwell Science, Oxford.

Dreyer, C.J., Preston, C.B. (1973) Abnormal behaviour patterns in dogs with cleft palates. S. Afr. J. Med. Sci. 38:13-16.

Duffell, S.J., Harper, P.A.W., Healy, P.J., Dennis, J.A. (1988) Congenital hypomyelinogenesis of Hereford calves. Vet. Rec. 123:423-4.

Earle, K.E., Smith P.M. (1993) A balanced diet for dogs and cats. In The Waltham book of companion animal nutrition (ed. I.Burger) Pergamon, Oxford p45-55.

Else, R.W., Hannant, D. (1979) Some epidemiological aspects of mammary neoplasia in the bitch. Vet. Rec. 104: 296-304.

Ernborg, B. (1986) Osteochondros och fragmententering av processus coronoideus I armbagsleden hos hund. Svensk. Vet. 38: 92-6.

Evans, J.M., White, K. (1988) The book of the bitch. Henston, Guildford. 230pp.

Faissler, D., Gaillard, C., Srenk, P., Graber, H., Heynold, Y., Jaggy, A. (1988) Genetic aspects of idiopathic epilepsy in Labrador retrievers. J. Small Animal pract. 39: 297-80
Falt, L., Swenson, L., Wilsson, E. (1982) cited by Mackenzie et al. (1986)

Farquhar, T., Bertram, J., Todhunter, R.J., Burton-Wurster, N., Lust, G. (1977) Variations in composition of cartilage from the shoulder joints of young adult dogs at risk for developing canine hip dysplasia. J. Am. Vet. Med. Assoc. 210:1483-5.

Ferber, D.B., Danciger, J.S., Aguirre, G. (1992) The beta subunit of cyclic phosphodiesterase in RNA is deficient in canine rod-cone dysplasia 1. Neuron. 9: 349-56.

Fison-Bates, Y. (1986) Bernese Mountain Dogs in New Zealand. NZ Kennel Gazette. Sept p 92-3.

Fluckiger, M., Lang, J., Binder, H., Busato, A., Boos, J. (1995) Die Bekampfung der Huftgelenksdysplasie in der Schweiz. Ein Ruckblick auf die vergangenen 24 Jahre. Schweiz. Arch. Tierheilk. 137: 243-50.

Glickman, L.T.,Glickman, N.W., Perez, C.M., Schellenberg, D.B., Lantz, G.C. (1994) Analysis of risk factors for gastric dilation and dilation-volvulus in dogs. J. Am. Vet. Med. Assoc. 204: 1465-71.

Glickman, L.T., Glickman, N.W., Schellenberg, D.B., Simpson, K., Lantz, G.C. (1997) Multiple risk factors for gastric dilation-volvulus syndrome in dogs: a practitioner/owner case-control study. J. Am. Anim. Hosp. Assoc. 33: 197-204.

Goddard, M.E., Beilharz, R.G. (1982) Genetic and environmental factors affecting the suitability of dogs as guide dogs for the blind. Theor. Appl. Genet. 62:97-102.

Griffiths, I.R., Duncan, I.D., McCulloch, M. Harvey, M.J.A. (1981) Shaking pups: a disorder of central myelination in the spaniel dog. J. Neurol. Sci. 50:423-33.
Grondalen, A.J. (1975) Tumores I skjelettsystemet. Norsk. Vet. 87: 30-7.

Grondalen, A.J. (1979a) Arthrosis with special reference to the elbow joint of rapidly growing dogs.1. a review of the literature. Nord. Vet. Med. 31:52-68.

Grondalen, A.J. (1979b) II. Occurrence, clinical and radiographic findings. Nord. Vet. Med. 31: 68-75.

Grondalen, A.J. (1979c) III. Ununited medial coronoid process of the ulna and osteochondritis dissecans of the humeral condyle. Nord. Vet. Med. 31: 520-7.

Grondalen, A.J.,Grondalen, T. (1981) V. A pathoanatomical investigation. Nord. Vet. Med. 33: 1-16.

Grondalen, A.J., Lingaas, F. (1991) Arthrosis in the elbow joint of rapidly growing dogs: a genetic investigation. J. Small Anim. Pract. 32: 460-4.

Grondalen, A.J., Rorvik, A.M. (1980) IV. A follow up investigation of operated dogs. Nord. Vet. Med. 32: 212-8.

Guthrie, S., Pidduck, H.G. (1990) Heritability of elbow osteochondrosis with a closed population of dogs. J. Small Anim. Pract. 31: 93-6.

Hall, S.J.G., Wallace, M.E. (1996) Canine epilepsy: a genetic counselling programme for Keeshonds. Vet. Rec. 138:358-60.

Hallgren, A. (1975) Skattning av mentalt avelsvarde hos hund. Svensk. Vet. 27: 447-453.

Hayes, H.M.jr. (1974) Congenital umbilical and inguinal hernias in cattle, horses, swine, dogs and cats: risk by breed and sex among hospital patients. Am. J. Vet. Res. 35: 839-42.

Heim, A. (1914) Die Schweizer Sennerhunde, Zurich.
Holmes, N.G. (1998) Canine genetic disease: the beginning of the end? Vet J. 155: 1-2

Jackson, F. (1994) Dog breeding: the theory and the practice. Crowood Press, Marlborough. 208 pp

Jennings, P.B. (1992) Epidemiology of gastric dilation-volvulus in the military working dog program. Mil. Med. 157: 369-71.

Jones, D.E., Joshua, J. (1982) Reproductive clinical problems in the dog. Wright, Bristol. 198pp.

Kaiser, G. (1971) Die Reproduktionsleistung der Haushunde in ihrer Beziehung zur Korpergrosse und zum Gewicht der Rassen. Z.Tierzucht.Zuchtbiol. 88:118068, 240-53, 316-40.

Kaneene, J.B., Mostosky, U.V., Padgett, G.A. (1997) Retrospective cohort study of changes in hip joint phenotype of dogs in the United States. J. Am. Vet. Med. Assoc. 211: 1542-44.

Kawakami, E., Tsutsui, T., Yamada, Y., Yamauchi, M. (1984) Cryptorchidism in the dog: occurrence of cryptorchidism and semen quality in the cryptorchid dog. Japan. J. Vet. Sci. 46: 303-8.

Kennel Club of Great Britain (1859) Stud Book. London.

Klingeborn, B. (1986) Indikationer pa en arftlig bakgrund till armbagsled – forandringar hos berner sennenhund. Svensk, Vet 38: 102-7.

Legrand-Defretin, V. Munday, H.S. (1993) Feeding dogs and cats for life. In The Waltham book of companion animal nutrition,(ed. I. Burger) Pergamon, Oxford p 57-68.

Leighton, E.A. (1997) Genetics of canine hip dysplasia. J. Am. Vet. Assoc. 210: 1474-9.

Lingaas, F. (1989) Generasjonsintervallet hos neon norske hunderaser. Norsk. Vet. 101: 15-18.

Lingaas, F., Heim, P. (1987) En genetisk undersokelse av hoftelddsdysplasi i norske hunderaser. Norsk. Vet. 99: 617-23.

Lust, G. (1997) An overview of the pathogenesis of canine hip dysplasia. J. Am. Vet. Med. Assoc. 210:1443-5.

Mackenzie, S.A., Oltenacu, E.A.B., Houpt, K.A. (1986) Canine behavioral genetics – a review. App. Anim. Behav. Sci. 15: 365-93.

Manwell, C., Baker, C.M.A. (1984) Domestication of the dog: hunter, food, bed-warmer or emotional object. Z. Tierzucht. Zuchtbiol. 101: 241-256.

Meric, S.M., Perman, V., Hardy, R.M. (1985) Corticosteroid responsive meningitis in ten dogs. J. Am. Anim. Hosp. Assoc. 21: 677-84.

Moore, P.F. (1984) Systemic histiocytosis of Bernese Mountain Dogs. Vet. Pathol. 21: 554-63.

Moore, P.F., Rosin, A. (1986) Malignant histiocytosis of Bernese Mountain Dogs. Vet. Pathol. 23: 1-10.

Morgenstern, R., Bartschi, M., Reinmann, M. (1997) La lutte contre la dysplasie du coude (DC) au sein du Club Suisse du Bouvier Bernois. In Handbook Schweizerischer Klub fur Berner Sennenhunde. p.117-21.

Morgenstern, R., Reinmann, M. (1997) La lutte contre la dysplasie des hanches (DH) au sein du Club Suisse du Bouvier Bernois. In Handbook Schweizerischer Klub fur Berner Sennenhunde p103-9.
Okkens, A.C., Dielman, S.J., Vogel, F. (1985) Proc. Voorjaarsdagen 26, Amsterdam.

Oliver, J.E. (1987) Seizure disorders and narcolepsy. In Veterinary Neurology (ed. J.E. Oliver, B.F.Horlein & I.G.Mathey.) 2nd ed. W.B.Saunders, Philadelphia. 285-302.

Olsen, S.J. (1985) Origins of the domestic dog: the fossil record. Univ. Arizona Press, Tucson.

Olsson, S.E., Bjurstrom, S., Ekman, S, Jonsson, L., Lindberg, R., Reiland, S. (1986) En epidemiologisk studie av tumorsjukdomar hos hund. Svensk Veterinartidning. 387: 212-24.

Orthopedic Foundation for Animals (1977) 30 Years of progress: OFA Data confirm dramatic improvements in dogs' hips. Press Release. OFA, Columbia, Mo.

Padgett, G.A., Madewell, B.R., Keller, E.T., Jodar, L.,Packard, M.E. (1995) Inheritance of histiocytosis in Bernese Mountain Dogs. J. Small Anim. Pract. 36: 93-8.

Palmer, A.C., Blakemore, W.F., Wallace, M.E., Wilkes, M.K. Hertage, M.E. Matic, S. (1987) Recognition of 'trembler', a hypomyelinating condition in the Bernese Mountain Dog. Vet. Rec. 120:609-12.

Paterson, S., Boydell,. P., Pike, R. (1995) Systemic histiocytosis in the Bernese Mountain Dog. J. Small Anim. Pract. 36: 233-6.
Pendergrass, T., Hayes, H.M. (1975) Cryptorchism and related defects in dogs: epidemiologic comparisons with man. Teratology 12: 51-6.
Peters, J.A. (1959) Canine breed ancestry. J. Am. Vet. Med. Assoc. 15:621-24.

Petersen-Jones, S.M. (1998) A review of research to elucidate the causes of the Generalized Progressive Retinal Atrophies. Vet. J. 155:5-18.

Pfleiderer-Hogner, M. (1979) Moglichkeiten der Zuchtwertschatzung beim Deutschen Schaferhund anhand der Schutzhundprufing 1. Dissertation.Vet. Med. Fac., University of Munich. 84pp.

Podberscek, A.L., Serpell, J.A. (1996) The English cocker spaniel: preliminary findings on aggressive behaviour. App. Anim. Behav. Sci. 47: 75-89.
Podberscek, A.L. Serpell, J.A. (1997) Aggressive behaviour in English cocker spaniels and the personality of their owners. Vet. Rec. 141:73-6.

Presthus, J. (1989) Aseptic Suppurative Meningitis in Bernese Mountain Dogs. Norsk. Vet. 101: 169-75.

References

Priester, W.A.(1979) Occurrence of mammary neoplasms in bitches in relation to breed, age, tumour type and geographical region from which reported. J. Small Anim.
 Pract. 20: 1-11.

Rahko, T. (1968) A statistical study of tumours of dogs. Acta Vet. Scand. 9: 328-49.

Robinson, R. (1973) Relationship between litter size and weight of dam in the dog. Vet. Rec. 92: 221-3.

Robinson, R. (1977) Genetic aspects of umbilical hernia incidence in cats and dogs. Vet. Rec.100: 9-10.

Romagnoli, S.E. (1991) Canine cryptorchidism. Vet Clinics N. Am. Small Anim. Pract. 21: 533-44.

Rosin A., Moore, P.F., Dubielzig, R. (1985) Malignant histiocytosis in Bernese Mountain Dogs. J. Am. Vet. Med. Assoc. 188:1041-45.

Schnelle, G.B. (1935) Some new diseases in dogs. Am. Kennel Gazette 52 (5) 25.
Schweizer Sennenhund-Verein fur Deutschland (1987-90) Zuchtbuch. SSV. Munich.

Scott, J.P., Fuller, J.L. (1965) Dog behaviour – the genetic basis. Chicago Univ. Press. Chicago.

Serpell J.A. ed. (1995) The Domestic Dog. Cambridge Univ. Press. Cambridge. x + 268pp.

Sevelius, E., Tidholm, A., Thoren-Tolling, K. (1990) Pyometra in the dog. J. Am. Anim. Hosp. Assoc. 26: 33-8.

Skrentny, T.T. (1964) Preliminary study of the inheritance of missing teeth in the dog. Wien. tierarztl. Mschr. 51: 231-45.

Slater, M.R., Scarlett, J.M., Donoghue, S., Kaderly, R.E., Bonnett, B.N., Cockshutt, J., Erb, H.N. (1992) Diet and exercise as potential risk factors for osteochondritis dissecans in dogs. Am. J. Vet. Res. 53: 2119-24.

Smith, G.K. (1997) Advances in diagnosing canine hip dysplasia. J. Am. Vet. Med. Assoc. 210: 1451-7.

Srenk, P. Jaggy, A., Gaillard, C., Busato, A., Horin, P. (1994) Genetische Grundlagen der idiopathischen Epilepsie beim Golden Retriever. Tierz. Praxis. 22: 574-8.

Studdert, V.P., Lavelle, R.B.,Beilharz, R.G., Mason, T.A. (1991) Clinical features and heritability of osteochondrosis of the elbow in Labrador retrievers. J. Small Anim. Pract. 32: 557-63.

Swenson, L. Audell, L, Hedhammar, A. (1997a) Prevalence and inheritance of and selection for hip dysplasia in seven breeds of dogs in Sweden and benefit: cost analysis of a screening and control program. J. Am. Vet. Med. Assoc. 210: 207-14.

Swenson, L. Audell, L., Hedhammar, A. (1997b) Prevalence and inheritance of and selection for elbow arthrosis in Bernese Mountain Dogs and Rottweilers in Sweden and benefit:cost analysis of a screening and control program. J. Am. Vet. Med. Assoc. 210:215-21.

Turba, E., Willer, S. (1987) Untersuchungen zu Vererbung von Hasenscharten und Wolfsrachen beim Deutschen Boxer. Monat. Veterinarmed. 42: 897-901.

Ubbink, G.J., Knol, B.W., Bouw, J. (1992) The relationship between homozygosity and the occurrence of specific diseases in bouvier Belge des flandres dogs in the Netherlands. Vet. Quart. 14: 137-40.

Van Haaften, B., Dielman, S.J., Okkens, A.C., Willemse, A.H. (1989) Timing the mating of dogs on the basis of blood progesterone concentration.

Vet. Rec. 125: 524-6.

Van Sluijs, F.J. (1991) Gastric dilation-volvulus in the dog: current views and a retrospective study in 160 patients. Tijschr. Diergeneeskd. 116: 112-20.

Van der Velden, N.A., de Weerdt, C.J., Brooymans-Schallenberg, J.H.C., Tielen, A.M. (1976) An abnormal behaviour trait in Bernese Mountain dogs (Berner Sennenhund) Tijdschr. Diergen. 101: 403-7.

Vila, C. (1997) USA Today Science Journal.

Von Tschudi, F. (1853) Das Thierleben der Alpenwert. Leipzig.
Walkowicz, C., Wilcox, B. (1994) Successful dog breeding (2nd ed) Howell, New York. xviii + 222pp.

Weber, W. (1955) Uber die mediane Nasenspalte beim Berner Sennenhund. Arch. Klaus-stift. VererbForsach 30:139-45.

Weber, W. (1959) Uber die Vererbung der medianen Nasenspalte beim Hund. Schweiz Arch.Tierhelk. 101: 378-81.

Wildt, D.F., Baas, E.D.J., Chakraborty, P.K., Wolfle, T.L., Stewart, A.P. (1982) Influence of inbreeding on reproductive performance, ejaculate quality and testicular volume in the dog. Theriogenology 17: 445-52.

Willis, M.B. (1986) Some provisional ideas on hypomyelinogenesis in the Bernese Mountain Dog. Mimeograph, Bernese Breeders Assoc.

Willis, M.B. (1989) Genetics of the Dog. Witherbys, London.xxii +417pp.

Willis, M.B. (1992) The German Shepherd Dog: a genetic history Witherbys, London. vii + 439pp.

Willis, M.B. (1997) A review of the progress in canine hip dysplasia control in Britain. J. Am. Vet. Med. Assoc. 210: 1480-2.

Wilsman, N.J., Van Sickle D.C. (1973) Weight change patterns as a basis for predicting survival in newborn Pointer pups. J. Am. Vet. Med. Assoc. 163: 971-5.

Wind, A.P. (1986) Elbow incongruity and developmental elbow diseases in the dog: Part I. J. Am. Anim. Hosp. Assoc. 22:711-24.

Wind, A.P. 1990) Etiology and Pathogenesis of elbow dysplasia: A hypothesis. Proc. 57th Annual meeting Am. Anim. Hosp. Assoc. 725-7.

Wind, A.P., Packard, M.E. (1986) Elbow incongruity and developmental elbow diseases in the dog: Part II. J. Am. Anim. Hosp. Assoc. 22:725-73.

Wouda, W., van Nes, J.J.(1986) Progressive ataxia due to central demyelination in Rottweiler dogs. Vet. Quarterly. 8: 89-97.

Appendix II
Books On The Bernese Mountain Dog

Bärtschi, M. and Spengler, H. (1992) Hunde sehen, zuchten, erleben, das Buch v Berner Sennenhund. Paul Haupt, Bern. 776pp (in German).

Bugmann, M. (1997) Bernese Mountain Dogs in Australia. Privately published. 70pp (Australian).

Chestnutt Smith, S. (1995) The new Bernese Mountain Dog. Howell, New York. xii + 259pp. (American).

Cochrane, D. (1982) The Bernese Mountain Dog. (2nd ed). Privately published. Alcester. xii+198pp. (UK).

Fechler, C. (1988) Berner Sennenhunde. Paul Parey. Hamburg. 104pp. (in German).

Galand G.(1990) Le Bouvier Bernois. Concraid Edition, Mons. 135pp (in French).

Gunter, B. (1993) Berner Sennenhund. Kynos Keine, Murlenbach. 133pp. (in German).

Iversen, A.M. (1994) Berner Sennen I Danmark. Forlaget Kongsvang. 117pp (in Danish).

Ludwig, G. (1995) The Bernese and other Mountain dogs. Barrons, New York (American, translated from the German) 65pp.

Ostermiller, L. (1993) Bernese Mountain Dogs. TFH Pub. New Jersey. 192pp. (American).

Paschoud, J-M. (1994) The Swiss canine breeds. Schweizerische Kynologische Gesellschaft, Bern. 99pp (in English).

Petch, P. (1992) The Bernese Mountain Dog. Dickson Price, Romney Marsh. 209pp (UK).

Russ, D. and Rogers, S. (1993) The beautiful Bernese Mountain Dogs; a complete American Handbook. Alpine, Loveland. xii + 235pp (American).

Symonds, J. (1989) The complete Bernese Mountain Dog. Ringpress, Lydney. 160pp (UK).

Stevens, P. (1984) De Berner Sennenhond en Nederland. Thieme & Co. Zutphen. 120pp (in Dutch).

INDEX

(The index to dogs refers only to animals mentioned and not to their parents or ancestors. They are indexed by affix with second affixes omitted. Dogs mentioned in tables are not indexed). Photo references are in italics. People are not indexed.

Index